THE BOOK OF THE WHITE MOUNTAINS

To Mother

Christmas, 1930

© *George F. Slade*

Mount Adams and Mount Madison

THE BOOK
OF THE
WHITE MOUNTAINS

BY
JOHN ANDERSON
AND
STEARNS MORSE

NEW YORK
MINTON, BALCH & COMPANY
1930

Printed in the United States of America by
J. J. LITTLE AND IVES COMPANY, NEW YORK

TO
STANLEY JOHNSON, ESQUIRE
CALIPH OF BATH AND
MANHATTAN

CONTENTS

CONTENTS

CONTENTS

ILLUSTRATIONS

11

THE BOOK OF THE WHITE MOUNTAINS

THE BOOK OF THE
WHITE MOUNTAINS

INTRODUCTORY

THOSE literate and careful tourists who go about the world, book in hand, must find a paradox of nature in the volumes prepared so that those who climb may read. By some antecedent miracle it seems that the topographical guides of our White Mountains achieved a degree of clairvoyance, since their works now appear to be actually older than the hills. Or perhaps they merely disclose that time is less corrosive on a mountain peak than in the library.

Wherefore, a survey of the New Hampshire ranges reveals that while the originals remain in fairly good condition, their literary duplicates are by no means in a suitable state of preservation. Those changes of calendar which spread splendid death across the hillside foliage, carry no promises of resurrection when they afflict the rootless leaves of print. When a leaf turns yellow, and dries, and turns red, and then scampers down the autumn gullies, there is assurance within the credulous memory of man that another will grow some day on that same limb. But when an adjective goes into its sere and yellow there is nothing for it but to await its vogue as an explicit antique.

It was a fashion among the writing pathfinders of the

White Mountains, as for that matter it may be among all mountain addicts, to match tall pinnacles with taller talk. Presumably a pigmy never grows so vain as when he stands upon something higher than himself, and it may be an open question as to which came first, the orator or the soap box. Perhaps they are mutually necessary. Whether from rarefied air or language men have been made giddy by the heights since first Pelion was piled on Ossa in that boastful attempt to reach the gods. Since then the gods have been wisely removed by cautious mankind from the demonstrable slopes of Olympus to the vaguer, and therefore safer, reaches of the empyrean.

In any case the ascent is as frequently imperilled by precipitous language as by the more obvious dangers of topography. Fastidious sightseers may be more easily frightened off by a sudden metaphor than by the most unexpected slide.

Too often these urgent but well intentioned cicerones have fallen into the errors which afflict so many sightseers. They show so much you can see nothing, and recall, indeed, the confusing exuberance of that famous guide in the Conciergerie who winds up his most opulent descriptions of walls, windows, doors, etc., with the honest but disheartening admission that in the old days they did not exist. Some day, perhaps, "Monsieur N'existe-pas" will inadvertently and fatally put himself into the past tense so that quiet will be restored among the visitors. They will perhaps welcome a little peace and risk willingly the mistakes that ensue from a grateful silence.

Naturally this is no suicidal argument for the abolition

of all guides. It is no plea against taking the tourist by the elbow, but merely the prayer that he may not be taken, instead, by the funnybone. The world is too full of complacent snobs admiring the wrong sights in preference to showing a decent ignorance. There are documented cases of self-satisfied travelers who will go to their deaths with the notion that the Bastille stood in the Place de la Concorde and that the New York Public Library is the Metropolitan Museum.

The point may be raised that it makes no difference, and that as long as you see what you think you see the essential curiosity of travel has been satisfied. It may be all very well to stay at home and see the world, but it gives hallucination the benefit of the doubt. After all, Molière's M. Jourdain was never so happy in his unconscious achievements as he was when he found out to his delight and amazement that he had been speaking prose all his life. Out of simple politeness it seems better and friendlier to meet even a mountain face to face, and call its right name, so it may be recognized at another meeting.

Speaking of faces brings to mind a group of tourists against which the wiles of the devil and the truth of Heaven fall alike on barren ground. These are the skeptics. They believe nothing, and cherish some inverted form of credulity in place of more normal illusions. One such of the breed will do for example. She was showing her son the Great Stone Face on Cannon Mountain, and he, inspired no doubt by inherited characteristics, asked how it got there.

"They say," said she, "that it just came there naturally in the rocks, but I have my doubts."

They were, when last seen, hunting over Echo Lake on a bushwacking expedition, trying, perhaps, to see the acoustics, though it is probable that she and her offspring do believe in waterfalls. The forces of gravity are so convincing that they explain to the stupidest how they are on earth, if not why.

Thus may appear the threefold object of this work, since it hopes to be reassuring to the resident and to the expert, informative to the stranger, and convincing to the skeptics. Against a certain selected background of previous works, and with all deference to tradition and legend, it volunteers modestly to make the White Mountains as accessible in print as roads and automobiles and magnificent hotels have made them in physical fact. When it quails before the majestic beauty of the scenery it casts itself upon the mercy of the beholders, and reserves the right to rely, with its tongue in its cheek, on the unbridled word festivals of its predecessors, as both warning and proof of what all of us have been spared.

Perhaps this scheme omits some of the time-honored features of such efforts, such features, for instance, as a discussion of the uses of mountains. Somewhere in his anthology of poetry, mistakenly published as a general physical and emotional White Mountain guide in 1860, the intrepid Starr King engages with quotations from Mr. Ruskin on the uses of mountains. He is full of such genial geologics as to the bulk of the Alps, and estimates how, if they were levelled, the material in them, spread over the continent of Europe, would raise its surface twenty feet higher than it is now above sea level.

Your present guides, unimpressed by these facts of lit-

erary legerdemain, propose to perform no such seismographic
miracles. For their immediate purposes it seems simplest and
best to assume that mountains are useful for going up and
coming down, and to proceed on this basis within the strictest
human limits. They agree to undertake proper and reasonable measurements, to suggest comparative sizes by the ordinary means, but they cannot, nay! dare not, stand the
Leviathan on its stern beside Mount Washington to demon-
strate the majestic eminence of that splendid peak. Aside
from a distaste for cowardly comparisons they refrain for the
reason that the spectacle could serve no useful purpose, and
on the further and more overwhelming ground that the
owners of the Leviathan might object.

Nor will they pry into the spiritual purposes to which
the mountains may be put, and here they beg leave humbly
to depart from the ritual of all save the most realistic of guide
books—that invaluably blunt and pointedly reticent volume
of the Appalachian Mountain Club. For the danger to previous commentators has proved greatest on peaks of fancy.
Their efforts, in retrospect, suggest too threateningly the
menace of getting off the ground while on some dizzy eminence. They perpetually expose their souls to the rigors of
high altitudes, without a decent coverage of dumb awe,
forgetful that in religion the garrulous convert has always
been its chief enemy.

There are occasions when the inarticulate should inherit
the earth. A trip through the mountains is one of them.
They are, willy-nilly, more considerate of their fellow creatures than the gushing egoists who wish all to see what they

see the way they see it. Incoherent "Ohs" and "Ahs" have been seriously underrated in a world where expression is altogether too easy and platitudes cheap at any price. There is much to be said for such tourists as one who exclaimed, on entering Michelangelo's chapel for the Medici, "Pretty good," and went away again. This is the essence of shrewdest criticism in the face of a masterpiece, even if it does raise the assumption that the truly sensitive tourist is the one who doesn't write a book on the White Mountains.

Your guides shrug off the implication, in the knowledge that they are not trying to improve upon nature—either human or otherwise. They dissent from the contention of Julius Ward's book that the spell of the mountains lies in "the conquest of nature over the forces of life," on the ground that they don't know what it means.

Equally, it seems that all such statements may be grouped under the vernacular scorn of "Ain't nature wonderful." "The joy," says Mr. Ward, "of being in the mountains is that every unused or waiting faculty of our higher nature is strained to the utmost to interpret them in the language of the spirit. . . . Great as is this gift to some, the use of the mountains to lift us into the higher moods of life is common to us all. Like the air and the sky and the clouds and the sunlight, no one can lay exclusive claims to them. The unlikeness begins in the fitness of the spirit to interpret them."

It seems possible to trust the mountains to speak for themselves, especially when we have before us the unblinking evidence of their verbal effect on others, in such goings on as the following from Mr. Ward's imaginative, though strictly non-Freudian, experiences:

"One goes to sleep with his arms around huge old Lafayette, as it were, and wakes to find Mount Cannon dancing before him in the mists and sunbeams of the next morning."

Or behold the spiritual intoxication of the impressionable Mr. King:

"See the early day pour down the upper slopes of the three easterly pyramids; then upon the broad forehead of the Profile Mountain, kindling its gloomy brows with radiance, and melting the azure of its temples into pale violet; and falling lower, staining with rose tints the cool mists of the ravines, till the Notch seems to expand, and the dark and rigid sides of it fall away as they lighten, and recede in soft perspective of buttressed wall and flushed tower,—and then say whether, to an eye that can never be satiated with the blue of a hyacinth, the purple of a fuchsia, and the blush of a rose, the gorgeousness ascribed to the mountains is a mere exercise in rhetoric or a fiction of the fancy."

With all salutes to Mr. King's gallantry in attempting the impossible, rhetoric still comes out somewhat behind the actuality, and there seems to be no use pelting a hillside with a thesaurus. That giddy faith in words is, at any rate, one faith that cannot move mountains. More cogent, though, is that it cannot even move the mountain's observer, and he is the only thing worth moving. Honestly and finally he must move of his own accord.

Wherefore it is probable that Mark Twain's impeccable

Harris was as good a guide as any. He it was, you may remember from "A Tramp Abroad," who acted as deputy when his chief decided that while a pedestrian tour of Europe would not be complete without a visit to the Furka Pass, the Rhone Glacier, the Finsteraarhorn, and the Wetterhorn, he felt himself personally unable to attend these sights, or exert himself.

"Of course that decided me at once to see them," he explains, "for I never allow myself to do things by halves, or in a slurring, slipshod way. I called in my agent and instructed him to go without delay and make a careful examination of these noted places on foot, and bring me back a written report for insertion in my book."

For all his odd and precarious hilarity of language Mr. Harris put down his route, as it behooves every guide to do, and it may clarify the plan of this present volume to give it brief outline. It purposes to go through the whole range covering the chief points of interest to a casual visitor, to indicate roads, trails, hotels, and where advisable to explain the legendary or traditional interest of various spots.

With this purpose in mind a design has been worked out to cover the whole, with as little retracing of steps as possible. In doing this a line has been borrowed from Robert Frost's "New Hampshire" which renders the pattern exceedingly clear.

"Anything I can say about New Hampshire
"Will serve almost as well about Vermont,
"Excepting that they differ in their mountains.
"The Vermont mountains stretch extended straight;
"New Hampshire mountains curl up in a coil."

As the table of contents indicates, the route begins to the south at the lower end of Franconia Notch, moves almost due north up the Notch, through Bethlehem, and into the North Country, including Dixville Notch, and mounts steadily as it goes along its spiral to the apex of the whole, the inner coil of the vast spring of mountains, the peak of Mount Washington.

Virtually every section of the mountains is easy of access and the range is dotted with accommodations to suit every taste and pocketbook. The entire area lies within a comparatively restricted territory, a fact which makes it more generally interesting, and creates the impression that Mount Washington is the highest peak east of the Rockies, because Mount Mitchell and two peaks in the Great Smokies, though actually superior, rise from a range that is much wider and higher than the New Hampshire country.

The White Mountains constitute a section of the country which is unrivalled in its variety of natural interests. It may be ventured that nowhere else, within so small a radius, is there such concentrated wealth of spectacular formation in peaks, valleys, and waterfall. Since the early exploration of the mountains they have grown steadily in popularity so that they have come to be a national resort. The climate, natural resources, and superb accommodations make an irresistible combination whether the visitor occupies a tent or the most luxurious hotel.

In covering them the present authors have relied upon their personal experiences and on a comprehensive research among other publications, in the wish to make their work as

useful as possible to all, whatever their interests. For those
who wish to make more extensive walking tours than are
indicated herein, the guide of the Appalachian Mountain
Club will be found invaluable with its carefully prepared data
on camping, climbing, and general outdoor practice. For
handy pocket consultation it is indispensable.

Other acknowledgments are due many who have, one
way and another, helped in the selection and preparation of
material. Special thanks for assistance are due to Stanley
Johnson, the Honorable Amos N. Blandin, J. Brooks Atkinson, D. D. Tuttle, Secretary of the New Hampshire State
Department of Publicity, to the studios of the Messrs. Conant,
Hunting, Slade, Merryman, and Shorey of Gorham, for the
use of certain photographs, and to Nathaniel L. Goodrich, the
Librarian of Dartmouth College, and to Nelson A. Rocke-
feller and the Dartmouth Outing Club, for generous assistance in obtaining special pictures.

And on the unequalled precedent of Herr Baedeker we
may quote the petition of Sir Richard Ros in his "Go lytel
Boke":

> "Where thou art wronge after her help to cal
> "The to correcte in any parte or al."

CHAPTER I

A GENERAL OUTLINE

A LTHOUGH the White Mountains are often and erroneously thought to include only the cluster of high peaks around Mount Washington, the term more properly applies to the whole range in Northern New Hampshire extending from north to south approximately forty miles, and embracing the surrounding territory to the same distance east and west. For present purposes the whole mountain country of New Hampshire will be considered, since the adjacent mountains and their notches afford some of the finest scenery of the region, and offer unique natural attractions that can be found nowhere else. Washington and its special lore are taken up in later chapters. This is an outline and a promise.

For the full grandeur of the central peaks it is, of course, necessary to move away from the gigantic canvas their panorama makes across the sky, and the view from Jefferson reveals the turbulent glory of the Presidential Range in its whole splendor.

It gives, too, the impression that explains the name—a name whose origin is lost in many legends, though all of them hold eloquent tribute to this mountain whiteness. Some of the Indians called them, or, as Starr King points out, more particularly Mount Washington, Agiocochook, and others. Waumbekketmethna, meaning literally white mountains, and others still, more imaginatively coupled their whiteness and their soaring grace in one figure, Kan Ran Vugarty, implying the whiteness of a seagull.

Less poetic explanations derive possibly from early explorations of the region when the first man to make the ascent of Mount Washington, Darby Field, an Irishman from Portsmouth, returned from a trip in 1632 with reports that the mountains were filled with "shining stones" that were thought to be diamonds until more cautious adventurers discovered that they were merely crystal.

Many others followed Field, lured on by his tales of dazzling wealth, and that first daring venture, told in Winthrop's Journal, is worth repeating on what is almost the three hundredth anniversary of its achievement.

Field, says the Journal, started off on his journey, "being accompanied with two Indians, and went to the top of the White Hill. He made his journey in eighteen days. His relation, at his return, was, that it was about 160 miles from Saco; that after forty miles travel he did, for the most part, ascend; and within twelve miles of the top was neither tree nor grass but low savins, which they went upon the top of sometimes; but a continual ascent upon rocks, on a ridge, between two valleys, filled with snow, out of which came two branches of the Saco River, which met at the foot of the hill where was an Indian town of some 200 inhabitants. Some of them accompanied him within eight miles of the top, but durst go no farther, telling him that no Indian ever dared to go higher,

Mounts Washington and Madison Over Peabody River, Glen Road

Tip-Top House, Mount Washington

and that he would die if he went. So they stayed there till his return and his two Indians took courage by his example and went with him. They went divers times through thick clouds, for a good space and within four miles of the top they had no clouds, but very cold. By the way among the rocks there were two ponds, one a blackish water and the other reddish. The top of all was plain, about sixty feet square. On the north side was such a precipice as they could scarcely discern the bottom. They had neither cloud nor wind on the top, but moderate heat. All the country about him seemed a level, except here and there a hill rising above the rest, and far beneath them. He saw, to the north, a great water which he judged to be 100 miles broad, but could see no land beyond it. The sea by Saco seemed as if it had been within twenty miles. He saw also a sea to the east which he judged to be the Gulf of Canada. He saw some great waters in parts of the west which he judged to be the great lake Canada River came out of. He found there much Muscovy glass; they could rive out pieces forty feet long and seven or eight broad."

Josselyn's "New England Rarities Discovered," which was published about forty years after the first ascent, estimated that the ridge of mountains "run Northwest and Northeast an hundred leagues, known by the name of the White Mountains, upon which lieth snow all the year, and is a landmark twenty miles off at sea" and those who venture into the North Country may be amused to know that, at the same time, he announced that "The country beyond these hills is daunting terrible, being full of rocky Hills, as thick as Mole Hills in a Meadow, and cloathed with infinite thick woods."

It was Josselyn, too, who first set down some of the general legends of the region, legends which embodied the ancient Indian belief that Washington was both Ararat and Carmel, and Sweetser, two centuries later, explained that the story was so widespread, and belief in it so implicit that "no hunter was bold enough to approach the sacred peaks, no war party dared to traverse their shadow defiles. These martial tribes of hardy and adventurous men lived for ages within sight of the mountains, and within a day's march of the deer-hunting glens and teeming brooks, but were restrained from visiting them by the ineffable awe which taught them to believe that such visits would be invasions of the shrine of the Great Spirit." Those who dared the dangers, he adds, were said to have been lost, condemned to wander forever "among the gloomy ravines, whence their despairing shrieks were borne from time to time to the valleys on the wings of stormy winds."

"Ask them," says Josselyn in his seventeenth century chronicle of the Indians, "whither they go when they dye, they will tell you, pointing with their finger to Heaven, beyond the white mountains, and they do hint at Noah's Floud, as may be conceived by a story they have received from Father to Son, time out of mind, that a great while agon their Countrey was drowned, and all the People and other Creatures in it, only one Powaw and his Webb foreseeing the Floud fled to the white mountains, carrying a hare along with them, and so escaped; after a while the Powaw sent the Hare away, who, not returning, emboldened thereby, they descended and lived many years after, and had many children from whom the

Countrie was filled again with Indians." The Indian version at least saved Noah a good deal of trouble, and leaves him fair tribute for incurable optimism if he was so favorably impressed by the fact that the Hare didn't get back.

Although Washington was set apart as the dwelling place of the Great Spirit the country about was populated by many large tribes, and extensive traces of their ancient encampments have been found on lakes and ponds and river banks.

Great sections of the mountains were occupied by the Sokokis and Anasahunticooks, tribes of the Abenakis, and they flourished mightily until a period just before the white settlers came, when vast numbers of them were carried off by a plague.

Morton in his "New English Canaan" describes the fearful ravage of disease in terms that are familiar from chronicles of similar plagues in London and Florence.

"The hand of God fell heavily upon them," he says, "with such a mortall stroake, that they died in heaps as they lay in their houses, and the living that were to shift for themselves, would run away and let them dy, and let their carkases ly above the ground without buriall. For in a place where many inhabited, there hath been but one left alive to tell what became of the rest; the living being (as it seems) not able to bury the dead. They were left for crowes, kites, and vermine to prey upon. And the bones and skulls, upon the severall places of their habitations, in that forest nere the Massachusetts, it seemed to me a new found Golgotha."

Gorges and Vines, who partially explored the region in 1616, added further light on the fearful death rate, explaining that the tribes suffered not only from the ravages of pestilence but from tribal wars caused by the death of Bashaba, or chief sachem, and his whole family at the hands of the Tarratines, a tribe living east of the Penobscot.

"In the midst of these evils," these explorers added, "the Englishmen passed with safety among them and slept in their cabins without suffering from the contagion."

Contemporary accounts and the traditions of a myth-loving race have left us names of a few great individuals of these tribes, left them picturesquely among the gloomy and forbidding lore of their people which hangs about these hills, and lend them the awesome legends which mountains everywhere evoke out of simple men overwhelmed by might and mystery. Ageless superstitions linger in the presence of complicated nature, and find here the counterparts of myths which take one form or another across the baffling ranges of the world, and echo among the Scottish highlands, through Dalecarlia and Norsland, Germany and into the east.

Chocorua's Curse is still immortalized by one of the smaller peaks in the region to the south of Washington, and remains one of the few surviving Indian names in a country that once abounded in them, before a craze for American historical personages changed the whole range to an outdoor Hall of Fame. Chocorua was a chieftain who seems to have been brutally slain upon a defenseless pinnacle of the mountain which bears his name, and his solemn vengeance is supposed to have poisoned the country about his hill.

Squando, a chief of the Sokokis is one of the first Indians mentioned by the explorers, who found him a "strange enthusiastical sagamore," who achieved a weird blending of savage beliefs with some scattered Christian dogma picked up from the first whites. He it was who is said to have fulfilled a bizarre compact with his God, who had appeared to him in the form of "a tall man in dark clothes" and told him that he would be the instrument of white extinction. How fanatically he felt his mission was revealed in the bloody massacres of 1675 and 1676.

But the most picturesque of these early monarchs of the hills was Assacumbit, also a chieftain of the Sokokis, whose ferocious cruelties toward the English settlers made him feared even among his own people, and endeared him to the French.

"He always carried a huge club," says Dr. Willey in his chatty chronicle of White Mountain lore published in 1856, "on which were notches denoting the number of English he had killed." Mather estimates the number at one hundred and fifty men, women, and children, adding with justifiable horror: "A bloody devil."

"He was particularly attached to the French," Dr. Willey continues, "and under some of their leaders won great renown. And so highly did the French esteem their ally that in 1705 Vaudreuil sent him to France. Here he was an object of great curiosity. At Versailles he was introduced to Louis XIV, surrounded by his splendid court. The king presented him with a beautiful sword, the undaunted chieftain remarking, as he held out his hand to receive it, 'This hand hath slain one hundred and forty of your Majesty's enemies in New England.'

"This so pleased the king that he knighted him, and commanded a pension of eight livres a day to be allowed him for life. On his return to America he wore upon his breast the insignia of his knighthood displayed in large letters.

"He was so 'exalted that he treated his countrymen in the most haughty and arrogant manner, murdering one and stabbing another, which so exasperated those of their relations that they sought revenge, and would have instantly executed it, but that he fled for protection to the French. Still faithful to his former masters, he accompanied Rouville in his attack upon Haverhill."

To geologists and botanists the mountains, naturally, offer special delights, though the casual visitor probably would take no more than a general interest in the subjects. Tales of a wealth of valuable minerals persisted into fairly recent times, preserving, usually, Indian traditions which had it that great treasures in precious stones were suspended from high precipices on great heights, and that carbuncles were seen so large and so splendid that even in darkness they shone with utmost brilliance. Indeed, so hard-headed a historian as Ethan A. Crawford recalls from memory the tales of a party that went in search of "a golden treasure, or carbuncle, which they said was under a large shelving rock, and would be difficult to obtain for they might fall and be dashed to pieces. Moreover, they thought it was guarded at night by an evil spirit, supposed to have been placed there by the Indians."

All of these reports are no doubt due to the rock formations which abound in gneiss, mica, schist, clay slate and

Mount Washington from Mount Adams

Franconia Notch from North Woodstock

quartzite, traversed in huge masses by veins of granite and greenstone, all giving the region the glint and lightness which was marked in the term "Crystal Hills" and which is not perpetuated in their present name. Few fossil remains have been found.

Some of the early explorations reveal statements that are as ingenuous as Indian beliefs, and the usually careful Josselyn, in his later work, corrects his statement that snow lies on the peaks all year, and says that "some suppose the White Mountains were first raised by earthquakes," adding the somewhat astonishing conclusion that "they are hollow, as may be guessed by the resounding of the rain upon the level of the top."

The noises which he thus attempts to account for have been mentioned by many travelers who reported that they heard sounds as of far-off guns. Some of these were, unquestionably, landslides which, at one time, occurred with comparative frequency, and many of the sound phenomena could obviously be accounted for by far-off thunder. They may even be part of that mysterious phenomenon which scientists have been unable to explain and which was known among the Indians as "Moodus noises."

The sound is precisely one of distant cannon, and occurs usually on days when the air is clear and still. There have been frequent reports of them in the hills of Northern Italy, where they are known as *brontidi,* and where they have been subjected to exhaustive inquiry by Prof. Tito Alippi, but without definite result. In India, they have been remarked by travelers for centuries and are called "Guns of Barisal" because of their high frequency in the delta of the Ganges, near the town of Barisal.

In winter the brilliance of frost phenomena is without equal. Frost is formed with great rapidity and its effect, when attached to the windward side of rocks and poles and buildings, is revealed in one of the striking illustrations of this book. It occurs when the wind is from the north or west and the mountains are covered with clouds, achieving forms that are marvels of intricate delicacy and lightness.

Fortunate visitors may be lucky enough to witness some of the other spectacular dramas of nature, for observers have seen such splendid effects as lightning through heavy snowstorms, and triple-rainbows, especially in August, which often remain for hours. There are also anthelia, or glories of light, and the specter of the Brocken, which, with all deference to the superstitions of Walpurgis night, is merely the shadow of a man thrown on fog, which can be seen, of course, only by the person who makes it.

Botanically the mountains afford specimens of flora which, with few exceptions, can be found elsewhere only in Arctic America, since on peaks in this region alone are conditions favorable to the growth of these plants.

"Of these Alpine areas," say the scientists who compiled "The Geology of New Hampshire," "Mount Washington and the adjacent peaks are the largest, being a treeless region eight miles long by two miles wide at its broadest part. These alpine plants are of great hardihood, and sometimes bloom amid ice and snow. In approaching these mountain summits one is first struck by the appearance of the firs and the spruces, which gradually become more and more dwarfish, at length rising but a few feet from the ground, the branches spreading out many feet and becoming thickly interwoven. These present a comparatively dense upper surface which is often firm enough to walk upon. At length these disappear wholly, and give place to the Lapland rhododendron, Labrador tea, dwarf birch, and alpine willows, all of which, after rising a few inches above the ground, spread out over the surface of the nearest rock, thereby gaining warmth, which enabled them to exist in spite of the tempest and the cold. These in their turn give place to the Greenland sandwort, the diapensia, the cassiope, and others, with arctic rushes, sedges, and lichens which flourish at the very summit."

In the four great valleys made by the Androscoggin, the Saco, the Merrimac, and the tributaries of the Connecticut, there are magnificent waterfalls, and scattered about the region are such fascinating natural formations as the Flume, the Old Man of the Mountain, and Echo Lake. They make up a territory that is rich in interest, and magnificent to the eye, a region whose background and traditions render it as alluring to those who have known it for years, as it is in the freshness of its appeal and the splendor of its natural beauty to one who beholds it for the first time.

With this general, if somewhat loosely drawn, picture of its whole extant in physical, historical, and legendary information, we may proceed through its notches and over its peaks in the inexhaustible wealth of interest and enchantment.

CHAPTER II

FRANCONIA NOTCH

SINCE Mount Washington broods over the spirit of the traveler through these mountains as serenely as it tops the physical world around it, visitors too often go to it first, and descend to the other wonder works from that eminence. Logically, though, it should be the climax of the whole; should be taken as the final movement of a vast crescendo. Some prelude is needed for approach, and Franconia Notch leads gently and suavely to the upper regions where Washington is piled in its great company of mountain giants.

In this way the route passes up the Pemigewasset Valley instead of down it from its head waters, as nearly all the guide book predecessors have done, and it has the added merit of being en route to the more majestic scenery beyond its northern gates.

More majestic, but not more pleasing, for the Franconia Range, taking its name from the township in which, for the most part, it is situated, affords a rare combination of grandeur and serenity. Its peaks are lower, and their slopes more wooded. Its perspectives are charming and more intimate than the tumultuously superb scenes in the upper hills, yet it suggests them delicately, as if announcing a quiet theme that is to be developed in larger orchestrations.

All audible travelers who have passed through this narrow lane along the Pemigewasset have attested its peculiar delights. Fredericka Bremer, the Swedish novelist, found the district more enchanting than the famous regions of Dalecarlia and Norsland in Sweden, and eloquently testified to the beauties of this locality.

"The scenery here is more picturesque, more playful and fantastic, has more cheerful diversity, and the affluence of wood and the beautiful foliage in the valleys is extraordinary: you walk or drive continually between the most lovely wild hedges of hazel, elm, sumach, sugar maple, yellow birch, fir trees, pines, and many other trees and shrubs, and on all sides is heard the singing and roaring of the mountain streams, clear as silver, through the passes of the hills."

And Starr King declared with something of the bluntness of authority that this district "contains more objects of interest to the mass of travelers than any other region of equal extent within the compass of the usual White Mountain tour."

For present purposes the trip through the Notch may begin at North Woodstock, where the Branch of the Pemigewasset, which rises to the east, joins the upper, or mainstream of the river. The Daniel Webster Highway runs alongside the river bank, crossing a small tributary just below Johnson, and bridging the main stream beyond The Flume. To the right are the Coolidges, Big and Little, their heights, respectively, 2,600 and 2,300 feet, named long ago among these presidential monuments by some forgotten stroke of clairvoyance.

The principal peaks of the range lie to the right in serried ranks, dominated at the upper end by Lafayette. Behind and to the left, over Kinsman Notch, looms the great flat-topped bulk of Moosilauke. For the five or six miles through the Notch proper the road curves only gently, affording superb vistas.

Nearest to the road beyond the confluence of the two streams is Mount Pemigewasset, a squat bulk *vis-à-vis* with Mount Flume, the first of the high peaks in the Notch, rising with its immediate neighbor, Mount Liberty, well above four thousand feet.

Since North Woodstock is the center of this interesting region, and since there are many nearby points which can be visited on short walks or drives from the town, it may be well to pause and survey the approaches to the Notch before going on. A small and well-arranged guide book to the points of local interest, together with a hotel directory, maps, and plans of panoramas from North Woodstock has been prepared by the North Woodstock Improvement Association. It is extremely compact, intelligent, and serviceable, a model indeed, which other towns could well afford to follow. The chief hotels are The Alpine, Deer Park, Mountain View Hotel and Cottages, Mount Adams Hotel and the Russell House.

The town grant was made in 1763 by the Colonial Governor, Benning Wentworth, to Eli Demerit, and it was then called Peeling, the first settlement having been made, according to some accounts, in 1773 by John Riant on Mount Cilley, an irregular height some four miles from the postoffice. Of this settlement nothing remains except the now overgrown outlines of a village street, and the foundations of a few houses. Many of the places hereabouts are called for some member of the Smith family which was so numerous in the neighborhood that a school superintendent reported in 1852 that "The Mount Cilley school is all Smiths." From the easy road to the height fine views may be had of Mount Washington and Mount Moosilauke.

This account of the town's history has it that the name "Peeling" became so objectionable to the inhabitants that they chafed under the appellation "Poor Peeling" and ultimately in 1840, after the Rev. Benjamin Ropes had preached two hours over time on the scornful text "Peeling," changed the name.

Justus Conrad, authority for these statements and author of a small pamphlet on the town, leaned previously to the opinion published in "The Granite Monthly" for July, 1897, that the original grant was made under the name Fairfield, and that the name Peeling was used in a legislative charter dated 1799. Records of the first town meeting indicate that it was held in 1800. It is assumed that when the present name was selected it was chosen from Scott's novel "Woodstock."

Naturally the whole of the Franconia Range is within easy traveling distance of the town, but the more strictly local points of interest include Agassiz Basin, an interesting formation of rocks and ledges worn by the Moosilauke Branch, Loon Pond, Russell Pond, and Lost River. It is also a convenient starting point for the trails over Kinsman and Moosilauke.

Few guide books of the region mention Lost River, yet it

is a spectacular phenomenon, about five miles northwest of
North Woodstock, on a reservation belonging to the Society
for the Protection of New Hampshire Forests.   Thousands
of tourists annually visit Lost River, and the fee of twenty-
five cents goes toward a fund for the maintenance of the
reservation, together with the hut, the keeper, and guides.
Simple lodgings are provided but it is best, on account of the
limited accommodations, to make reservations.

The "lost" river derives its name from the unusual fact
that the Moosilauke Branch disappears completely, here and
there, along its course over a bed composed of enormous
rocks. These rocks form huge caves of peculiar shapes, which
may be visited down ladders, though only under the super-
vision of an accredited guide. Within one of the caves the
water falls twenty feet. Some primeval spruce trees may be
seen on the bluff above.

Lost River is as unforgettably weird as any natural phenomenon is likely to seem, especially if it arouses those stub-
born apprehensions, nursed by imaginative theologists, that
Hell lies somewhere in the terrestrial cellar. It is as cavernous
and menacing and spectacular as all that: something out of
Doré cut immortally into vast illustration of solid rock.

Of many writers who expend their vocabularies on other
sections of the mountains, only one, Karl Pomeroy Harrington, supervisor of trails for the Appalachian Mountain Club,
devotes much space to the wonders of Lost River. In "Walks
and Climbs in the White Mountains," he says:

"As the visitor approaches the pellucid waters of the
little stream, it looks as innocent as any rivulet in the moun-

© *Moosilauke Studio*

Franconia Notch from Fairview Hotel

© *Moosilauke Studio*

The Flume

tains, and gives no promise of the rush, the turmoil, the gloom, the unknown depths of the temporary burial awaiting it. But a chaotic jumble on monstrous rocks lies just below; and within fifty feet the brook has disappeared beneath them as completely as if there were no water course for a hundred miles. Now and then it will emerge at one or another level, or you can hear the splashing or fall or the gurgle of slower movement in some choked up passage below you. But as you wander down among the caves and over the boulders and along the precipitous sides of the gorge for an hour or more you seldom see any signs of a normal brook. It is either lost entirely or lost to view most of the time, from the 'Cave of the Ships' to 'Titan's Workshop.'

"What peculiar spell the uncanny place throws over the visitor it is not so easy to explain. Doubtless there is a complex of curiosity, rashness, the excitement of exploration, the passion for 'doing stunts' and that mysterious fondness that the human animal exhibits—possibly inherited from lower mammalian ancestors—for hiding in dark places."

Mr. Harrington is utterly right about the failure of photography to reproduce the strange effects of this wayward river, and its capricious bed. The vague gloom of the place defies the most attentive lenses, even as the persuasive spell of the place eludes ready definition. Its compulsion is a thing of mystery out of geological accidents, as if these dim caves imprisoned an old secret of creation within their dank walls.

"How picture," Mr. Harrington asks, "the mysterious tenuousness of the light in the 'Hall of Forgetfulness' or the Lethean fog rising from the impassable waters? How photograph the thrilling glimpse of the plunging cataract into un-known depths as you lean over the smooth ledge worn into incalculable curves by the rush of waters ages ago? How reproduce on any plate, be it never so sensitive, the tangible gloom of that far-away cavern which a modern-theological imagination has dubbed 'The Abode of the Lost Souls.'

"On a bright day the sharp contrasts between light and shade can occasionally be secured in a photograph, as one balances oneself on the side of a ledge at an angle of forty-five degrees. But what will you do with a camera while de-scending 'the chimney' or traveling from one dark hole to another by the use of the portion of your anatomy which corresponds to that upon which the serpent has uniformly progressed since his egress from the garden of Eden?"

Well, for our part, we leave such feats to more intrepid, or more photographically exigent visitors, on the cowardly theory that if the Lost River ever suddenly finds itself it isn't going to do anyone any good to have a camera with them down "the chimney."

But it is a grand sight to see, and tourists would do well to take this side jaunt off the beaten track.

The Beaver Brook Trail up Moosilauke leaves the west side of the Kinsman Notch road about half a mile beyond Lost River, just south of the public camp ground at Beaver Meadows. In the main the early portion follows Beaver Brook, which plunges down the mountain in beautiful cas-cades. Here the trail is very steep but the ascent is somewhat facilitated by ladders. About two thirds of the way up it skirts the edges of Jobildunk Ravine (named, according to legend, for three men named Joe, Bill, and Duncan), a glacial ravine which gives one a foretaste of the more rugged glacial cirques on Mount Washington. The distance from the Kinsman Notch road to the Tip-Top House (operated by the Dartmouth Outing Club) is not quite four miles. The Tip-Top House is a house of stone and wood, opened in 1860 with appropriate ceremonies, which has the distinction of being the only summit habitation in the White Mountains proper besides the one on Washington. Moosilauke is 4,811 feet above sea level.

The ascent of Moosilauke by those who approach it from the west (from the Connecticut Valley, for instance, or the Lake Tarleton Club, or from the Boston and Maine railroad line from Concord to Woodsville) is best made by means of the Glencliff Trail. This is one of the links of the official Dartmouth Outing Club route from Hanover to Mount Washington. The beginning of the trail can be reached by highway and country road easily accessible to automobiles in summer and starts at the Great Bear Cabin of the D.O.C. It goes up rather steeply through beautiful spruce woods until on the south peak of Moosilauke, about a mile from the top, it joins the old carriage road from Warren. (This is the road, Drake tells us, whose miles the builder lengthened or shortened in the Einsteinian manner, according as the going was good or bad: the easy first mile, for example, was stretched by the guide-posts to a mile and a quarter; in this fashion the two and a half miles of roughest going was shortened by the guide-posts to one and three-quarters miles. A happy deception, certainly, but of little use now since the road is practically impassable to vehicles.) The distance from the

Great Bear Cabin to the summit is about three and a half miles.

The easiest trail up the mountain is the Benton Trail which may be reached by continuing on the Kinsman Notch road down into Wildwood and then turning to the left on the road to Parker's. This road, however, was badly washed in the flood of 1927 and is still, probably, rather dubious for automobiles.

Those, however, who like to go off the beaten track (especially if their goal happens to be the Connecticut Valley) can hardly do better than continue on down the Wild Ammonoosuc, turning to the left two or three miles from Wildwood to go up into the little town of Benton. They will be rewarded by backward views of Kinsman and the Franconia Range and of the long gentle curve which makes of Moosilauke so distinctive a mountain; and ahead of them by a distant view of the Connecticut Valley and the Green Mountains.

Since Moosilauke is almost isolated it affords a superb view which has the great advantage of being easily accessible, and which is considered by some to be the finest view in the whole section. Mr. O'Kane, indeed, in his admirable volume, quotes Dr. Washington Gladden as saying that "I give my hearty preference to Moosilauke over every mountain whose top I have climbed. The view from Washington is vast, but vague; the view from Lafayette is noble, but it shows little of the sweet restfulness of the Connecticut Valley; on Moosilauke we get all forms of grandeur and all types of beauty."

From the summit of Moosilauke Mount Washington may

be found to the northeast by sighting along a line drawn to the right of Mount Liberty, the more northerly of two mountains of similar shape across Franconia Notch, and to the left of Mount Bond, some six miles beyond Liberty. Once this commanding landmark is identified the observer can readily find the others. Mount Jefferson is to the left of Washington and Adams back of Jefferson.

To the north stretch the long wooded slopes of Mount Kinsman (4,377 feet), which may be reached along the trail mentioned above, where the path turns to the right of the State Road, near Lost River Cabin. From Kinsman the trail leads across the ridge to Mount Cannon, and the upper end of Profile Notch. Parties proceeding generally by motor return to North Woodstock and proceed thence up the valley of the Pemigewasset.

Four miles north of North Woodstock the traveler reaches Indian Head, in the town of Lincoln, near the southern end of Franconia Notch and about a mile south of the entrance to the Flume.

It is one of those natural formations in the rocks which Fredericka Bremer must have meant in her mention of the peculiarities of the region.

The highway passes a small cleared space where there is a refreshment stand, and usually a few small bears tethered to stumps in the ground, and one of the locally encouraged pastimes is giving the bears a concoction sold at the booth as "Bear Special." For the better part of a mile along the road the Indian head is visible against the Western sky, along the southern slope of Mount Pemigewasset, though the best view is obtainable from the steel tower (fee) moved from Apthorp in 1921. The tower also yields surpassing views of the Franconia Range, walling the valley in to the eastward.

Except the Profile, few of the formations supposed to resemble human or animal forms so definitely live up to expectations. The face against the sky is that of a head slightly reclining in "stoical repose" and it gazes down the valley. In former days, though the resemblance to an Indian head was marked, its perfection was marred by a growth of trees near the southern extremity, or chin. In 1901 this growth was burned off in a forest fire, so the head emerged, cleanly shaven, and perfect in its outlines.

Chief Pemigewasset is said to have used the summit of his name-mountain as lookout down the valley on a perpetual watch for tribal enemies. The actual measurements of the gigantic features are: 98 feet from forehead to chin; 17 feet across forehead (up and down, not breadth), 42 feet along the nose, and 23 feet along the upper lip, and 16 down the chin. The top of the head is 1,330 feet above the level of the highway.

This region was settled, apparently about the time North Woodstock was, by David Guernsey, or Garnsey, and his family. On the site of the souvenir store there was a block house where, in 1807, he and a number of others repulsed a bloody attack by the Abenaki Indians. Chronicles say that ultimately in these small battles all but twelve of the Abenakis were killed, and they moved to Canada, whence their more peaceful descendants come now and then on gentle missions of selling souvenirs to the passersby. When the block-house was torn down in 1892 by Guernsey's grandson, arrow heads were found lodged in the walls.

It was Guernsey's removal from Plymouth which led, incidentally, to the discovery of the next point of interest along the road, the Flume, by his wife. She was, according to all reports, a native of Dublin, who moved, at the age of 93, to this spot with her husband and lived hereabouts to the hearty age of 108.

Though credited by later tellers of the tale with certainly excusable senile dementia, she had wits enough about her to know that the Flume was something extraordinary, and when she found it one day while wandering, or perhaps fishing in the woods, she reported it to the family, and it soon became the center of great interest. As many as three thousand persons have visited it in a day.

Near the Flume is the Pool, a large cauldron-shaped formation in the Pemigewasset River, which can be reached by a short path off the main highway just north of the Flume restaurant. The river falls into a basin about forty feet deep and approximately a hundred feet across. The water leaps over a rocky cascade, churned by many fragments, and the whole is surrounded by high cliffs which cast the scene into heavy gloom, lightened, on a bright day, by the glint of sun on foliage above. It seems oppressively quiet, in spite of the noise of the waters, as if some secret wood cult kept here a shrine of silence, which casts its spell upon those who penetrate this weird fastness in the rocks.

Although the Flume is reached first by the road going

north it is worth the short retracing of steps to see it after
visiting the Pool. It, too, lies on the east side of the road, a
short distance away on Flume Brook, which runs through a
narrow gorge, and presents one of the most interesting sights
in the whole region, a natural pass whose peaceful aspect
thinly veils the violence with which the rock was sundered
to create it.

A private carriage road, on which automobiles are prohibited, turns off the main highway to the right at the site
of the old Flume House and runs about half a mile to the
lower end of the Flume, where there is a souvenir store, and
where parties start up the short walk into the canyon. The best
time of day to visit the place is in the morning, and visitors
should carry light wraps against the dampness.

This fissure is simply a huge gash in the side of Mount
Flume, about 700 feet long over its greatest extent and
flanked by sheer perpendicular walls ranging from fifty to
seventy feet in height and separated along the whole length
by distances of from twelve to twenty feet.

Flume Brook, which makes a charming cascade at the
upper end, particularly worth seeing after heavy rains, runs
through the gorge leaving narrow ledges of rock, as a natural
footpath, along one side.

At first the almost level rock is covered by a thin sheet
of water, as if it were wrapped in gelatin paper, that glistens
as it moves in almost unrippled transparency. As the corridor
narrows the visitor takes to a narrow plank walk along the
side, over the rock between the high walls that are covered
with moss and dank growth, over which water from the top

© *Moosilauke Studio*

Franconia Notch from Forest Hills Hotel

Profile Lake and Eagle Cliff

seeps in thin patches. The effect is fascinating and the scene full of a weird beauty.

Near the upper end and across the narrowest part a huge boulder was wedged until the great slide of 1883, when an avalanche caused by a cloudburst on Mount Liberty swept through the gorge, and littered the lower end with a mass of débris, thereby upsetting Starr King's rhapsodic prediction, made only thirteen years before, concerning this great egg-shaped boulder "As unpleasant to look at, if the nerves are irresolute, as the sword of Damocles, and yet held by a grasp out of which it will not slip for centuries."

Returning to the highway the journey proceeds again northward, past the little path leading to the Pool, over a bridge where the road crosses the Pemigewasset. About a mile and a half beyond the Flume house site is the Basin, at the juncture of Cascade Brook and the main stream. Enthusiasts would have all visitors approach the Basin from the cascades above it, though the process may be a little trying for casual visitors. The small stream foams down a series of bright falls and over level rocks to the pool which was rubbed in the rocks, no doubt, by the violent erosion of boulders when the streams were larger and avalanches more frequent.

It is a deep pit worn in the solid granite beneath the ledge, about fifty feet in diameter and perhaps twelve feet deep. The bottom is strewn with smooth round rocks, worn by ages of movement, and on the lower rim, where the water runs out, is a curious indention in the rock strikingly like the impression of a gigantic foot.

Two miles farther along the highway is Lonesome Lake

Clearing, or Lafayette Place, from which superb views of the south face of Cannon Mountain, guardian of the western side of the Notch, across from Mount Lafayette, and from whose southeast wall the Old Man of the Mountain keeps his unceasing vigil.

From Lafayette Place a path leads to Lonesome Lake, formerly called Tamarack Pond, a small sheet of water, where Cascade Brook rises, and from whose shores magnificent views of the range on the eastern side of the Notch may be had. The lake is 2,750 feet above sea level, and lies on the southern ribs of Mount Cannon. The best views may be obtained from the southwest shore.

The ascent to the lake is gentle and along a well-graded path, and towards the top the cliffs on the other side of the river begin to rear their heads above the surroundings. To the left Mount Lafayette and Mount Lincoln range upwards, while to the south of them Mount Liberty holds the skyline in majestic panorama. It is the first vantage point on this upward trip presenting the splendors of distant peaks, and it gives an accurate idea of the narrow gorge, beyond which the range lifts in blue-gray solemnity. The immense solitude of the little tarn, ringed by heavy forest, imparts at once the feeling of the whole region, and accents particularly the remoteness which gives the lake its name. W. C. Prime once owned a cabin on the lake, visited often by General McClellan.

We go back to the highway and continue, as the vast walls of the Notch come closer together to form at last the huge gateway to the north. A few miles farther along we approach

Profile Lake, with Cannon Mountain on the left, and Mount Lafayette on the right. Here we see one of the most beautiful vistas of the region, where Eagle Cliff juts out like a huge promontory from Lafayette, of which it is a great spur, though it is partly separated from the mountain by a ravine. From the clearing the cliff is supposed to resemble a recumbent elephant. The Cliff, which derives its name from the fact that eagles, long since departed, used to nest high up on its crags, is 3,466 feet above sea level. From Profile House site, which it closely approaches, it presents a mighty screen for sunset colors, and when low hanging clouds cast their shadows over its face, the effect is magnificent.

From a point near Profile Lake the precipitous walls of Cannon Mountain disclose one of the sights for which the region is noted everywhere—the Profile, or Old Man of the Mountain, a vast stone visage which has been immortalized by Hawthorne in the story bought by Whittier for "The National Era" for twenty-five dollars, and rhapsodized over by all who have ever seen this gigantic physiognomy thrust out in splendid calm from the sheer wall of the mountain.

Before standing in either awe or skepticism before it, it is well to take our bearings. Profile Lake, formerly Ferrin's Pond, and "Old Man's Washbowl," to the left of the main road, is nearly surrounded by forests, and it is worth the visitor's while to row out to get the effect of the surrounding hills. Behind lies the range which flanks the Notch to the eastward, and beyond, past Echo Lake, are a few lower summits from which, presently, we may look back down the Notch upon one of the grand vistas of the whole region.

The effect of the great Profile naturally depends, as does any beauty that lies in the eye of the beholder, upon the vision of the visitor, but certainly none can gainsay the somehow unbelievable fact that here are carved out the inescapable features of a man.

"Men," said a boastful commentator quoted by Dr. Willey, "put out signs representing their different trades; jewelers hang out a monster watch; shoemakers, a huge boot; and, up in Franconia, God Almighty has hung out a sign that in New England He makes men."

Against its majestic wonder there has been, of record, only one voice lifted and that by the usually susceptible, and previously quoted Swedish novelist, Fredericka Bremer. After spending some time in the mountains, as part of her tour of the United States in 1851, she wrote:

"The peculiarity of these so-called White Mountains is the gigantic human profiles which, in many places, look out from the mountains with a precision and perfect regularity of outline which is quite astonishing. They have very much amused me, and I have sketched several of them in my rambles. We have our quarters here (Lafayette House—built in 1835 and destroyed by fire in 1911) very close to one of these countenances which has long been known under the name of the "Old Man of the Mountain." It has not any nobility in its features, but resembles an old man in a bad humor and with a nightcap on his head, who is looking out from the mountain half inquisitive. Far below the old giant's face is an enchanting little lake, resembling a bright oval toilet-glass, inclosed in a verdant frame of leafage. The Old Man of the Mountain looks out gloomily over this quiet lake, and the clouds float far below his chin."

The first published account of the Profile was in the American Journal of Science and Arts, for July, 1828, when General Martin Field contributed a short letter describing the phenomenon.

Though it is little known, another literary tribute to the remarkable visage is contained in "Christus Judex," a legendary tale by Edward Roth, which tells of the search of an Italian painter Casola for a suitable model for the face of Christ for an altar piece portraying Christ in judgment. After vain searches the painter at last hears that a dying missionary told of having seen such a face in a mountain wilderness in America, where he had preached among the Indians. Visiting the spot, Casola found the fulfillment of his vision.

Cannon Mountain, whose scarred sides produce this startling silhouette, is 4,107 feet above sea level, and takes its name from another peculiar natural formation which graces its summit, a stone so arranged horizontally that from the site of the former hotel it suggests the form of a cannon. Climbers who take the path, plainly marked by a sign to the northwest of the hotel site, will be rewarded by superb views. The trail is steep for more than a mile, and comes out through a growth of low fir, to the lower summit, at a height of 3,898 feet. From there another trail leads northeast over the ledges to the Cannon, affording an excellent vantage point.

Mr. Ward has attested to the beauties from this eminence in lyrical ecstasy; though he managed to control himself:

"The cliff is bare and almost white on the tiptop. There is an unfettered sweep of the wind, and one could realize up here in a storm what it is to be where the winds exhaust their strength The view is best down the valley and over toward the side of Mount Lafayette. There is a charm about the Pemigewasset Valley as it stretches out at the south which grows upon one the longer he stays in it. One sees nothing but wooded hills, and the feeling of absolute wildness, necessary to enjoy the mountain scenery to the full, is constantly called forth. A few rods below is the Profile of the Old Man of the Mountain, but it is not safe to go near enough to make his familiar acquaintance. He is an unfeeling, old weather-beaten character, and was never known to exert himself to save one who had lost his footing in coming too near him. The keenest enjoyment here is to lie on the bare cliffs, and let the rest of the world take care of itself."

The Profile is the chief feature of the region, or (barring the pun) the chief features. It is on the upper ledges of the mountain, some 1,200 feet above the surface of the lake, and it was discovered, according to all available records, in 1805 by Francis Whitcomb and Luke Brooks, two road workmen who noticed the face while washing their hands in the lake. Legends claim that it was worshipped by the Indians as some deity of the mountains, but the contention, while plausible, is without support.

The original discoverers thought it looked like Thomas Jefferson, who was then president, and certainly there is more than contemporary political allegiance to support the claim.

The Profile is best seen about four in the afternoon in summer. It is composed of three separate masses of rock, and from the point on the road, about a quarter of a mile away from the face, the component parts are distinguishable, one forming the forehead, the middle layer forming nose and upper lip, and the third the chin. Only at one particular place, readily found by the natural laws of perspective, if no other way is handy, are they brought into proper relation. Any movement from the spot distorts the countenance, and in moving down the road it becomes as Oakes says in his "Scenery of the White Mountains," "a toothless old woman in a mob cap." The length of the Profile, from forehead to chin, is about eighty feet, somewhat less than Hawthorne's exuberant description in "Twice-told Tales."

"It seemed," he said, "as if an enormous giant, or Titan, had sculptured his own likeness on the precipice. There was the broad arch of the forehead, a hundred feet in height; the nose with its long bridge; and the vast lips, which, if they could have spoken, would have rolled their thunder accents from one end of the valley to the other."

There is an incontestable grandeur about his grim and craggy old face whose expression, depending somewhat on the time of day, is not of fatigue so much as of noble serenity, touched with a certain vague melancholy.

Mr. King becomes quite clinical on the subject:

"The upper portion of the mouth looks a little weak,

as though the front teeth had decayed and the granite lip had consequently fallen in." It must have been a monstrous toothache.

"Those who can see it with a thundercloud behind," he continues, after this impertinent interruption, "and the slaty scud of sky driving thin across it, will carry away the grandest impression which it ever makes on the beholder's mind. But when, after an August shower, late in the afternoon, the mists that arise from the forest below congregate around it, and, smitten with sunshine, break as they drift against its nervous outline, and hiding the mass of the mountain which over-hangs, isolate it with a thin halo, the countenance, awful but benignant, is 'as if a mighty angel were sitting among the hills, and enrobing himself in a cloud vesture of gold and purple.' "

Though the Old Man of the Mountain was originally a work of nature it has been preserved from nature's own de-struction by civilization in what was probably the largest face-lifting operation ever done. Several years ago it was dis-covered that the ledges which compose the profile were in danger of slipping off down into the lake below to the great detriment of the Old Man's physiognomy. By great ingenuity, however, and at no little hazard, chains were imbedded in the rocks which threatened by sliding to destroy the famous pro-file so that they are now safely anchored to the main ledges of Mt. Cannon. The account of this public-spirited enterprise is printed in a little pamphlet by Guy Roberts entitled: "The Profile and How It was Saved."

Leaving the Old Man gazing thus sadly out across the

lake in his ancient meditations we move a little further on to
Echo Lake, "the only sheet of water that nestles near any one
of the higher White Mountains."

Those who distrust the guardians of such phenomena all
over the world will have here a chance to vent their incredulity
to their hearts' content. If they doubt the Whispering Gallery
in Washington, or suspect that the implacable Italian guide
to the Baptistery in Pisa really has an accomplice hidden in
the dome to toss back his jovial (for a price) yohoos, here is
their picnic. For at that rate Echo Lake must have a whole
battalion of mocking mimics at its call.

Let us dip, if not into its chill waters, at least into Mr.
King's warmer vocabulary:

"See what colors or forms it is stained with or hides!
The little segment of beach it repeats. The rocks around it it
sets below as part of the wall of its under stillness. The climbing trees and the shadow of the steep shore make a large section of its borders dim with dusky green. The sky hues, blue
or gray, brilliant or sober, dull or joyous, it clothes itself with.
It answers to the temper of the wind, with smiling ripples,
or slaty churlishness, or heaving petulance. It is glad in the
colors of sunrise, and pensive as the flames of sunset cool in
the west. . . . It takes the moods of the mountain, woods,
and firmament into its own being, softly flashes their joy, or is
saturated with their grief, and repeats to them their experience, as the heart of a friend returns the color of our fortunes and our moods."

Some will say that it is best seen in the afternoon and
others in the morning. Certainly the morning, if early enough,

yields its special glories as the valley mists rise and catch the shimmering light across the surface of the lake.

But for once, in these matters, and in spite of the beauties of the views, here is a curiosity that, unlike children, must be heard and not seen.

WATERVILLE

Perhaps the inevitably accurate guide book could be written only for a Ferris Wheel which is guaranteed to start and stop at the same place and hold its parties intact until they are dismissed. But roads lead everywhere, notches have two ends, and all travelers are of various minds. If these pages are headed north and it is the reader's wish to go south go south he shall, if possible, without stripping these typographical gears. Nor need he, like Hamlet's crab, move backward, since each section is treated, where possible, from a local center, so that those who wish to reverse the order of the book will find the whole grouped under appropriate headings in the index.

Thus the Waterville section is included in this chapter operating out of North Woodstock, so the traveler can take it going up or coming down at his convenience.

For true mountain connoisseurs there is no more delightful and charming region in the mountains than the Waterville Valley, which may be reached by a good dirt road from West Campton, about fourteen miles south of North Woodstock. The road follows the Mad River for about fifteen miles to the Waterville Inn, situated at an elevation of 1,500 feet at the bottom of the great bowl made by the encircling Waterville Mountains from Tecumseh (4,008 feet) on the west to Sandwich Mountain (3,999 feet) on the south. Waterville is one of those isolated one-man townships which Ethan Allen Crawford tells about so amusingly in his history as sending their only citizen to represent them in the legislature. It was first settled about 1820. "By 1831," Mr. A. L. Goodrich tells us in "The Waterville Valley Guide" published in 1916, "seventeen poll taxes were assessed and twenty acres of improved land taxed, but the cold rocky soil of this high, northern valley offered few inducements for farming and by 1833 eleven of the seventeen men, two of the three horses, and four of the fourteen cows had disappeared." It is doubtful if the present permanent population exceeds the population of 1833 but the summer popularity of this picturesque pocket in the mountains may be indicated by the account of the opening in 1860 of the first hotel, operated by Nathaniel Greeley, who, as long ago as 1833 had begun to take summer boarders. At this opening there were a thousand people present, forming a procession two miles long.

That hotel burned but its present-day successor is the Waterville Inn and cottages operated by the Waterville Valley Association. This association, together with the A.M.C., keeps over thirty miles of path cleared in the valley. The circle of mountains from Tecumseh to Sandwich Mountain includes Osceola (4,352 feet), Tripyramid (a long mountain with three peaks, the highest of which is 4,189 feet), and Whiteface (4,057 feet). The whole region is now a part of the National Forest. For the confirmed tramper there are a U. S. Forest trail through the Waterville Gap to North Woodstock (fourteen miles) and the A.M.C. Livermore Trail to Mount Carrigain and the Crawford Notch. The distance of this latter trail from the Waterville Inn to the Sawyer River Station of the Maine Central in Crawford Notch is about fifteen miles.

But we return to the ordered route of this journey and resume our course at the head of Notch, to examine with some special attention, the contours of Mount Lafayette.

CHAPTER III

LAFAYETTE—TRAILS AND SUMMIT

MOUNT LAFAYETTE is the lesser Washington of the White Mountains, the dominant peak of the Franconia Range, whose summit rises 5,269 feet, or within an approximate thousand of its greater neighbor. Standing at the northern end of the wall which flanks the Pemigewasset on the east its eminence affords magnificent views to the south, looking down the valley toward Plymouth, to the east and south to the Sandwich group, where Chocorua lifts its spire-like crest, to the majesty of Mount Washington north of them. The Green Mountains rim the horizon to the west, and in the north may be seen the Canada hills. Nearer at hand, the peak provides a close-up of the scarred sides of Cannon Mountain across the Notch, and immediately south of Lafayette soars the peak of Lincoln, to a height of 5,098 feet. For this immediate region Lafayette is the top of the world. Until 1824-25 when General Lafayette made a visit to the United States, the mountain was called Great Haystack. Little Haystack lies beyond Lincoln.

Three trails lead to the summit, one from the Profile House site, where once stood one of the great hotels of the region, the other over the Franconia Ridge from the south, and the third, the Garfield Ridge trail, from the northeast.

Since the first is the shortest from the highway, and therefore probably more appealing to those making the general trip by motor, it will be the route of this guide, though both the others offer special beauties to more energetic climbers who approach Lafayette from the surrounding mountains.

From a point opposite the former Profile House tennis courts the Greenleaf Trail leads east and enters the woods, descending gently until it crosses a brook, where the ascent begins by easy stages up the zigzag paths of Eagle Cliff. This path is named for the late Col. C. H. Greenleaf, and has been taken over by the Appalachian Mountain Club, which has already made many improvements.* The distance to the summit over the trail is nearly four miles, and should be covered in about three and a half hours.

The path continues under the frowning bulk of Eagle Cliff and affords not only a glimpse of the Profile but some very charming views of the Notch. In the configuration of the land Eagle Cliff stands out from Lafayette, with a gorge between, broken by a smaller spur, with some interesting rock formations and great caves. In a generally easterly direction the trail moves through the pass, and after a good level stretch begins precipitately the hard pull across the steep slope on the northwest flank of the mountain. Many loose stones impede the way, and in wet weather afford extremely insecure footing. A mile above the pass there is a spring, ten yards to the left of the trail.

"Half a mile farther up the mountain," says the inde-

---

* The A.M.C. has just completed a large hut on the shores of the Eagle Lakes, a mile and a quarter below the summit, which will probably be open for the accommodation of trampers beginning with the season of 1930.

fatigable Mr. Ward, "I found myself near one of the sources of the Ammonoosuc, which was roaring from the depths of a chasm that lay a thousand feet below where I was ascending. The overhanging spurs of Mount Lafayette glistened in the morning sunshine" [with Mark Twain you are supposed to arise early for this business of the mountains] "where the springs had moistened the lichened crags and no vegetation hide their nakedness. The path now began to show the severity of the climate. The timber line grew less and less, and the stunted spruces and the courageous birches began to hand over their sway to the hardier vegetation. Next the scrub spruces showed their scraggy heads, as much to say, 'We have a hard time of it too, but we never give up.' By this time I had arisen above the spur which reaches out of the Notch and overhangs the carriage road that passes through it. I could now see where I was. The Pemigewasset Valley stretched out below like a part of paradise, and the half-clothed peaks of Lafayette and its adjoining mountains commanded the horizon. Mount Cannon with its summit looking like a man's face covered with scabs, lifted up its huge front, but did not conceal the other peaks rising up in its rear. Away beyond its reach to the southwest rose the apparently round-topped Moosilauke, concealing the Connecticut Valley over which it stands sentinel. Snugly ensconced in the embrace of Mount Cannon lay Lonesome Lake" [for which Mr. Ward has a special and rhetorical fondness] "looking as if it were the child of the wilderness as indeed it was. Climbing up through the scrub you come out upon the bare peak, where the Greenland sandwort makes the spaces between the rocks look like an Alpine garden. Here the ruggedness of the mountain is every moment more impressive. You go up a few rods and look back only to find that the world is constantly growing larger behind you.

"At last you come up to the tiny spring that oozes out from the last cliff below the crown of the peak." [Actually about 300 yards.] "Presently I resumed my course to the brow of the mountain. The view for the day was not the best one could have desired, but you have to be satisfied with what you can get when you make these ventures." [An admirable psychology for any undertaking in the mountains.] "The mountains have no resources for displays to order. You take them as you find them, and it is this or nothing. But the view is simply grand, even when you cannot see Mount Washington, and Mount Mansfield is hidden in the haze."

Mr. Ward's philosophical acceptance of defeat at the hands of the elements is touching, but not altogether convincing to one, frailly typical, perhaps, of all climbers, who rail at the unfairness to those who struggle up to a peak only to find themselves shut out from the striking features of the view. An amateur can only attest to the profundity of curses laid upon those thick vapors which have, upon a time, swirled up the gorges of the Alps to hide the Jungfrau, or the Matterhorn, or suddenly dropped impenetrably before Mount Washington. You might as well pretend that it makes no difference if the curtain does not go up on the play. Decorous tourists will put the best face possible upon their disappointment, but let them feel that it is a disappointment. If their tempers are bad, let them assure themselves in advance of a clear day.

© *George F. Slade*

Paradise Falls, Lost River

The Old Man of the Mountains

When the climber has caught his breath, lost either by the exertion of the ascent or the first gasp over the view, he will find it profitable before looking too closely at the panorama, to study his own position, and the contours of Lafayette.

The summit is a thin ridge, sloping off abruptly into wide chasms, and along it runs a peculiar narrow indention, which is supposed to have been caused by the feet of many animals passing along the ridge. From the north and south sides of the main peak narrow ridges extend, that on the north to a distance of about half a mile, where it terminates in a subordinate peak, rising to a height of 5,075 feet. On the right is White Cross Ravine, of which superb views may be had.

From the map it is easy enough to assemble the panoramas and identify the better known mountains, as soon as the general bearings are taken. Out of the apparent confusion details slowly impress themselves on the overwhelmed vision, shapes stand out, lines are carefully followed to indicate distances beyond which other mountains pile up, and presently the whole picture yields its familiar features.

It is well to make, at first, a casual and comprehensive survey on all points of the compass, seizing upon obvious landmarks and working from them later as each section is examined more carefully. Naturally the first point to be sought is Washington, which lies to the northeast beyond the Twin Range, its great dome appearing over the nearer Twin Range. On clear days the house is visible, as are also the railway tracks.

Turning through about 35 degrees and facing southeast the observer will find at once the dominant spire-like summit of Chocorua, white and solitary. Directly south are Haystack and Liberty, and the Pemigewasset Valley. To the southwest, a little to the left of the nearer Kinsman, may be seen the long bulk of Moosilauke. To the west Mount Cannon breaks the expanse with its nearby summit, but beyond its north flank is Sugar Hill, and northeast of Sugar Hill, on an almost direct northerly line from Lafayette is Mount Agassiz. This completes the circle of the horizon, and permits a more careful survey of individual features.

Looking again in the direction of Mount Washington, but nearer at hand, the observer will find a little to the left of a straight line between Lafayette and Washington the conelike summit of Garfield (4,519) about two-thirds of a mile distant. Beyond Mount Garfield, and slightly to the right, or east of it, may be seen the Twin Mountains. Still further off, and almost directly east of Lafayette two peaks stand well above the immediate hills. The more northerly of the two is Mount Guyot, 4,589 feet, and the other is Mount Bond, 4,709 feet.

A little to the left of Guyot's summit is Mount Willey (4,260) southernmost of five peaks which flank the Saco River on the west side of Crawford Notch. Mount Tom, as seen from Lafayette, is at the other end of the chain, and between the two is the peak of Mount Field (4,300).

Beyond this chain is the Presidential Range, with Mount Webster visible over the flank of Willey, Mount Clinton slightly to the north, and over Field, Mount Pleasant over the south Twin, while to the left of Pleasant may be descried Franklin, dominated by the higher crest of Monroe. Piled behind them is Washington, and to the left of Washington Mount Clay, distinguished by its rolling humps, and Jefferson, with a faint gash in its peak. To the left of Jefferson is the eminence of Mount Adams, though its lower part is hidden behind the ridges on the southwest.

A little to the right of a line on Mount Willey is Crawford, 3,100 feet in height, and to the left of Crawford is Stairs Mountain, the highest peak of its immediate region. Between Crawford and Stairs is Mount Resolution. Slightly to the right of Crawford is the flat top of Iron Mountain, while in a line directly over Mount Bond, and over the right of Iron Mountain, is Kearsarge or Pequaket.

Slightly to the right of Crawford and nearer is Mount Bemis at the northeast end of a short chain composed, in the order of their appearance, of Bemis (3,710), Nancy (3,810), Anderson (3,725), Lowell (3,780), Vose Spur (3,855) and Carrigain (4,647).

Over the notch of the pyramidal Mount Lowell may be seen the north peak of Moat Mountain, and Tremont and Bear Mountains are between Moat and Carrigain, as they appear on this flattened panorama.

Next to Carrigain, and almost in line with Chocorua, is Mount Hancock, and next it, though further off is Kancamagus, over whose left flank is Passaconaway. Next in line is Tripyramid, and then Whiteface. To the right, but nearer Kancamagus, is Osceola, over whose right flank may be seen the long ridge of the Sandwich Mountain, formerly called Sandwich Dome, and Black Mountain. Nearer Osceola, and on its right, is Mount Tecumseh, where the hills fall away until another segment of the great circumference soars again with the view almost directly south.

This view, composed across the majestic contours of Haystack and Liberty, embraces Mount Flume and the immediate valley of the Pemigewasset and runs off on its southernmost rim to the Ragged Mountains and Monadnock. Toward Moosilauke in the southwest, but much nearer, is Mount Pemigewasset on the west side of Franconia Notch. Above it, moving the range of vision northward, is Kinsman, and on the long slope lies the twinkling surface of Lonesome Lake.

On the right of Eagle Cliff, which here juts out across the view, is a part of Echo Lake, and still further to the right, beyond the north flank of Mount Cannon, is Sugar Hill, and over it the hills of Lyman and Hunt's Mountain of the Gardner range. Far beyond is Camel's Hump in Vermont, and to the right of Hunt's Mountain, and still farther off, is Mount Mansfield. Next in the shifting panorama spread out beneath this great vantage point come the pretty, swelling valleys of the Gale and Ammonoosuc, the former turning almost at right angles at Franconia village, of which a small part may be seen, with a long stretch of the Littleton road.

The remaining sector embraces the northerly horizon, and the view is across the agreeable variety of the valley of Gale River to Mount Agassiz (2,401 feet), and to the right of it Mount Cleveland. Beyond the valley of the Ammonoosuc in the narrow strip of land between that river and the Connecticut are a few low hills, Morse Hill, Dalton, and even farther are the Dixville peaks.

To the right of Mount Agassiz and much nearer is Beech

© *George F. Slade*

Mount Lafayette from Sugar Hill

Echo Lake, Franconia Notch

Hill, in Bethlehem, while to the north-northeast is Mount Starr King, Cherry Mountain and the Pilot Mountains.

This completes the circuit of the skyline. Motorists unwilling to continue the ventures across the ridge return to the highway. More ambitious climbers may prefer to follow the trail either to the north or south along the ridge. To the north the Garfield Ridge trail traverses the sharp crest that joins Lafayette to South Twin Mountain, winds to the northeast, after passing the subordinate peak (5,075 feet) and descends to the timber line. After some descent the trail climbs gradually, passing, near the foot of the cone, Garfield Pond.

"Here the Garfield Pond Cut-off diverges to the left," says the Appalachian Mountain Club Guide, "passes the outlet of the Pond and in about three-quarters of a mile reaches the United States Forest Service Mount Garfield trail. At the east end of the Pond a side trail diverges to the right for about 150 yards to the old Garfield Pond Shelter built by the A.M.C. in 1917 and accommodating six persons. The old shelter is still usable, but a new one was built in 1925, several hundred feet nearer the Pond. It accommodates eight or ten. Elizabeth Spring lies near the Pond. The trail then climbs the cone to within a few rods of the bare summit, which is reached by a short side path to the right. At this junction the direct trail of the U. S. Forest Service to the state highway forks to the left. Continuing, the Garfield trail descends to the northeast and east to avoid some bad ledges directly east of the cone."

Mount Garfield is 4,519 feet in height and until 1881 was known as one of the Franconia Haystacks, or simply as Haystack. In that year, when President Garfield was assassinated, its name was changed by the selectmen of Franconia. Excellent views may be obtained from the summit, which is quite bare.

Particularly fine views of the Notch may be obtained from Artist Bluff and Bald Mountain, situated closely together to the northwest of Echo Lake, and hence commanding not only superb vistas of the country to the northward, but offering a splendid vantage point for the range down the Valley of the Pemigewasset.

From the Profile House site, up Bald Mountain, and across to Artist Bluff, returning by the shore of Echo Lake the whole trip is about three miles. The path begins where a road joins the highway on the left fork beyond Echo Lake. About half a mile along the cart-road a path diverges to the left and ascends through open woods, for about an eighth of a mile to the summit. To return by way of Artist Bluff retrace the path to the cart-path, turn to the left on this, and then follow a path to the right leading southeast. It runs about a quarter of a mile to the summit of the bluff, from which the descent is made down the south slope to the road at the north end of Echo Lake.

As the point of departure by motor into the upper country beyond Franconia Notch, Echo Lake marks the divergence of the road. Midway on its west shore the road divides, the Daniel Webster Highway continuing along the shore of the lake, crosses several small streams running into Gale River, and follows more or less closely the route on the abandoned railroad branch which used to run to Bethlehem and upon which, in this 1930 moment, there is a plan to build a new highway. Beyond Abbot Hill, where the highway crosses Gale River proper is a Public Camp Ground. The highway continues east, and the road which branches off near the camp ground almost at a right angle, goes north to Bethlehem Junction, through Maplewood, and to Bethlehem, one of the chief tourist centers of the region.

The road to the left at Echo Lake leads down the Three Mile Hill into Franconia, one of the most famous and picturesque of White Mountain villages, which lies along the broad meadow at the foot of the Franconia Range through which the Gale River, taking its rise on the northern slopes of Mount Lafayette and the Twins, makes its way. From Franconia Village a road to the right leads to Bethlehem; the way straight through the village leads to Littleton; turning sharply to the left just beyond the picturesque ruins of the Franconia Iron Works the road rises sharply to Sugar Hill.

Sugar Hill, which can also be approached by a beautifully winding road from the Ammonoosuc Valley at Lisbon, has perhaps the most magnificent views of the Franconia and Presidential Ranges in the mountains. Its high altitude (over 1,600 feet) and its closeness to the Franconia Range make the view of Lafayette, Cannon, and Kinsman to the east particularly impressive. Twenty-five miles to the northeast is the blue sweep of the Presidential Range. The Look-off, at the highest point, the Sunset Hill House, with the wide expanse of sloping field before it affording a foreground for its superb view, and Pecketts-on-Sugar Hill, which was one of the first hotels to cater to winter custom, are three of the best known hotels in the mountains.

CHAPTER IV

BETHLEHEM AND VICINITY

IN A modest pamphlet of 1880 entitled: "The White Mountain Village of Bethlehem as a Resort for Health and Pleasure," the author records his indebtedness to "The White Mountain Echo" and its accomplished editor, Mr. Markenfield Addey, "for almost the whole of the chapter on railroads, steamer, and other methods of approach to Bethlehem."

"The number of routes by which Bethlehem may be reached," begins the accomplished Mr. Addey, "are so numerous that the tourist is liable to labor under what the French style an *embarras des richesses*. Railroads from every direction seem to center in this neighborhood." He proceeds to list these converging railroads. To be sure, at the end of his chapter, he reveals the fact that no one of them comes nearer than three miles from Bethlehem proper and that the rest of one's journey must be by stage, but no matter: Mr. Addey in his chapter lists prominently nine different railroads (and taps the Grand Trunk) and five steamship lines (though one of them is on Lake Champlain) by which Bethlehem may be—approximately—reached. Happily, however, for the tourist of the nineteen thirties, the Interstate Commerce Commission and the motor car have done their work;

72

the waters have receded considerably, leaving Bethlehem Street at present high and dry (and there is ample evidence, as will perhaps later appear, that Bethlehem Street, fifty or one hundred years ago, could not boast of its present eminence above sea level); and Mr. Addey's chapter, therefore, has shrunk to a page or two: we can ignore the railroads and steamers, the other methods of approach will not detain us long.

For Bethlehem Junction (on the Boston and Maine's White Mountain Division between Woodsville and Fabyan) has become Bethlehem again and the spur line to Maplewood and the other line along the mountain-side up into the Franconia Notch, along which daily in summer a brave little engine chugged its way to the Profile House, have for years been discontinued. Shank's mare or the automobile, therefore, remain the usual methods of approach. And as we blithely coil in upon the mountains from the south, there are, roughly speaking, three ways of entering upon the long plateau known as Bethlehem Street.

One may take the lonely road from Echo Lake in the Franconia Notch to Twin Mountain and, branching off to the left (to follow the line of the abandoned railroad) enter Bethlehem from the east. Or one may take the road from Franconia Village which skirts the west slope of Mount Agassiz and come into the center of the Street. Or one may come up from the south, along the Ammonoosuc valley, through Bath, Lisbon, and Littleton and approach the Street from the west. This is the historical route, the one by which the settlers came and is, perhaps, the one we had better take since it gives us a chance to say something about Littleton, a village which oughtn't to go unmentioned in any respectable book of the White Mountains.

Littleton is a pleasant and lively village of several thousand people whose Main Street stretches along the Ammonoosuc River, now somewhat tamed after its turbulent descent off the western slope of Mount Washington. Roads lead abruptly up out of it on either side of the river and some of the most gorgeous views of the Franconias and the Presidential Peaks in the mountains can be had only a mile or two out from the Main Street, from the Skyline Cabin, say, of the Dartmouth Outing Club on the western side of the river or from Mount Eustis just above the village on the east.

From Littleton westward it is only a matter of twenty-five miles or so, across the Connecticut and through the town of Waterford to St. Johnsbury, the metropolis of northeastern Vermont. And if the traveler finds himself wandering in this direction or approaching the White Mountains, perchance, from Vermont, he cannot do better than to turn aside for a couple of hours at the Connecticut and visit the Lower Development of Fifteen Miles Falls, at present probably the largest power development in New England. The Connecticut River, in these fifteen miles, drops some three hundred and seventy feet and the drop is to be divided between the upper and the lower dam. The lower dam, at East Barnet, Vermont, and North Monroe, New Hampshire, is to be opened in October, 1930. Its height is about one hundred and seventy feet and it stretches across the Connecticut, an enormous mass of solidly packed earth on the New Hampshire side, a bulwark of white concrete on the Vermont side, where the bed-rock granite was close enough to the surface to permit of sinking the concrete wall into it. From the distributing station at the foot of the dam a double row of steel towers in the best modernistic manner carries the high tension wires (of 220,000 voltage) along a straight slit through the woods up and over the long Gardner Range that divides the Connecticut from the Ammonoosuc River, to Concord and the South. The figures as to kilowatts, horsepower, and tons of material stagger the mind in quite the most up-to-date fashion: the curious traveler, statistically inclined, can get them all from the offices of the New England Power Association on the Vermont side of the dam.

Nor is this all. An upper dam is projected, several miles up the river, in height equal to the lower one. This dam will impound the waters of the Connecticut in a reservoir which will be, in effect, a long artificial lake some miles in extent, burying roads and here and there a hamlet or so in the manner of such developments. But this, for two such guides as we, nostalgic of the past, is compounding far too much with the mere mechanics of modern civilization. Already the spirits of the Rev. Starr King and the Rev. Simeon Bolles are rustling in their graves. We must snatch ourselves back to Littleton, like a child's rubber ball at the end of an elastic, before the night descends and catches us in the hollow of the Connecticut with Bethlehem still on its plateau twenty miles away. . .

As one crosses the railroad track at Littleton for the Bethlehem road one passes a large apartment house on the right which was, some fifty years ago, the factory where were turned out those stereoscopic views that graced the parlors of all refined homes before the movies broke up the home. The authorities tell us that the manufacturers, the Kilburn Brothers, turned out every year over three hundred thousand stereoscopic views of American and foreign scenery. And this, too, in a day when word-painting was a much finer art than it is in ours.

But we are still bound for Bethlehem, five miles away. The road is for the most part a gradual ascent. (If one wants to take a little more time one can take the road to the right for Franconia and then branch back on to the Bethlehem highway through the beautiful roads of the Glessner estate. On each side of these roads—where they lie in the open—are huge stone walls which show the stuff of which the region is made; much of the way they lie through lovely woods.) Just before it reaches Bethlehem the road dips down into a little valley and . . . .

But let us substitute for our car, smoothly rolling off the miles on its speedometer, the more dignified advent of Lot Woodbury and his family who came hither in March, 1794, from Roylston, Massachusetts. (The Woodbury family departed from Roylston under a cloud, as it were; at least, their chronicler tells us that "no pleasing story was rehearsed or jovial language used, no merry peals of laughter or songs of mirthful import saluted the ear, but solemnity bended over this little group of anxious friends, for their hearts were sad and their eyes were filled with flowing tears." We wish we might dwell longer with the "bending solemnity" of this scene but, after all, our major concern—as it was Lot Woodbury's—is to get to Bethlehem, New Hampshire; we have no

© *Walter R. Merryman*

Mount Moosilauke Summit from South Peak

Moosilauke and Lake Tarleton

right, not even the right of history, to include Roylston, Massachusetts, within the purlieus of the White Mountains.) Well, then, let us imagine ourselves to have traversed in the mind Lot's long journey on the ox-sled, a journey "surrounded by the same general scenery . . . while the sameness of the teamster's voice and language, the likeness of the cries and prattling noise of the little ones and calm, soothing voice of the fond, careful mother all combined to make their long tedious journey a monotonous one." But—"in due time they reached the brook in the little valley about a mile west of Bethlehem Street" [and this is where we have joined them] "and began to ascend the hill. The oxen, weary and worn by the heavy load they had drawn and great distance they had come, moved on mindful of the fact that the end was near, but by much and constant urging with a vigorous given imperative command of 'Gee Star,' 'Haw Line,' or 'Wake up, my boy,' which awoke many slumbering echoes, the jaded team was induced to obey the driver's voice and to move on, stopping every four rods to rest. . . ."

Happy, perhaps, that town which has no history. Thrice happy that which has a historian like the Rev. Simeon Bolles. Halting the telepathic yet reluctant oxen, restraining the eager tourist of the twentieth century, about to catch his first glimpse of the Range from Bethlehem Street, we must perforce pause to pay tribute to Bethlehem's historian.

A clergyman, manifestly, and incidentally (by happy chance an advertisement in his history gives us this information) the concocter of "Nature's Own Remedy" for certain of the impoliter human ailments, the Rev. Simeon Bolles seems to have possessed a major historical talent—comparable, say, to that of Herodotus and not inferior to the Greek's in imaginative faculty—and a historical style modeled partly upon his own sermons and partly upon the narratives of J. Fenimore Cooper. "The style of writing may vary," he says in his preface, "but the facts presented lose none of their legitimate importance or interest." He is too modest: the variety of the style compensates completely for the relative scarcity of facts in his little work. To the genius of a Herodotus, then, to the style of a Cooper, the Rev. Simeon Bolles, so long ago as 1883, adds the speculative profundity of a Spengler. To illustrate adequately these phases of his three-fold talent we can do no otherwise than make extensive quotation from his first chapter.

"While some parts of our country," begins the Rev. Simeon Bolles, "are furnishing conclusive proof, in the form of mounds, fortifications and other relics of various kinds, that a race were dwellers in the Western World long before and superior to the red man in development, if not by nature, we have no proof that Bethlehem was ever inhabited or even known to exist by any human being prior to the existence of the North American Indian; and we fail to find conclusive evidence that the red man ever chose this spot for a permanent home. No doubt the uncultivated children of the forest (being lovers of nature), came at times to hunt and fish or to enjoy a few weeks of pleasure in nature's wild retreat, and it may be that these commodious structures that furnish pleasant homes for the many tourists who annually visit this lovely spot, have been erected on the same grounds that were once utilized by the red man on which to construct his wigwam. Who can say that on the same identical spot beneath the overhanging branches of some forest king, in twilight hour, a wood-nymph being the only witness, the dark-skinned warrior did not woo and win his dusky mate?

"While the mound builders were unconsciously making records that would reveal the fact to future generations that they once existed, that which is now Bethlehem was clothed with primeval upland grandeur beautified by nature's own adornments. No sound of the woodman's axe, no crack of the hunter's rifle, no merry laugh of happy children were heard and no familiar bell awoke the echoes of Sabbath morning calling the people to church. The morning and evening stars saw no change and setting sun bid adieu (not a final farewell), kissing tree-tops and hillside with his departing rays to greet them again on the morrow. Thus things continued without any essential change during periods of unknown length. Could an observer have been permitted to look upon this enchanting spot from his home on some planet far off in the regions in space, his thoughts might have been something like the following: 'Thou Invisible One! Why such lavish display of Thy creative power in that uninhabited region with gradual sloping grounds, more conspicuous elevations, plats and valleys covered with forest kings with giant forms interspersed with various specimens of the floral kingdom? No human beings enjoy the beauties of this favored spot for none are there. Why is it thus?' Echo repeats, 'Why?' and the sound dies away in ethereal space."

But not for long. (Here we must condense the clergyman's

logic somewhat.) It seems that, over the cycle of the centuries, a time had come in America when "crowded cities, close application to business and unhealthy climate necessitated rest, a change of scenery and atmosphere. While causes were creating a necessity for such a change, causes were preparing places where such changes could be obtained. Civilization was on the march. . . ."

In other words, the Creator was about to found in Bethlehem an asylum for all the sneezes of the world.

But enough of philosophic speculation—now for a lyric passage so that we may see what the Rev. Simeon Bolles can do at his best. For—

"At this point we leave the subject and go back to an earlier date in the history of the town.

"It was early dawn in the beautiful morning when the feathered tribe were stopped and startled in the midst of their early songs, wild beasts were disturbed in their lairs and old Bruin sat upon his haunches, while the nimble squirrel ascended to the top-most branch of some stately tree to understand, if possible, the meaning of those strange sounds and wonderful sights; but being new to them they could not solve the mystery, for they now beheld for the first time, the camp of the white man with its ascending smoke; they heard the sound of the woodman's axe as stroke after stroke was vigorously applied, and the meaning of all this was that the wild occupants of the forest could no longer hold undisputed sway over that part of nature's wild domain; and more, it was the precursor of important events, a link in the long chain of cause and effect by which the Creator governs the world. It

Franconia Notch from Artist's Bluff

The Cascades Above the Flume, Franconia Notch

was a harbinger of the day when Bruin must live a more retired life or retreat before the advancing tide . . ." [when
the necessary but abridging asterisks are deadly insults to our
historian's periods] . . . "when school and meeting houses
should dot the place, standing like so many guardian angels
to protect the best interests of society, when railroads, telegraph and telephone would connect this town with Boston
and other great cities, when Bethlehem Street would witness
the coming and going of the majestic iron horse" [and here
he becomes a prophet—how could he know, in 1883, about
its going?] "when this locality would become a theme of
conversation in all parts of the civilized world and thousands
be attracted hither by its natural scenery and the wonderful
power of its atmosphere to restore health to suffering invalids.
. . . Looking far back into the past and peering away into
the comparatively unknown future, who can define or limit
the resources and ability of Bethlehem to accommodate
guests, or the demand that shall be made upon her? Who can
tell what the ultimatum will be?"

Thus the first chapter. But we cannot quote the whole
history. We wish we could—this book would be so much the
better for it. We can only give you an inkling, here and there,
of the treasure lost to American literature because of the ob-
scurity of the author. . . . This picture, for instance, of the
interior of a cabin that over a hundred years ago "might have
been seen in Bethlehem": "no carpeted floors or walls adorned
with paint, paper or works of art, and no center table laden
with poems, histories or popular novels, organs and pianos
were alike strangers in this woodland but happy home. Now

additional joy has been added to former happiness and new pleasures suffuse the entire household. New hopes and fears have found a place in their meditations and conflicting emotions reveal their existence in looks and actions. Welcome sights greet the eyes of happy parents and pleasant scenes come like music to the ear. A babe was born. . . ." We have sneaked in thus, at unawares, the first birth in Bethlehem but we shall spare our readers the first death and the account of "the acquaintance which commenced at the junction of the two roads [and] finally ended [ambiguous phrase for a clergyman!] in marriage relations."

But here is a passage revelatory of the Rev. Simeon Bolles's lyric power and also of the sober organ tones of the dialogue of our ancestors:

"It was the month of June, bright stars were preparing to veil their nightly splendors and ajar were the warning gates through which, softly and silently, were creeping rays of mellow light—harbingers of coming day—when a man of medium size, with a knapsack strapped to his back and trusty gun on his shoulder, stepped upon the threshold of a small log cabin surrounded on all sides by primeval forests. He was strong and muscular, and care had left its mark on his honest but sunburnt face. His garments, though made of coarse material, showed the skill of well-trained hands; his hat, though somewhat worn, gave evidence of having seen better days. He stopped a moment, as if to speak to some one within, and then stepping forth into the open air, in a low tone soliloquized thus: 'It looks a little like rain. That belt of reddish color stretched across the eastern sky foretells a change in weather, or I have failed to read correctly signs that precede coming storms in this hilly region.' "

Our soliloquizer was not mistaken. Nevertheless, he had time to walk to the nearest grist mill at Bath (twenty-five miles away) and almost home again with a peck of corn meal on his back before the storm broke—a providential storm for our historian, who loved nothing better than a storm. But we will spare our readers this description, in which the lightning's vivid glare, howling wind, terrific thunder, giant trees, "the forest stripped of its foliage and hurled in all directions, broken branches filling the air with their mutilated forms," fell in a grand and sublime confusion upon our poor unfortunate's head—just as he "entered the humble cabin from which he came at early dawn." Or rather, we will save it: we may be in more urgent need of this description (or other meteorological masterpieces of Mr. Bolles) when later we find ourselves exposed to the elements on the Presidential Range.

But let us take shelter from the storm long enough, at least, to let Mr. Bolles's muse tell us something of the virtues of the early Bethlehemites. A young lady, for instance, of those days who could not "skillfully use the cards, convert toe and flax into yarn, weave it into cloth and make it into garments, patch, darn, or, milk a cow" was regarded as most inadequately prepared for life. Nor were the young men less industriously versatile. (And here we feel that the stern pastor was writing with one eye upon those pampered minions of the idle rich who, paradoxically enough, were even then making Bethlehem what she was in the eighties.) "No money-grasping misers, rich in land, stock and government bonds to domineer; no self-conceited petty tyrant to look upon the honest laboring class as mud-sills of society; no idlers infested those industrious homes. No dandy, with artificial polish, his lily-white hands covered with fancy colored kid gloves and clothed in all the styles belonging to his kind, was present to live on the earnings of honest toil, there being no necessity for that class of men." (This is the period, remember, which John Held, Jr., is immortalizing.) No, the early Bethlehemites were honest horny-handed sons of toil: "peaceful and quiet were their hours of slumber, undisturbed by those frightful demons that might arise from idleness, overeating too richly prepared food, or a conscience disturbed by many crimes."

And yet, alas!—did our clear-eyed historian perhaps suspect it, we wonder?—already a canker was nibbling at the rose. The social element, destined to be at once the town's immortal glory and her ultimate desolation, was insidiously at work, there among the rude cabins of the Street. In a magnificent passage whose wealth, even plethora, of metaphor leads one to guess that somewhere in the convolutions of the Rev. Simeon Bolles's brain hovered the specter of a premonitory dismay (or perhaps it was too richly prepared food) he describes the "social element" in Bethlehem in its earliest and purest manifestation. "When, at times," he says, "weary and despondent from many cares and heavy burdens, as any mortal would be in like circumstances, the social element would come to their rescue, like the green oasis to the weary traveler in a barren land, or when fear for a moment would

Frost Feathers on Mount Moosilauke

Photograph by Dartmouth Outing Club

Photograph by Dartmouth Outing Club

Beaver Brook Trail, Mount Moosilauke

reign supreme and their frail bark seemed to be at the mercy of every rolling wave on life's stormy sea, a social chat would be to them like a fertile gem in mid ocean to a storm-tossed mariner."

But Mount Washington and the Range have long been waiting for us over the rim of the hill as we paused here in the primeval forest with the Rev. Simeon Bolles. We ask your pardon, we are shamefully conscious of our dilatoriness. We can only say that the Range and the Street are there for all to see whereas the fertile gems of Mr. Bolles have been waiting for years for lapidaries—or shall we saw midwives?—like ourselves to give their fecundity a happy delivery.

And now, at long last, Bethlehem Street lies stretched before us. In 1858, according to Mr. Eastman, there were two fine churches, five large sawmills, one or two starch factories. A year later Starr King was lamenting the lack of attractive public houses in this village whose "horizon is fretted with mountains." We have seen from our historian that by 1883 this condition was rectified. Today the town boasts thirty hotels—at least so those roadside signs all over the state used to announce laconically before a wise New Hampshire legislature prohibited the roadside bally-hoo. We have not counted them but we do not doubt the number. For a mile they stretch along this street with the magnificent view, from The Alpine and Upland Terrace on the west to the Maplewood Club in splendid isolation on the east.

For fifty or sixty summers, now, thousands of people have been coming to Bethlehem. Perhaps it is the climate. Bethlehem has an altitude of 1,500 feet and those noxious proteins which the latest science tells us breed hay fever do not flourish in its brisk clear air. Apparently, in such a climate, it is impossible to die. One physician, making extensive researches over a period of two years in the late seventies, was able to rout out only one demise—that of a lady who, unfortunately for the town's vital statistics, arrived there in the last stages of consumption, too weak, alas, to be shipped off home to die. Or perhaps it may be the view. Or perhaps it is just gregariousness. At any rate, Bethlehem is the most populous resort in the mountains.

Bethlehem Street of a summer's night is not quite Coney Island. Nevertheless it is a lively place. In the trees on the upper side of the road are the lights of most of the hotels from which sounds of jazz float out into the night air. Opposite are the brightly lighted soda fountains serving their indigestible but non-intoxicating concoctions, and the movie palace. (There is even an outdoor swimming lake fed, we suppose, by those chill springs on the hillside which have been the town's boast for fifty years and drained, doubtless, by that excellent drainage which has been its equal boast—from fifteen hundred feet you can get quite a fall.) White-flanneled dandies (without "fancy colored gloves," however) stroll and pet with girls diaphanously clad. The street is brightly lighted; white lines to guide the traffic glare in the best manner, a traffic cop is on duty. And "über allen Gipfeln stinkt Benzine." There is left, however, a faintly shivering mystery in the sound of the cars hurtling down the leaf-covered road beyond the Maplewood into the loneliness of the road to Wing Road and the Range and of the still lonelier road back up into the Franconia Notch. And all around the mountains loom shadowy.

In the daytime, too, they are there. "No village commands so grand a panorama," says Starr King. Within limits he is right. From the golf links below the Maplewood the golfer gets the whole sweep of the Presidential Range (if a golfer looks up from his tee for any other reason than to follow the ball). It is much the same sweep that one gets from Sugar Hill, except that it is about ten miles nearer. On a clear day the smoke of the trains creeping up Jacob's Ladder can be clearly discerned. (For some unknown reason to see those trains seems to tourists very important.) To the right of the southern peaks is the dip which is the gateway to Crawford Notch. Further right are the Twins and the wilderness behind. Blocking the east the rugged bulk of Lafayette thrusts itself into the sky. If the day is clear and the beholder is not wedded to golf, he can climb Mount Agassiz (named for the famous naturalist who came here in 1847, exploring for glacial moraines and finding them) which rises some five hundred feet into the sky behind the Street to the west. There, from a steel observatory, he gets the same panorama, with Moosilauke, the Ammonoosuc valley, and the Green Mountains into the bargain. Or, he can take car and in a half hour or so be in the Franconia Notch for a climb up Lafayette. Or in a little longer time he can be at the Base Station for the noon trip to the Summit. All this has the twentieth century done for the inheritors of Starr King and the Rev. Simeon Bolles.

Yet sometimes two twentieth century guides like to medi-

tate in an elegiac strain on Bethlehem in its hey-day, fifty or
sixty years ago. Then her fame was scarcely second to the
fame of Saratoga. Her hotels, to be sure, were lacking in the
Victorian grandeur of the United States or the American
House at that famous spa, but they did very well in their
modest way. And in front of them was the famous plank
walk, two miles in length, along which strolled the gentlemen in their top hats, morning coats and the fancy colored
gloves that aroused Mr. Bolles's ministerial ire, and the ladies
with their dainty parasols, perching hats (like those Queen
Mary wears), leg-o'-mutton sleeves, wasp waists and billow-
ing skirts. Or there was croquet on the hotel lawns. Or one
might, perhaps, catch a glimpse of Lucy Larcom, William
Dean Howells, or other of the Boston literati. For other
diversion, there was an hour's drive "around the Heater."
(And the driver would point out the place where the coach
from Bethlehem to the Profile House overturned and crushed
a little boy under the baggage.) Or of a Sunday, one might
drive over to Twin Mountain to hear Henry Ward Beecher
preach under a tent. At any rate there were no honking cars,
no stench of gasoline. Only the musical horn of a tally-ho as
the horses pranced off down the Street for the Franconia
Notch. And they would tell you how, in '69 President Grant
sat on the box while Edmund Cox drove his six horses over
the eleven miles from the Sinclair to the Profile House in
fifty-eight minutes. There was speed! . . .

But we romanticize. Cherry Mountain, the Whitefield
Plain and Jefferson are waiting to be explored.

CHAPTER V

JEFFERSON AND THE NORTH COUNTRY

FROM Bethlehem to Jefferson there is a choice of routes, but let us pass (or whiz) down by the Maplewood, and through Twin Mountain where at the Twin Mountain House, as we have said, Henry Ward Beecher maintained for so many years a sort of summer Plymouth Church to which people came from miles around. At Carroll the long bulk of Cherry Mountain stretching north divides our route into two. On the right there is a lovely country road which will lead us more directly into Jefferson. This road, too, is perhaps of more historical and sentimental interest since it is part of the famous Cherry Mountain Road from Gorham to the Notch whose praises Starr King sang. But as we shall rejoin it later let us, for the present, stick to the main road. This will lead us to Whitefield and the Whitefield plain, where was opened in the summer of 1929 the first major airport in the White Mountain region. On the west the bulk of Dalton Mountain separates Whitefield from the Connecticut River, on the east the railroad steadily rises to the Jefferson plateau. But we still hold to the black asphalt and the white concrete, succumbing to no alluring bosky temptation to right or left, thus perversely turning our backs upon the Presidential peaks, of which, from Whitefield, there is a superb view. But we may look upon the gentler slope of Mount Prospect and if we are not driving ourselves there is no traffic law against taking fleeting glimpses to the rear. Then Prospect shuts us off from the Range, for the moment, and suddenly we find ourselves at Lancaster and the Connecticut.

Lancaster is the shire town of Coos County. Starr King was of the opinion, in 1859, that if the Grand Trunk railroad had only come to Lancaster it would have been a great rival of North Conway, that, though "there is no single meadow-view in Lancaster equal to the intervale of North Conway" still the Connecticut is far superior to the Saco. And so on. In a subtended poem he even intimates that were it not for white church-spire and cottage smoke taking the place of "dome and turret hoary" it might almost be the valley of the Arno. But having been in Lancaster in the winter he knows better than that. Nevertheless, in spite of his somewhat complicated comparisons, Starr King is right: the views from Lancaster are charming—to the northeast the gentle, long-curving Pilot range; to the westward the curving Connecticut and the hills of Vermont; south the Franconias; southeast-ward, perhaps fifteen miles as the crow flies, the looming Range. We shall have to confess that we have not seen it, as Starr King did, at sunrise and at sunset, in August, in winter, and in March. But perhaps it is just as well, for if we had we might well have been compelled as he was to dip our brushes "into as exquisite ambers, plum tints, gold, and purple" as would be needed "to interpret the baptism of the evening upon Mont Blanc, or the morning glow upon the Jungfrau."

But we must leave the paint pots. We can, of course, having once turned our backs upon the magnetic range, pursue our way northward along the river, through Northumberland and under the shadows of the Percys to Colebrook and Dixville Notch and so back to Gorham. But we have elected for the moment to turn back to Jefferson and the Range.

Between Jefferson and Bethlehem there was, in the thriving eighties, considerable friendly rivalry. We suppose they have risen above it now. After all, by car, they are scarcely an hour apart and by airplane—well, perhaps both equally insignificant. But in the eighties they took their altitudes seriously and the natives of each resort prided themselves on looking *down* into the other. Which were right? We shall not attempt to settle the ancient argument. The figures of the Geological Survey are now available but though, of course, these of all figures are the least mendacious the decision still depends upon whereabouts in each of these mountain villages the beholder takes his stance. Shall we say, as old Uncle Amos Wilson said of his yoke of oxen, that one of them is just as high as the other and if anything, a leetle mite higher?

Historically, perhaps, Jefferson has a slight advantage. For, though it can boast no historian like the Rev. Simeon Bolles, its recorded history antedates that of Bethlehem by about twenty years and it is more or less the center of a region much richer in legend.

Both Jefferson and Carroll—the town to the south, which was the home of the famous Crawford family and to which we shall finally return before our ascent of Mount Washington—are in Coos County, that county which includes within its southern borders the entire Presidential Range and stretches northward between Maine and the Connecticut River to the Canadian line. Coos is pronounced by the natives as two very distinct syllables. In the older days it was variously spelled, Cohos and Cowasse being the favorite orthographies. Indian philology, so far as this region and its historians are concerned, is, we suspect, somewhat imaginative. This being so we can believe the statement of Benjamin Willey as well as any: "Coos," he says, "is a habitable county in the northern part of New Hampshire, meaning crooked; and Coos was the name of the Connecticut River, near Lancaster." At any rate, it is true that the Connecticut River near Lancaster is crooked. Mr. Willey, it seems, is rather sensitive about the county's habitability. He assures us that "it is neither too mountainous to be cultivated, nor too sterile to be productive. It is not covered with perpetual snow; and, though its climate is somewhat cold in winter, its inhabitants are healthy and long-lived." He concludes, somewhat distantly: "We know that this is not the opinion which has been formed in the minds of most in respect to it." But so long as it is reasonably mountainous, tourists, being notoriously selfish, will scarcely worry about the possible sterility of the soil.

Coos or Coös or Cohos or Cowasse or Crooked, then, was set off from Grafton County (one of the five original New Hampshire counties) in 1803. But before that the name was applied loosely to the whole northern mountain region of New Hampshire. Long before it was settled it was a favorite

Eagle Cliff, Mount Lafayette and Echo Lake

Cherry Mountain from Jefferson

hunting and roaming ground for the Indians and for those Ishmaels who wearied of the effete civilization of the settlements in the older colonies. There is recorded in the Grafton County Registry a rather curious deed of a large tract of land roughly corresponding to the present lines of Coos County (though the generous grantors flung in a little of what is now Maine and Canada for good measure). The grantors are Philip (his mark) Indian Chief, Molley (her mark) Messell, and Mooseleck (her mark) Sussop; the grantees certain gentlemen nominated in full at the beginning of the bond but thereafter called familiarly, by Chief Philip: Thomas, John, Jonathan and Nathan, "all my peculiar friends."

Something peculiar there must have been about the transaction. The deed is dated in 1796 but there is no further evidence that the four named gentlemen entered upon possession of the region—at least to the exclusion of many other settlers. One can only hope that Philip and his squaws got their consideration, which was "free liberty to hunt all sorts of wild game on any of the foregoing territories, and taking fish in any of the waters thereof for myself my heirs and *sucksessors* & all Indian tribes forever, also liberty of planting four bushels of corn & beans."

Or one has another dark suspicion.

Ethan Allen Crawford tells us in his "History of the White Mountains" that during the Revolution his grandmother, Hannah Rosebrook, lived alone at Guildhall (in the New Hampshire Grants, just across the Connecticut .from Northumberland) and was often visited by the Indians. "By disposing of their furs," he says, "they would provide themselves with a plenty of what they called uncupy, or spirit, which they carried in bladders, taken from moose, and, at times, they would have a great drunk. This troubled her much, knowing their savage dispositions; she, fearing she would offend them and incur their displeasure, bore with them; at one time, however, she became decided and cleared her house of them, all but one, and she was so far gone under the influence of the spirit, or liquor, that she lay motionless upon the floor; grandmother took her by the hair of her head, and with the strength of her feelings, dragged her out of doors; and the squaw by being put in motion, came to herself so much that she had the use of her limbs; she drew her toma-hawk and aimed it at grandmother, who had just closed the door after her, when this tomahawk came so near as to take off the wooden thumb-piece from the door handle; thus she providentially made her escape."

Now Thomas, the first of Chief Philip's "peculiar friends," was Thomas Eames of Northumberland; his deed is dated some fifteen years later than the time when Hannah Rosebrook was living alone across the river in Guildhall. The habits established among the Indian squaws doubtless grew on them with time. Is it impossible that Thomas and his three cronies secured the deed to this vast and desirable tract from Philip and his squaws at some moment when these three were auspiciously under the influence of uncupy or spirits? May they not even have themselves provided the uncupy or spirits? One's imagination leaps. We are aware that our theory is rather ingenious than plausible. However, history is silent, and in the silence of history why may not the imagination soar? Dare one even speculate—perhaps the squaw whom the intrepid Hannah Rosebrook hauled out of doors "with the strength of her feelings" was either Molley Messell or Mooseleck Sussop. If so, we must look upon this deprivation of their lands, however fraudulent, as a judgment visited upon them by God. But of course it may have been some other squaw.

The most romantic story of the region is the story of the raid of Rogers' Rangers on the Indian village of St. Francis and the disastrous retreat of part of them through what is now lower Coos.

Historians, alas, are not always exact, but from Jeremy Belknap's history and Spaulding's "Historical Relics" (checked by Mr. Kilbourne's admirable "Chronicles of the White Mountains") it is possible to remold this episode fairly close to the heart's desire. In the fall of 1759, then, it appears that Major Robert Rogers with a force of about two hundred Rangers was ordered north by General Amherst from the fortress at Crown Point on Lake Champlain to destroy the Indian village of St. Francis de Sales which lay in the St. Lawrence region southwest of Quebec. After a fatiguing march of twenty-one days the major came within sight of the place, reconnoitered, visited the village with two officers in disguise while "the Indians were engaged in a grand dance" and early the next morning ordered the attack. "The dawn of day disclosed a horrid scene; and an edge was given to the fury of the assailants by the sight of several hundred scalps of their countrymen, elevated on poles, and waving in the air." After the massacre the Rangers plundered the church of its golden candlesticks and "a silver image weighing ten pounds," burnt the village and beat a hasty retreat up the St. Francis River with the intention of striking the Connecticut in upper Cohos and following it down to Number 4 (now Charlestown in the southern part of New Hampshire) which was then the northernmost settlement on the Connecticut River. But the enraged Indians turned the colonial retreat into a miniature retreat from Moscow. East of Memphremagog the Rangers scattered, the main body after many vicissitudes at last reaching its destination at Charlestown.

But for others the fateful prophecy uttered by an old Indian as they plundered the church: *The Great Spirit will scatter darkness upon the path of the pale-faces!* was only too true. Remains of some of the Rangers are said to have been found at the head of Fifteen Miles Falls. Another group of nine men at last delivered themselves over to an Indian runner who offered to lead them down through the great pass of Waumbekketmethna—The Crystal Hills. He led them up the valley of the Singrawack River (what is now Israel's River in Jefferson) toward the frowning mountains. At their foot he left them, giving their leader who carried the treasure from the plundered church, a birch bark map. Apparently the Indian also poisoned him with a scratch from a rattlesnake's fang administered on the back of his hand as the leader took the map. At any rate, as the "pain pressed madness into his brain" he flung himself from a high rock and "was dashed to pieces." Panicstricken by the loss of their leader they buried him and the booty in a rude cave; wan-

Mounts Madison and Adams from Randolph

Starr King Range from Cherry Mountain

dering about in the wilderness only one of them survived the "rigorous storms of approaching winter." "This ragged and forlorn-looking mortal had with him six knives, and in his bloody knapsack was a piece of human flesh, of which for the last eight days he declared he had eaten to support the flickering spark of life that now but faintly burned within him."

Tradition records various traces of this ill-fated expedition. According to one report the skeletons and remains of this group were found by early hunters in one of the wild ravines from which Israel's River takes its rise. The golden candlesticks are reputed to have been found near Lake Memphremagog in 1816: whether they are still in existence we know not. Another legend of this same saga is perhaps the nearest the White Mountains have to offer to the Catskill legend of Rip Van Winkle. A hunter, camping one night far up among the mountains, was troubled in his "dreamy restlessness" by a strange noise and a still thick mist that glittered in the moonlight about the summit of a craggy mountain. Let Spaulding's words tell the tale: "The hunter's nerves were like steel, but a fanciful influence changed the mist to a great stone church, and within this was an altar, where from a sparkling censer rose a curling wreath of incense-smoke, and around it lights dispersed a mellow glow, by which in groups before that altar appeared a tribe of savages kneeling in profound silence. A change came in the wind; a song loud and long rose as a voice-offering to the Great Spirit; then glittering church-spire, church and altar, vanished, and down the steep rock trailed a long line of strange-looking men, in solemn silence. Before all, as borne by some airy sprite, sported a glittering image of silver, which in the deep shadows changed to a fairy shape, and, with sparkling wings, disappeared in the rent rocks. A loud laugh of brutal triumph, combined with the strange vision, startled to consciousness the hunter; and, musing on what had passed, he rekindled his fire by the light of morning over the eastern mountains."

And on still another occasion still another hunter was startled from his deep slumber by a voice crying from out a great storm: *"That pagan treasure from St. Francis may not remain a secret to adventure till the Great Spirit's thunder dies on the crags of Agiochook."* But whatever the true significance of this rather cryptic utterance may have been at any rate the silver image of St. Francis has never been found nor has the thunder of the Great Spirit permanently departed from the crags of the Presidential Range.

Such were the goings-on in the regions about Jefferson before the soberer and more respectable Anglo-Saxons came to settle there. It is high time, perhaps, that we left this "misty mid region of Weir" and came down to the rugged *terra firma* of Jefferson again.

Jefferson—or Dartmouth, as it was originally called—was granted by the Crown in 1765 with the usual reservations of white pine for the masting of the Royal Navy. In 1773 (nearly twenty years before its rival, Bethlehem, was settled) Colonel Whipple arrived, a man of no mean ability, whose genius as a realtor was perhaps somewhat wasted on that lonely terrain and leisurely century. By his prowess he obtained possession of the whole town from the original grantees, and parceled it out by the astute method adopted in the twentieth century by the chain stores) of giving away fifty acres with every purchase of an equal acreage. For years Jefferson was distinctly a one man town but, from all accounts, Whipple was a benevolent despot. In fact, he must have been a good Democrat, for in 1796 the town legally adopted the name of the distinguished author of the Declaration of Independence.

Barren educational facilities, destitution of religious privileges, and inhabitants goitrous from a lack of salt, characterized the early life of Jefferson (in contrast, perhaps, to the sociability of Bethlehem), but the only episode that need concern tourists has to do with *"the first white woman of the town . . . whose story has been told in every book published concerning the White Mountains."* Well, let this book be no exception. Barton or Livermore or Rogers—authorities differ as to her last name—her first name was indubitably Nancy. Imported as a cook by the redoubtable Colonel Whipple she soon fell prey to the charms of one of his male servants. "The wretch, having molded her affections completely to his purpose, agreed to go to Portsmouth and be married." Nancy went to Lancaster, to prepare for their lonely journey and while she was gone the lover, "false to the common feelings of humanity," but with his eye distinctly out for the main chance decamped with Nancy's two years' savings. When she learned of her lover's treachery the indomitable girl set out to follow him, despite the warnings of her friends and a light snow that had already obliterated her lover's tracks on the blazed path that led down through the White Mountain Notch to the nearest settlement thirty miles below. Through the night she pressed on. In early morning, far down in the Notch she came upon the ashes of his camp-fire, still warm. A little further on, near the brook that today bears her name, her frozen body was found by the searching party from Jefferson which set out the next day to rescue her. This pathetic story is perhaps the most celebrated of all White Mountain lore; not unsurprisingly it has formed the basis of many a short story, poem and ballad of more or less dubious artistic merit. It is a pleasure, therefore, to record that the perfidious lover, hearing of her horrible death, "became insane, and after a few weeks died a raving madman."

But enough for history. The geographical claims of Jefferson are clamoring for our attention. For after all, Colonel Whipple, and the Rangers, and Nancy, and "Granny Stalbird" (the second woman in Jefferson) have little to do with motorists and their clouds of dust. And yet, despite the state roads, and the cleared intervale, the golf courses, the hostelries, the topography of Jefferson is scarcely changed after a hundred years, for these mountains are of granite and were built to stay. True, in 1885, in the southwest corner of the town, a freshet started a million tons of earth hurtling down the mountain-side for two miles and the Cherry Mountain Slide is still a memory for the citizens but the scar on its slope that marks its passage might, for all a tourist knows, have been there from the beginning of time.

Jefferson is a long sloping plateau which stretches up to Mount Starr King in the northeastern corner of the Township. Very fitting it is that the young clergyman (he was only thirty-five years old when "The White Hills" was published and he died three years later in California), who lamented in 1859 that there was as yet no large public house in Jefferson, should have his name immortalized by the beautiful mountain behind the Waumbek, one of the most famous hostelries in the White Mountain region. Strictly speaking, Starr King and an edge of the Pliny Range are the only mountains within the borders of Jefferson itself—that is why, of course, the unimpeded view from the Hill down across the lovely sloping fields and pastures toward the long-lying Cherry Mountain on the south, toward Mount Dartmouth and the bulking masses of the Range on the east, is so charmingly impressive.

It was on Cherry Mountain, by the way, that Timothy Nash while out hunting one day in 1771 climbed a tree and discovered the old Indian trail down through the Notch (although Ethan Allen Crawford places this historic event on Mount Mitten, to the southeast, and clinches the matter by averring that it was by his loss of a mitten there that this mountain got its name).

It is fitting, of course, that the mountain which appears to greatest advantage in the Range is Mount Jefferson, which is the nearest. Clay and Washington curve away to the east from the beholder. Starr King, anticipating Mr. Frost and ourselves, compares it to a snake that playfully raises "its wary head for a moment by a curve that is the poetry of rest."

In fact, the beauty and majesty of this view have gone rather dizzily to the heads of commentators. Ward, writing in 1890 and never forgetting that he has a long line of poets to out-rhapsodize says that from Jefferson Hill "the huge peaks are invested with flashes of color that change every moment, and open their sides and kiss their summits and awaken their emotions"—which seems like taking a deucedly unfair advantage. Could it have been something like this that was Nancy's undoing?

Drake soars even higher. Ascribing an extraordinary muscular agility to the eye he tells us how it (the eye) "dives into the cool ravines; it seeks to penetrate, like the birds, the profound silence of the forests. It toils slowly up the broken crags, or loiters by the cascades, hanging like athletes from dizzy brinks. It shrinks, it admires, it questions; it is grave, gay, or thoughtful by turns." In fact, meditating upon these astounding antics of the eye, he leaps to this solemn moral conclusion: "I do not believe," he says, "the man lives who, looking up to those mountains as in the face of the Deity, can deliberately utter a falsehood: the lie would choke him." This is why we have been so timid about advancing some of the historical data in the earlier part of this chapter; we have no desire to be choked.

But, after all, it was Starr King of course who, in the words of Mr. Drake, was most "capable of detecting intuitively what was hid from common eyes." We earlier half promised the reader to traverse the historic Cherry Mountain Road from Gorham to the Notch with Starr King. Asking his pardon, we shall reverse his direction since we are, in a rambling sort of way, headed toward Gorham and the Glen. We shall pass over Starr King's debate with himself as to the relative merits of this drive and the approach to the Notch and the Glen by way of Jackson and Bartlett. The horse was a leisurely animal; gasoline has made both routes possible, in fact, the whole circuit of the mountains, in one day and thus saved argument.

As we go toward Gorham, then, the Franconias, the Twins, Cherry Mountain are behind us. On our right is the snake's head of Mount Washington, gradually disappearing as we go east. Jefferson, with its Castellated Ridge, Adams and King's Ravine, Madison and the lesser Adamses loom nearer and nearer. The view of Adams is indeed sublime. We can certainly agree with Starr King in one respect. "The forms of the mountains are nobler on this side than on the side towards the old Fabyan place near the Notch." Nobler? We cannot say. More impressive they certainly are, perhaps because they are in echelon—though that may not be the reason, either.

For we shall have to admit that travel in a motor car does not permit us to analyze our aesthetic responses so minutely as it was possible for Starr King to do in the fifties behind his jogging horse. Why this obsession with jewelry, for instance? (The mystery of the great carbuncle which Hawthorne tells about—the fertile gem of sociability of the Rev. Simeon Bolles —now Starr King has got the craze.) His description of the great ravine of Mount Adams—was it for this it was named for him, we wonder—reads like the jewelry section of a Sears Roebuck catalogue. "A long, narrow, leaping stream gleams aloft—a chain of diamonds dropped from the neck down the bosom of the mountain." The sun shines and "you see a broad wrapper adorned from the collar downwards with flashing gems." (He enlarges on this theme with a quotation about the diamonds on Arthur's crown from "Idylls of the

King.") Diamond after diamond wakes into glow—the Koh-i-noor appears. . . . But after all, he concludes, "the 'great carbuncles' of the mountains are its splendors that feed and quicken the sentiment of beauty." For ourselves we prefer something a little less garish—the mountains without their jewels. The play of somber shadow and color upon their rugged flanks is more impressive.

But Starr King has time to play with color, too. He expatiates upon it. What would one do without it, he wonders. "If it were possible to mold in plaster of Paris an exact duplicate of Mont Blanc, and the range of which it is the head, and to set the model in place of the removed Alps, surrounding the whole with untinted air, the necessity of color to expression would need no further argument." But such legerdemain, thank God, is as impossible on the northern side of the Presidential Range as it is in Switzerland.

And so we can glory in the magnificent view of the northern peaks from Randolph Hill. Here, as Drake says, rather intimately, "you hold the great northern peaks admiringly at arm's length, as you would an old friend. Putting an imaginary hand on each broad shoulder, you scan them from head to foot. They submit calmly. . . ." We should not advise this gesture—they might not submit. Nevertheless, the view is grand: the bulk of Madison in the foreground, hardly a stone's throw across the valley, if *we* may be permitted a little hyperbole, the vaster bulk of Adams behind. For the mountain climber the challenge to the ascent from this side of the Range is almost overpowering. But we have not yet any license to climb the Range. Much about the base of it still remains to be explored. And before we go on to circle it through Gorham and the Glen we must say a word or so about the North Country.

The North Country is the tip end of the peninsula of New Hampshire that stretches north of the Presidential Range to Canada between the boundaries of Maine and Vermont. From the Range to the tip of New Hampshire the distance is sixty-five miles; at the Range the distance across from east to west is about forty miles, at the tip about fifteen. The wilderness character of this region may be indicated by the fact that there are only two main thoroughfares traversing the width of it, one from Berlin to Groveton, following the line of the Grand Trunk, and one across from Errol to Colebrook through the Dixville Notch. It is a region of forests, streams and lakes—Umbagog Lake, leaking over into Maine on the east, and the Connecticut Lakes in the upper tip. It is a tramper's, fisherman's, and hunter's paradise but not for the regular tourist, except on the beaten paths.

It is only within comparatively recent years that this region has been popular with tourists—for this popularity we doubtless have Mr. Ford and his fellow-manufacturers to thank. Starr King seems to have penetrated no further north than Milan. To that town, however, he drove from Gorham and described the view from it of the Presidential Range in most enthusiastic terms. His successors, for the most part, seem not to have gone even as far as that. Drake seems to have limited himself by the title of his book: "The Heart of the White Mountains." It would require considerable physiological dexterity to include Dixville within the heart.

Eastman, however, in his White Mountain Guide of 1858 included the region. At that time, Dixville Notch, the chief scenic attraction, could be reached by rail only from the east, from Portland through Gorham on the Atlantic and St. Lawrence which carried one as far as North Stratford. At North Stratford one took a stage to Colebrook where one put up for the night in the Monadnoc House in the shadow "of a massive and majestic mountain which the inhabitants call Monadnoc" that lay across the Connecticut in Vermont. Thence, rising early the next morning, one took the ten mile drive up into Dixville Notch where, in the Clear Stream Meadows at the eastern end, was a solitary farmer's house.

Nowadays the approach is not vastly different. It is possible to approach Colebrook from the west by rail, using the Boston and Maine and the Maine Central railroads. And one may still put up in the Monadnock House (with an extra "k" for this day of simplified spelling). And one may take a bus from Colebrook to the Notch, or even, we suppose, a carriage. But this mode of approach is for the old-fashioned. The vast majority, of course, will come by car: from the east through Gorham, Berlin and Milan (in New Hampshire adjacent metropolises, no matter how far apart they may keep them still in Europe) and Errol; from the west through Lancaster and Colebrook.

From Colebrook the road winds along the lovely valley of the Mohawk River to the western gateway of the Notch. There, on the shore of Lake Gloriette, a beautiful little body of water (in three sections, joined together by drives) made by damming the Mohawk River as it issues from the Notch, is situated the Balsams, the northernmost of the famous White Mountain hotels. Continuing, one enters the Notch proper which curves southeast for nearly two miles between Mount Sanguinari (named, they will tell you, for the garnet color it takes in the sunset) on the north and Mount Gloriette on the south. The Notch, at its highest point, is nearly 2000 feet in altitude; Mount Gloriette rises precipitously above it for some six or seven hundred feet more. Devotees of the White Mountains have their favorites among the notches and one has to speak softly lest sensibilities be wounded. Even the blindest partisan, however, will scarcely deny that Dixville Notch is the wildest and most picturesque of them all. The Notch itself is narrower, and the sharpness of the pinnacles, the steepness of Table Rock, rising just south of the Balsams and the lake give this Notch a decidedly Alpine character (Alpine in miniature, of course, though geologists assure us that not so many thousands of years ago these pinnacles were twice their present height). There is a grand view of the Notch to be obtained from Table Rock, to which a trail leads from the highway. In the old days, apparently, this was a rather precarious climb. Mr. Eastman avers that hands and feet were necessary; in fact, he says, if it had not been for a young lady (who belonged to Boston and was a model traveler) the gentlemen of his party would have been discouraged ere they had reached the top. The top is a platform, scarcely more than six feet wide at its narrowest, with a sheer drop of seven hundred feet, and a view into Maine, Vermont, and Canada. Ten miles north are the Connecticut Lakes, chief source of the Connecticut and the dwelling-place of fabulous trout; to the east is Lake Umbagog. The mountains about the Notch can be reached by trails: Mount Dixville, to the south, is the highest with an altitude of 3118 feet; on the northeast is Mount Sanguinari, on the north, less than a mile to its two summits from the Balsams, is Mount Abenaki.

The confirmed sportsman will hardly resist penetrating further into the wilderness to the north, into the Diamond Pond territory and the region of the Connecticut Lakes. In this latter region we approach a no-man's land. From 1832-35 this was the "Republic of Indian Stream" with constitution, council, assembly and courts of its own. In the "Indian Stream War" of 1835-6 it was occupied by the New Hampshire militia; in 1842 it was finally awarded to the State of New Hampshire by the Ashburton treaty. But we are getting dangerously close to the Canadian border for a book on the White Mountains. Let us turn, then, through the Notch southeastward, out from the spiky cliffs which hem it in, into the Clear Stream Meadows through which the road will take us back to Errol, the famous Italian and Prussian cities, and Gorham underneath the great Range which is our final goal.

CHAPTER VI

GORHAM AND THE GLEN

FROM the days when adventurous mariners, cruising in the early seventeenth century along the coast of New England, first noticed the gull-like mountain tops against the far northwestern sky until the latter part of the last century the Waumbekketmethna seem to have faced the sea. Comparatively recently they have executed a volte-face. Or perhaps the process has been gradual. It began, we suspect, when the redoubtable Ethan Allen Crawford established his hostelry on the western side of the range in 1819. The opening of the Mount Washington Railroad in 1869 and the popularity of Bethlehem and Sugar Hill as resorts, in the seventies and eighties, with their panoramic upland views of the Range doubtless hastened the somersault, or whatever the geological upheaval was. Now that the geographical center of the country is situated not far from Topeka, Kansas, and the center of population is creeping toward the Mississippi River (if it has not already swum across) we may say, with all due respect to Conway and the beautiful Intervale region, that Mount Washington has pretty definitely, with the rest of the country, turned its back upon Europe and the ocean. (With the exception, of course, of that large minority

109

of the population which still keeps the trans-Atlantic lanes open for travel.)

However this may be, it is at any rate certain that around 1850 the most popular approach to the White Mountains was through Gorham and the Glen. Starr King had nothing but words of highest praise for the approach along the Androscoggin intervale from Bethel, Maine, to Gorham, and in spite of the westward march of the center of population it still remains beautiful.

Beautiful as this approach is, however, the mid-century popularity of the Gorham region was probably due, like all the major movements and events of history, to economic reasons. For Gorham was the first village within easy distance of the mountains to boast a railroad service. In 1852, a year before a correspondent in the New York *Herald* expressed the pious hope that "no railroad should ever be constructed farther into these mountains than Littleton" (in this same year the Northern Railroad *had* reached Littleton, twenty-five miles west of Mount Washington), the Atlantic and St. Lawrence Railroad had reached Gorham on its ambitious way from Portland to Island Pond, Vermont (Gorham is ninety-two miles northwest of Portland). In July of the next year this railroad had amalgamated with another line extending from Montreal and the first train from Montreal to Portland arrived there to the ringing of bells and a salute of thirty-one guns. A month later this route, in the beaten way of railroads, was leased to the Grand Trunk Railway for 999 years. (The lease has not yet expired.)

The history of Gorham previous to the coming of the

railroad is similar to that of the other mountain towns and it has had no Simeon Bolles to immortalize it in song and story. Granted, as a part of Shelburne, in 1771, with the usual reservations for the masting of the royal navy, it was settled to the usual accompaniment of hardships and privations endured by the intrepid early settlers. In 1781 it was the victim of a massacre by an Indian party returning to Canada after raiding Bethel and Gilead in Maine. The inhabitants, after listening to the delighted whoops of the Indians from the comparative safety of Hark Hill, fled to Fryeburg, Maine, in the morning, a distance of fifty-nine miles, where they remained until the Indians had returned to Canada.

In the days before the white man came for permanent occupancy this region was evidently the rather unhappy hunting ground of an Indian brave named Pealsucep, whose sad story Spaulding recounts in his "Historical Relics of the White Mountains." Pealsucep dwelt happily by the shores of a little lake with his squaw and little boy until one day while he was off hunting in the forest his wigwam was visited by a pale-face sailor. The sailor was evidently on a tout: he amused himself by tossing the little boy out into the lake and watching him swim ashore; he offered the squaw a drink and then departed. The boy sickened and died; Pealsucep in wrath and jealousy averted his affections from the faithful spouse until she too had pined away. Overcome by grief and ostracized by the other members of his tribe, Pealsucep built a funeral pyre for wife and child, took their ashes, and departed for the abode of the Great Spirit, coming mysteriously forth now and again to visit vengeance upon the hated pale-faces and living, after all the other members of his tribe had vanished before advancing civilization, until 1779 in "the shadow of the Great Spirit's home." But this is dubious history.

Gorham itself (until 1836 called the Shelburne addition) was, even among White Mountain towns, a singularly rough and unproductive region. The village, situated at the junction of the Peabody and Androscoggin rivers in a narrow valley, is about the only level place in the whole township (except where Moose River stretches west toward Randolph and Jefferson) and is scarcely adapted to extensive farming. Consequently it was not until the coming of the railroad in 1852 that the region took on life. "People," says Mr. Willey, "for a moment were dumb with astonishment. . . . That the cars should actually carry visitors to the mountains was something which every one had supposed would take place in the far-off future, but not until they themselves had ceased to travel; but it was actually so." And business men could actually visit the mountains and attend to their business, by telegraph, at the same time. For with the coming of the railroad one of the most famous of mountain hostelries, from a historical point of view, was established. This was the White Mountain Station House which, like the old Pemigewasset at Plymouth, served as both station and hotel. Becoming later the Alpine House, under the management of Col. John R. Hitchcock, proprietor also of the Summit and Tip-top Houses on Washington, it was for twenty years the rendezvous of enthusiastic mountaineers. Fire destroyed it in 1872 and the second Alpine House was closed in 1905 and later moved across the street and incorporated into the present Mount

Dixville Notch

Carter-Moriah and Presidentials Over Gorham

Madison House. Today, with its sawmills and railroad re-
pair shops, Gorham is quite different from the solitary Alpine
House of seventy years ago, which existed, with its accommodations for two hundred and fifty guests, for the scenery
alone.

But Gorham is still the center of gorgeous scenery. Northward is the valley of the Androscoggin, with the Alpine Cascades and Berlin five miles up the river. In 1859 Starr King
could say: "We do not think that in New England there is
any passage of river passion that will compare with the Berlin
Falls. . . . Who can tire of gazing at the amber flood?"
Now the paper mills along the banks somewhat impede the
view and the amber flood is sulphite-stained. What would
Starr King say of this passage of river passion now? Nothing,
perhaps. At any rate the present beholder can gaze upon the
paper mills and be sure that his Sunday supplement is safe
for some time to come (even though the paper business in
northern New Hampshire is not what it used to be).

We have already mentioned the views from Shelburne,
to the east as one approaches this region. And we have spoken
of the view from Randolph Hill in the township on the west
(originally called Durand but named in 1824 for the Vir-
ginia statesman, the friend of Jefferson). Of the famous Ravine House at Appalachia, for several years now the summer
and winter haunt of mountaineers, and of the famous trails
leading from the township of Randolph up over the northern
peaks we shall have much to say in the chapters on the Range.

"Gorham," says Starr King, "is the place to see the more
rugged sculpturing and the Titanic brawn of the hills. Turn-

ing from North Conway to the Androscoggin Valley is some-what like turning from a volume of Tennyson to the pages of Carlyle." To a generation which knows not Carlyle and reads little of Tennyson this comparison may not be especially en-lightening. The cold figures given by Mr. Eastman in his guide book may be more instructive. He points out, in a somewhat complicated mathematical computation, that since Gorham is only 800 feet above sea-level and Carter Dome about 5000 "the summit of Carter is really higher, as seen from Gorham, than Mount Lafayette, the highest of the Franconia range, is from the lovely Echo Lake." By the same token, of course, the peaks of the Range are higher by over a thousand feet from Gorham than they are from the Glen or Bretton Woods, where the altitude is 1,600 feet. (And, this being the age of Einstein, we should like to speculate on the actual height of the highest point in the United States, Mount Whitney, with its fourteen thousand feet, seen from the floor of Death Val-ley, six hundred feet below sea-level. But the floor of Death Valley is no place to be—besides it is over three thousand miles away—so let us admit that things are what they seem.)

Before taking trails from Gorham or ascending to the Glen, let us regale ourselves with a general description of the various peaks from Gorham as quoted by the Rev. Benjamin Willey from a "writer in the Boston *Transcript*." (Our pas-sage turns out to be nothing less than the first draft of the same description from Starr King's book; the first draft, however, is much more ebullient: let us stick to that.) It is evening, we, with Starr King's first version, are taking a drive. Nature, who pours the wine of her beauty twice a day is pouring it now. But—"her richest flasks are reserved for the dessert-hour of the day's feast. Then they are bountifully poured. Herr Alexander and Wizard Anderson, when they perform the trick of turning many liquors from one bottle, to an astonished crowd, meanly parody the magic of the evening sun shedding over these hills the most various juices of light from his single urn. Those strong, substantial, twin majesties, Madison and Jefferson, have a steady preference for a brown-sherry hue; the Androscoggin Hills take to the lighter and sparkling yellows, hocks and champagne; but the clarets, the red hermitage, and the deep purple Burgundies, are reserved for the ridge of Mount Moriah. This wine for the eye does not interfere with the temperance pledge; and the visual flavor is so delicious, that one is eager all through the day for the evening repast."

Such were the advantages of writing about the White Mountains in a less arid era. Thus fortified, we can consider ourselves prepared to undertake any ascent from this starting-point—and there are many enchanting trails, excluding for the time being those that lead up the Presidential peaks. On the north of Gorham Village is Mount Hayes (named not for Rutherford B. Hayes, as might be supposed, in this executive region, but for a famous landlady of the old Alpine House), the ascent of which may easily be made in an hour and which Starr King has described as "the chair set by the Creator at the proper distance and angle to appreciate and enjoy Mount Washington. "In the Creator's estimate of this globe," he continues, "is it not probable that Mount Washington is a picture, rather than some thousands of cubic rods of rock?" Well, the beholder may judge for himself. It is, indeed, true that Mount Washington, from this point, is thrown into a rather splendid isolation.

Another favorite climb is the climb to the top of Pine Mountain, which may be taken as the last northern outpost of the Presidential Range. Pine Mountain lies in the peninsula formed at its tip by the Androscoggin, on the northwest by Moose River, along which the railroad and highway run from Jefferson to Gorham, and Peabody River on the east. The summit can be reached directly from Gorham in two hours, easily (the distance is two mountain miles); or from the Mount Madison Mineral Spring, three miles west of Gorham on the Randolph highway and one mile in from the highway. Starting from here one may take a trail at the right of the railway bridge across the river and climb the mile to the summit by an easy trail, or one may proceed back toward Gorham along the railway track for half a mile and then take the trail to the right by a small waterfall. This is a little longer but goes through woods and comes out upon the northern and higher summit. Pine Mountain was, as its name would indicate to the alert mind, originally pine-clad, but a devastating forest fire has denuded it, not only of trees but even of soil, so that the gougings of the glacier are distinctly traceable in its rugged rock summit. Though the mountain is not particularly lovely in itself the view is compensating. Westerly the view extends up the Moose River Valley toward Jefferson; northerly up the Androscoggin Valley toward Berlin and beyond, easterly down the Androscoggin after it has crooked about at Gorham toward Maine; on the southeast the Peabody River up into the Glen and the bold peaks of the Carter-Moriah Range. To the southwest the granitic expanse of the big Range blocks out the sky: rising nearly three thousand feet higher, four miles distant through the air, is the bulk of Mount Madison, which hides Adams and Jefferson but allows the summit of Washington to be visible at its left.

Perhaps approaching in popularity the Presidential peaks themselves among enthusiastic trampers are the mountains of the Carter-Moriah Range, not only for the magnificent views of their more rugged companions across the valley which may be obtained from them but also for their own wild picturesqueness. Geographically considered this range ought properly to be said to begin at Mount Winthrop, which lies south of the Androscoggin in Shelburne. (This is the mountain up whose steep white ledge, so the story goes, a certain Moses Ingalls glided barefoot like a cat, thus winning the best lot of land in the township. The Ingalls family was one of great repute in the region: Moses's father was a pious and godly man; his brother was an early temperance advocate, organizing a famous "Cold Water Army" of youths and maidens; the account of Moses's feat is doubtless, therefore, true.) For the mountaineer, however, the range begins properly with Mount Moriah.

Mount Moriah, named by an early settler "because its shape or position coincided with some conception he had formed of its Scripture namesake"—our limited knowledge of Old Testament exegesis prevents us from discerning just what the conception could have been—was one of the earliest mountains to be popular with travelers because of its proximity to Gorham. There is a trail—once euphemistically called a bridle path—leading from Gorham (over Mount Surprise, a fire-denuded mountain of about half its height) to the summit. The altitude of Moriah is 4,500 feet and the view is a surpassing one: Umbagog and the mountains of Maine to the north, southeast the outlying spurs of the White Mountains sloping down to Sebago Lake and the Maine seaboard. To the south stretches the Carter Range: Imp, North Carter, Middle Carter, South Carter, Mount Hight, the truncated peak of— obese, Mr. Drake calls it—Carter Dome, which is the highest peak of the ridge with an elevation of 4,800 feet; then the sharp dip of Carter Notch, with Mount Wildcat on the further side, and the lesser peaks curving away to the right down into Pinkham Notch. Directly south are the hills of Bartlett and Conway; Moat Mountain; Chocorua and Winnepesaukee on the far southern horizon. To the west, of course, is the vast wall of the Range: this panorama had perhaps better be left for the summit of Carter Dome.

One may go on down south over the ridge, over the Imp, Carter and Carter Dome to the Carter Notch. The distance from Moriah is nearly ten mountain miles. The favorite method of approach, however, is from the Glen House whither, by swift anticipation, we may now imagine ourselves to be. A trail leads directly east from the Glen to Mount Hight, or a mile from the Glen one may turn to the left along Nineteen Mile Brook (this trail also starts two miles north of the Glen House on the road at the junction of Nineteen Mile Brook with the Peabody River). This path leads along the right of the brook directly up into the Notch. There is a di-

verging path, to the left, a mile up from the junction of the
Glen House and Nineteen Mile Brook trail to the summit of
Carter Dome or, if one chooses, one may ascend the Dome
from the Notch itself. Continuing up toward the Notch, one
may catch glimpses of the Dome through the trees ahead. At
the highest point of the trail there is another diverging path,
to the right this time, which leads to the summit of Mount
Wildcat and over the lower peaks to Pinkham Notch. Descending sharply straight ahead, you come immediately upon
the Notch itself, the sharp cleft between Carter Dome on the
northeast and Wildcat rising abruptly on the west.

Carter Notch is the highest of the Notches; its altitude is
3,500 feet. It is also the wildest, for civilization, at least in
macadam form, has not penetrated. But it is not wholly
abandoned: there are two charming little lakes in the cleft in
the hills and on the far border of the smaller one is a stone hut
of the Appalachian Mountain Club where rest, lodging, and
simple refreshment for the weary hiker may be obtained. The
hiker, if he has come from the Glen House, has come nearly
four mountain miles. The trail up Carter Dome from the
Notch leads off at the right from the lakes. From this point to
the Dome the distance is about a mile and a half, the first part
abrupt, the latter part more gradual. The Dome is over 4,800
feet high; it is six miles as the crow (or bee) flies to the top
of Mount Washington. These figures may give one some idea
of the impressive panorama of the Range to be seen from its
broad summit. The view in other directions is, of course, not
essentially different from the view from Moriah. To the west
the whole extent of the Range seems to shut out the sky. At

the fire-warden's lookout tower on the summit one can identify the peaks. At the right of the vast semi-circle is the pointed cone of Madison, next is Adams with the lesser Adamses grouped about it; then come the rounded summit of Jefferson, the rounded hummocks of Mount Clay and Washington itself, with the lesser southern peaks fading away to the southwest. It is the view of the great glacial ravines in the flanks of the Range that is especially prodigious. To the left is the steep cirque of Tuckerman's, to the right the still steeper Huntington Ravine. To the right of Huntington is the Chandler Ridge, along the top of which is the white zigzagging carriage road. Beyond the Ridge is partially visible the Great Gulf, the vast ravine between Chandler Ridge and Jefferson. It is almost as good as an airplane view: perhaps better, one has at least the advantage of being able to take it in at leisure.

Leaving the Notch one has a choice of two other routes. One may leave by the Wildcat River Trail which leads out through the interesting dike of glacial boulders behind the hut down to a road four and a half miles away which leads one to Jackson, about nine miles from the Notch. Or one may take the rather rough trail over Wildcat and the lesser peaks down into Pinkham Notch by Glen Ellis Falls three miles below the Glen House. This trail affords magnificent glimpses of the Presidential Range and is, from the hut to the Pinkham Notch road, about six miles in length.

But let us return to Gorham for a less strenuous exploration of the Glen.

The Glen is the narrow valley lying between the Carter

© *George F. Slade*

Mounts Jefferson, Adams, and Madison from the Glen

Carter Notch from the Glen

Mountains and the great Range. Through it flows the rushing Peabody River. The upper branch of this river, according to ancient legend, sprang spontaneously from the loins of the Range. We certainly cannot be expected to vouch for the truth of this, although a certain Mr. Peabody of Andover, Massachusetts, related the event and averred that the Indian cabin in which he was spending the night was swept away in the spontaneous deluge which was both birth and baptism— for the river has taken Mr. Peabody's name. The beautiful road winds up from Gorham eight miles to the Glen House, the altitude of which is 1,600 feet. A little more than halfway from Gorham is the Dolly Copp Camp Ground. From the road at the bottom of the valley one gets glimpses through the trees of the Carter Mountains to the left and the Range to the right. In winter, it appears, the sex of the Presidents can be more clearly determined. At any rate, Starr King speaks of Washington, on one wintry drive, as "bulging into the cold and brilliant blue with irregular whiteness" while "Madison, in more feminine symmetry, displayed a fresh view of sloping shoulders clasped to the waist in ermine." Masculine, feminine, or neuter (as we are inclined to think they probably are, after all) they are there most majestically. The sense of their imminence is greater here than anywhere else in the whole circuit of the range. Leaving the road about two miles from the Glen House (if anyone can stop a car long enough nowadays to leave the road) one may see the curious rock formation on the left known as the Imp. Starr King would say, we suppose, that the Imp was the Glen's attempt —unsuccessful—to burlesque the Old Man of the Mountains.

It is a somewhat sad comment upon the amusing egoism of human nature—this irrepressible attempt to see the human physiognomy in every irregular rock formation.

In his guide book of 1858 Eastman describes the Glen House as "one of the largest and grandest Hotels of the White Mountain region." It has a grand portico. Over this is a balcony. It has a noble dining hall "calculated to seat two hundred persons." The withdrawing rooms, fronting the mountains, are spacious and airy. This was the first establishment, under the management of Mr. J. M. Thompson. Later it was enlarged, again and again. It enjoyed a long season of prosperity. In 1884 it burned to the ground. In 1887 it had been replaced by a commodious structure, capable of housing five hundred guests, built in English cottage style with a veranda along the entire front, gables, and turrets at the corners—a reasonably sober example of what Victorian architecture could do. In 1893 it burned again. Now there is nothing left of all this grandeur but the purely humdrum facilities for tending to the wants of pedestrians and to restive automotive tourists, who may perchance stop for a night to ascend Mount Washington by the carriage road.

The carriage road was the first civilized means of ascending the mountain. Projected in 1853 when the Mount Washington Road Company was chartered with a capital of fifty thousand dollars, by 1856 four miles of it had been completed to the Ledge just above the Halfway House. Then the original company failed, the Mount Washington Summit Road Company was incorporated, and the road completed in 1861, when it was opened for travel on August 8th. It is admirably built, winding up the Chandler Ridge with a comparatively easy gradient—in its eight miles it makes an ascent of forty-six hundred feet, the average grade being one foot in eight, the steepest, one foot in six. On the precipitous curves it is well banked with stones. So far as we know there has been only one major casualty connected with passage up and down. That was in 1880 when a six horse mountain-wagon was overturned a mile below the Halfway House and one woman killed, five other passengers injured. This accident was due not to any fault in the construction of the road but to the accidental collision of the driver with some liquor on the summit of the mountain.

A prospectus of the carriages quoted by Mr. Willey sounds rather marvelous. They are to be of omnibus form, and drawn by four horses. "The passengers will not sit facing each other, nor facing the front, but half way between these two positions. A separate seat is arranged for each passenger, and each carriage has only twelve seats inside. The body of the carriage is so arranged as to be raised in front in ascending, and in the rear in descending the mountains, so as to always keep the body on a level." There are to be foot brakes, operating much like railroad-car brakes. There is to be a safety strap by which "the motion of the horses may be arrested by any one of the passengers, if necessary." It was doubtless this unholy device which drove the drivers to liquor.

On August 31, 1899, the first automobile ascent was made in a steamer by Mr. and Mrs. F. O. Stanley of Newton, Massachusetts. Four years later the first officially timed ascent took one hour and forty-six minutes. In the following years

Mount Washington was the Mecca for the famous Glidden Tours which, with great trial and tribulation, accomplished the mazing feat of covering several hundred miles on each yearly expedition by virtue of taking the winter off for repairs. "Climbs to the Clouds" occurred. In 1905 the best time was made in 20 minutes, 58 2-5 seconds. Since then we do not know what has happened—the record is doubtless broken every summer. Possibly the record-breakers sometimes stop to look at the view. The Glen House Company operates specially geared cars at reasonable prices for the ascent. There is a reasonable toll charge for private cars. It is impossible now to drive in New Hampshire without meeting almost hourly cars labelled with the boastful placard: "This car has climbed Mount Washington." Well, who cares?

But to return to other times.

It is a little shocking to observe how the Glen, for all its beauty, has given a decidedly peevish tone to the mountains' clergymen-historians. Starr King, for instance, takes the Glen as a text upon which to lecture the Creator on his failure to provide the White Mountain region with sufficient lakes. He goes even further. He presumes to advise. "If we had full power over the scenery near the highest range to alter or amend it," he says, "we should order a lake to appear forthwith in 'The Glen'. . . . To be able to sail about over a liquid mirror covering the whole gorge of the Peabody River in front of the Glen House;—to see the clouds sweeping under you in a mighty bowl of blue and catch the Narcissus of the Range, Mount Madison, secluded from his fellows, gazing at his own symmetry . . . to skim along in the shadow of

Washington, observing the heavy roll of his shoulder like an arrested wave. . . ."

But alas, it was not to be. The Creator had other designs. There were the Alps and the Adirondacks and Banff to supply with water. But Starr King, in his peevishness, seems not to have thought of that.

The Rev. Julius Ward is even more critical. The Creator has distinctly made of this region a test: here "the problem is to conquer the whole mountain wall and make it a teacher of the human spirit. It is a hard task." Not, however, one beyond the powers of Mr. Ward. If Milton could evolve the epic of Paradise Lost out of negative conditions so could the Creator evolve a creative technique to fit this place. He did: "the rise and fall of man are repeated in their summits and ravines." But Paradise Lost is a strain on mortal man. So does the watching of this huge mountain wall make the Rev. Julius Ward weary. "There was a constant strain about it. The effort was beyond me . . . the opening is so limited and the height of the range so imposing that the eye is like Noah's dove when the bird first flew out of the ark upon the waste of waters; it has nothing but the immense height of wall to rest upon. This is partly why the view at the Glen is often painfully depressing."

One would think that the Creator might have had more consideration for the eye and sensibilities of Rev. Julius Ward. But no, it was not the Creator's, it was Mr. Ward's error. "I had seen the mountain side face to face, and not as Nature intended it to be seen. It has been studied out of relation." Seen from the proper place the barriers break down. We wish we had time and space to record fully Mr. Ward's return to sanity and his acceptance of the Creator's plans for the Glen. . .

The road goes on down by the Glen House through Pinkham Notch. Three miles below the Glen House on the left is Glen Ellis Falls, one of the most beautiful waterfalls in the mountains. Below Glen Ellis, on the right, are the Crystal Cascades. Mr. Drake takes three pages to describe their shifting colors and shades. But we shall spare you those. Through Pinkham Notch the road leads down, down, down to Jackson and the Conway Intervale whence we may turn to look back—and it will be a nostalgic look, you may be sure—at the lofty remoteness of Washington against the sky.

CHAPTER VII

THE SACO VALLEY AND CHOCORUA

IN THIS whole upheaval making up the mountains of New Hampshire, which Robert Frost says "curl up in a coil," the southern rim is called the Sandwich Range. If the region is reduced to another figure it will be seen that it makes an approximate triangle, so that taking Mount Washington as the peak, its sides come down to the West, Franconia Range, and on the east through Crawford Notch, and the Carter-Moriah Range. The Sandwich Range is the base, a region of comparatively low peaks but with views that are excelled by none in the section, on the valid principle that you do not stand on top of a picture to see it. The village center of this region is Conway, with its neighboring towns of North Conway, and Intervale.

Conway is the oldest White Mountain town, an important summer colony, and the center of a group of artists who perpetuate the enthusiasm if not the technique of those earlier painters who settled about North Conway and Artists' Brook and christened the place somewhat self-consciously "The Barbizon of America." Their canvases of the country round about, particularly views of and from Chocorua, may be found in many public collections as examples of the "Hudson River School." Meadows and peaks are, in the summer, still dotted with umbrellas, though they shelter from the sun heads with far different ideas of art.

If, as many do, you reverse the order of this book and approach the mountains through the eastern gateway Chocorua stands out a mighty and striking sentinel as the road, following generally the line of the railway, skirts Chocorua Lake and runs on to Conway.

Indian remains found in Conway attest its early settling by the aborigines, who called it Pegwagget, and town records show that its charter was granted by Governor Wentworth in 1765, a year after the first settlement, to Daniel Foster and others "on condition that each grantee should pay a rent, if it were demanded, of one ear of Indian corn annually for ten years, and, after the end of that period, of one shilling proclamation money for every hundred acres."

The town derives its name, according to historians, from Walpole's friend, Henry Seymour Conway, commander in chief of the British army and a champion of American liberty.

In the early organization of the town the land was divided into sixty-nine parcels, with the understanding that each grantee or his heirs would, for a period of five years, cultivate five acres for every fifty in his holding.

Soon after this first settlement was made, the reports of the fertility of the soil brought many new settlers, especially from Portsmouth, Concord, Durham, and Exeter, and in the year following the original grant Foster and some of the others built a small settlement five miles north of Conway, on a long terrace about thirty feet above the intervales of the Saco

The White Mountains from Conway

© Hunting Studio

The White Mountains from Intervale

River and approximately a mile from its banks, which they called North Conway.

Conway's historical preëminence is due to the fact that its organization was never allowed to lapse, as was the case with many early settlements, so that its record is continuous from the original grant and the first town meeting.

The town lies at the juncture of two roads to the north of Pequaket Pond, and just southeast of the confluence of the Swift and Saco Rivers.

But it was the redoubtable Darby Field, first scaler of Washington, who first set white foot in the region, and therefore he was the first to come out singing praises which have been echoed by everyone ever since. He says he "found ten falls on that river [the Saco] to stop boats, and there were two thousands of acres on rich meadow to Pegwagget, an Indian town."

On the heels of his enthusiastic reports many settlers made their way to the region, and many tales are still told of their terrible hardships, typical enough of all the early settlers of this territory. Among them was one Elijah Dinsmore and his wife, whose names are connected with almost incredible fortitude in fighting the wilderness, since they traveled from Lee on snowshoes in the dead of winter, a distance of eighty miles, with a huge pack containing all their belongings. They spent their nights in the open, and slept upon the "cold, cold snow."

An expedient of the settler's family common among pioneers is told by Mr. Willey, whose information came naturally at first hand, and he reports the extreme measures taken by the stoical invaders, to sustain their strength in the absence of food.

"A wide strap of some skin," he writes, "was fastened around them. Each day as they grew more emaciated and thin, the strap being drawn the straiter. Often the buckle was drawn almost to the last hole, the wearer anxiously eyeing and counting the number of holes, beyond which was complete prostration.

"One persevering man, named Emery (Enoch, or Humphrey, it is not known which), had actually buckled into the last hole, and, hardly able to stand, tottered around expecting on the morrow to be unable to rise. A neighbor, in nearly as bad condition as himself crept to his door, and informed him that a moose was not far from his cabin. The poor neighbor himself would have killed him had he had a gun. The intelligence brought a little strength to Emery, and could his strap be drawn a little tighter they yet might live. They cut a new hole, and with all their strength, the skeleton men tightening the strengthening strap. As noiseless as a shadow he crept out, and, steadying his aim with great effort, killed the moose. Together the two famished men sat down to their repast, and before the close of the following day, *it is said,* their straps would hardly reach round them." One can only salute Mr. Willey for discreet italics. They are his.

After the Revolutionary War, or by 1783, Conway had become more numerously settled than any other inland town in the state, and its inhabitants had begun to relieve their early circumstances by engaging in the lumber business. They relied, of course, to a great extent upon hunting for their sustenance, though their rock and maple trees furnished them an abundance of sugar.

These were eked out by bread and other foodstuffs for which their timber was exchanged after they had floated the logs and masts down the Saco to its mouth. Wild geese and ducks and fish abounded in the ponds and rivers, so that after the first years of hardship they lived comfortably enough, and soon developed the fertile fields.

From such beginnings most of these little villages have sprung, and bear witness in their present inhabitants to the dauntless valor of their forebears.

But, while Conway is famous in the history of the region, it is North Conway that has been celebrated in paint, and prose, and poetry, since this lovely village, dreaming in its elm-feathered meadows beside its brook, seems the embodiment of the irresistible charm of that simple human dignity that wrestled with these great mountains and bent them, even a little, to man's use.

From its gentle terrace, left no doubt as memento of the former river bed when the Saco subsided to its present confines, it presents many views of rarest enchantment. To the east it is bounded by a ridge of the Green Hills, called Rattlesnake Ridge, while to the west, across the Saco, the long mass of the Moats, North, Middle, and South, wall it in and lend it the spectacular depth of their shadows for splendid sunset. Northward Mount Washington stands across the jumbled mass of intervening peaks while nearer Kearsarge, or Pequaket, looms in mighty bulk. Chocorua's peak barely peeps over the shut-in horizon line to the southeast.

It was the calm and pervasive beauty of this town, nestling in its unique position, which led the impressionable Mr. King to find it "a little quotation from Arcadia, or a suburb of Paradise."

"Who can tell," he asks in an ecstatic moment, "how it is that the trees here seem of more aristocratic elegance—that the shadows are more delicately pencilled—that the curves of the brooks are more seductive than elsewhere? Why do the nights seem more tender and less solemn? What has touched the ledgy rocks with a grace that softens the impression of sublimity and age? What has made the 'twilight parks' of pine dim with a pensive rather than a melancholy dusk? Certainly there is to be seen in New England no other region so swathed in dreamy charm."

Who, indeed, can answer for this gentle spell that is laid at sundown across this valley with a quivering splendor of light. That quiet miracle leaves the beholder breathless in many a mountain village with its glint of light on trees and the sharp stencils of shadow across the green. Then it is that New England mountains touch their suavest moments of radiant grandeur and make an impression that is never to be forgotten, or found elsewhere, save, perhaps, in those luminous afternoons, after a sun-baked day among the cypress hills of Italy, though Mr. King, an ardent partisan, would yield no place even to that mellow magic.

Naturally, walking about the country around North Conway affords serene delight for those less strenuous sightseers who would behold the marvels of the scenery without the exhaustive effort of climbing. Short walks may be taken over the Green Hills, which lie to the east of North Conway, particularly Middle Mountain (1,850 feet) for which the trail starts behind the Forest Glen Inn, follows the driveway to the north of the hotel; and to Peaked Mountain (1,730 feet) a bare rocky eminence to the north of Middle Mountain, which may be reached by starting along the Middle Mountain trail and diverging off to the left just beyond the point where the main trail crosses a small brook.

On the other side of the Saco the peaks are higher, but not difficult. Moat Mountain, or Middle Moat (2,760 feet) lies almost directly opposite North Conway, and since all three have been burned off, and are all connected by a path which leads along the ridge, they present splendid vantage points.

From North Conway, or Intervale, the usual route to North Moat, the highest summit of the three (3,195 feet) starts from Lucy's Baths, or Diana's Baths, a point three miles from North Conway, easily reached by automobile. The baths are made by a small stream flowing out from the north peak of Middle Moat, which here runs over a nearly level floor of granite before dropping ten feet into a deep basin. The main path leaves the clearing close to the baths by a wide logging road which follows the bank of the brook a short distance and then forks. The right branch is the trail to North Moat Mountain. For Middle Moat the same path branches to the left about half a mile beyond the Baths, just before crossing Cedar Brook. Local maps, indicating these trails more fully, are easily obtainable.

Other interesting walks about North Conway take the

visitor to White Horse and Cathedral Ledges, Echo Lake, Thompson's Falls, Humphrey Ledge, Dolloff Bluff, and Pitman's Arch.

White Horse and Cathedral Ledges are the best known and most notable of a series of bluffs surrounding the base of Moat Mountain. The present roads from Diana's Baths to Cathedral Ledge and from Echo Lake to White Horse Ledge were established by the late Viscount Bryce when he was Ambassador from the Court of St. James to the United States, to replace older roads that had been made virtually impassable by lumbering. The path extends from the Lucy Farm and forks to reach the two ledges.

White Horse Ledge is 1,455 feet in height and derives its name from the supposed likeness of a spot on its face to a white horse. If you see the resemblance it is clear gain. Cathedral Ledge, as may be readily imagined, testifies to a great arch beneath the overhanging cliffs. Echo Lake, from across whose waters many photographs have been taken of the duplicated contours of White Horse Ledge, lies beneath that bluff. Thompson's Falls are behind White Horse, on a tributary of the Saco. Humphrey's Ledge connects Moat Mountain with Mount Attitash, sometimes called West Moat, and affords a very beautiful view, while Dolloff Bluff is a cliff on the southwest of Humphrey's Bluff, but higher. Pitman's Arch is an immense cavern beyond Cathedral Ledge, some two hundred feet above the road, and from it a magnificent view of the meadows along the river, and of parts of the village, may be had.

In all these rambles in the neighborhood of North Conway, though, the pictures lie in sudden glimpses, quick compositions made in the eye of the attentive walker who catches a glimpse here of Washington framed between elms, or of the nearer hills, caught beyond an undulant field, over the roof-line of some house. It makes it all an intimate and beguiling place, endless in its scenic fascinations, easy rapture for those who bring with them the seeing eye and the understanding heart.

If we seem, somehow, to have sidetracked Chocorua it is only seeming, for there is no sidetracking that insistent guard whose height is no measure of its interest.

Chocorua has been climbed, hymned and painted more probably than any mountain hereabouts except Washington, and that majority may depend on some missing precincts. For Chocorua holds its place by its sheer personality. If there is one physical superlative that can be used about it Mr. King uses it when he calls it the sharpest, and even that dubious flattery must give place to Adams if not others. It is, as Dr. Crothers says in his preface to "The White Hills in Poetry," "every inch a mountain."

It is the easternmost peak of the Sandwich Range, and indeed, on the earliest extant maps of that range, it is the only peak to have a name. Its cone-like pinnacle is reached by no less than six trails, and its precipitous slope and its bare summit give it an impression of greater altitude than the 3,508 feet it can actually claim.

In almost any panorama from the better known peaks of the region it lifts its readily identifiable top, and from it superb views may be had of the country all about.

Whittier thought it "the most beautiful and striking of all the New Hampshire Hills" and attested his enthusiasm for the region in many poems, notably "Among the Hills," "Voyage of the Jettie" and "Sunset on the Bearcamp" besides a frolicsome, and originally anonymous verse called "How They Climbed Chocorua" which Lucy Larcom read to the assembled climbers whose names were mentioned in the stanzas. Thomas Cole, who was one of the first American painters to enshrine the glories of the region on canvas climbed Chocorua about 1824 and found it "mighty and sublime" though "too extended and map-like for the canvas." His painting of "Chocorua's Curse" is famous.

"Chocorua is not as big as the Matterhorn," says Dr. Crothers. "But the principle is the same. It is every inch a mountain. And you have actually climbed Chocorua, while you only looked at the Matterhorn from the hotel."

There is, as a matter of sudden fact, the peculiar pleasure of all the White Mountains. They bring mountain climbing into something approaching human possibility, a delight to be indulged in by a majority of visitors, instead of yielding their summits only to a dauntless few who must turn professional before achieving the conquest of higher and more perilous peaks. They are everybody's mountains. They belong no less to those who walk a stretch off the road to frame some distant peak in graceful fringes of elm, than to those who stalk their most isolated summits.

It is that very pervasive fact which must impress every watchful tourist, thereby belying the name that is given to them. Though Josselyn, in his earliest commentary, boldly stated that "snow lieth upon them all the year" more careful exploration led him to correct the statement and to admit, what all the world may see with relief, that it is not so.

"If that were true," says J. Brooks Atkinson in his charming and engagingly philosophic "Skyline Promenades," which should be in every meditative travel kit, then " 'White Mountains' might be a truthful term suggestive of glaciers, ice-capped peaks, broad expanses of snow, Arctic winds and cloud banners streaming from sharp summits. Of such glorious, sparkling quality is their beauty on sharp days in the winter. And ascents by snow shoes and ice-creepers deserve well some frigid description. I once saw them in April from Monadnock, seventy-five miles south; 'White Hills' they were then, too, great mounds of white looming on the horizon, Arctic enough in appearance, while the landscape around Monadnock was of that drab tone which just precedes the first delicate tinges of verdure.

"But the frequent assertion that the White Mountains bear that name because even in summer the summit rocks of the Presidential Range are white, or whitish-gray, or appear so by reason of atmospheric conditions, is not strictly in accordance with the facts and seems a beggarly way to justify a vain boast. Does not this summoning of evidence betray the braggart? It doth protest too much; if the name were fitting these explanations would be superfluous.

"No; 'White Mountains' implies summits so lofty as to bear perpetual snows. The occasional snow-squalls which flurry over the summit of Mount Washington in the summer scarcely come within that category; and the snow-bank which lies in Tuckerman Ravine long after the June flowers have bloomed and faded vanishes as a rule before August is done. I confess that when I first visited these New Hampshire hills as a boy I was disappointed. Spurred on by the name 'White Mountains' my imagination had sprung to ambitious conclusions which their height does not warrant.

"We must not beat our breasts over the height of these mountains. What is the 6,000 feet of Mt. Washington to the 29,000 of Mt. Everest, the 20,000 of Mt. McKinley, the 15,-000 of Mont Blanc, the 14,000 of the Matterhorn or Rainier?

" 'Why, these are mere foothills!' exclaim tourists in New Hampshire to whom mountains mean the Rockies or Alps. Bless us! Of course they are foothills. Those who have stood on the summit of the Gönergrat above Zermatt and looked in awe upon Monte Rosa, the Lyskamm, the sharp, defiant Matterhorn, the Weisshorn and other peaks far to the north, all sparkling with fresh-fallen snow, vast distances of white capped, jagged peaks, snaky glaciers in every crevice, deep gorges, turbulent, foaming streams—whoever sees these peaks knows that *they* are the true 'white' mountains.

"We should do ourselves more credit and celebrate the beauties of our New England hills more effectively if we said less about their comprising the 'Switzerland of America' and devoted our attention to their special characteristics— if, like Lord Bryce, we commended them for their friendliness, placidity, and accessibility. To me also those are their chief virtues."

They are the special virtues of this shining challenge that is Chocorua—a challenge that is also an invitation. Its slopes have been pelted with adjectives, and its trails worn by many footprints. Sweetser, who calls it himself, "probably the most picturesque and beautiful of the mountains of New England" finds that Mr. King has saluted its splendor by no less varied and comprehensive descriptions than "defiant, jagged, gaunt and grisly, tired, haggard, rocky, desolate, craggy-peaked, ghost-like, crouching, proud, gallant, steel-hooded, rugged, torn, lonely, proud-peaked, solemn, and haughty." It is catalogue enough for any dictionarian, and more than ample for those who try their strength against its somber buttresses. His Thesaurus, at any rate, testifies to its many-sidedness, and the variety of aspects which it presents from every point on the horizon. It seems always different, yet unmistakably itself.

Geologically, according to scientists, the peak was formed of a crystalline labradorite called Chocorua granite "which was erupted during the great cataclysm of the Labrador period. It stood upon the site of one of the islands of porphyritic gneiss which constituted the first dry land in New Hampshire, emerging from the ocean at the dawn of geological history. Sharp as is the present peak, it is but the dwarfed remnant of the colossal spire which stood here before the glacial currents swept and ground it away. This action shows why we have no pinnacles of rock such as abound in the Alps. The Swiss glaciers have plowed around these pinnacles and left them standing; but the American continental drift was of such vast proportions that the needles disappeared as if they were pebbles in the path of an ordinary river of ice."

Having thus stood about this inviting pinnacle, pointing

to it from every quarter, and standing here conversing at its very foot, we may examine the ways of scaling its steep sides. Six routes twist across these steep slopes, so that travelers from any point of the compass may be accommodated at least to the first footway.

Most climbers take either the Piper Trail, marked at half mile intervals by the Chocorua Mountain Club, and named for Joshua Piper, who blazed it many years ago, or the Hammond Trail, which is the most direct, and takes about seven hours to the summit and return to Chocorua Village, where it begins. The period allows for about an hour on the peak. Liberty Trail, or Brook Trail may be taken from Tamworth, approaching through the greater distance in a generally northeasterly direction, while from the opposite side of Chocorua the Champney Falls Trail begins at a spot, marked by a sign, on the highway between Conway and Passaconaway. The Bee Line Trail is the direct route between Chocorua and Mount Paugus to the west. The Wetamoo Trail is really a link between the Piper and Hammond Trails, since it branches from the former to the left, just before the Piper Trail reaches an old sap house near its outset, and joins the Hammond Trail about two hours up, beyond an immense boulder. Other lesser known and more inaccessible trails ascend the slopes, or join these at various places, but for such variations it is well to consult the A.M.C. or local guides.

To reach the Piper Trail from Conway the highway is followed southeast to Knowles Pond, which it skirts. At Clement Inn, formerly the Piper House, the trail begins, by a cart-road across a brook to the old house, and proceeds through a pasture. The path crosses Chocorua Brook, and the grade is fairly easy for three-quarters of a mile, when the incline becomes rapidly steeper. About a quarter of a mile before the trail reaches the first ledges Camp Upweekis is reached, on the left, while on the right is a short side trail to Camp Penacock. From this point the summit rises some six hundred feet above a fringe of woods, to the ultimate tip. The last half mile of the trail is through a bare area, without trees, and over ledges. "Great God of Russia!" exclaimed Mr. Atkinson at this point on peak, "What a trail!" It may well go for all last long pulls needing more stable Gods than those of Russia.

The Hammond Trail leaves the main road a mile and a half to the north of Chocorua Lake, where another road, less smooth but still accessible to motor cars, branches off to the right (coming down from Conway), crosses Chocorua Brook, and ends near a farmhouse. On the right of the road, just before it reaches a brook, the trail begins, crosses the brook again as a slender foot path, passes through beech and birch trees, and maples and some scattered evergreens, and ascends a ridge called Bald Mountain. From the lower slopes there are fine views over Chocorua Lake, toward the mountains off to the south—Ossipee, Whittier, Bearcamp, and the lesser hills of the Sandwich Range. Beyond the crest of this spur the path dips through ravines and over jutting crags, all plainly marked, and reaches the base of the cone that forms the summit. On the upper stretches there are short level places in the path—grateful easements to the climber.

Since many motorists may approach the peak along the

road from Conway to Passaconaway it may be well to outline this course briefly. It leaves the highway about three miles east of Swift River Inn, where Twin Brook crosses the road, and just beyond the Bolles Trail, which begins some 250 yards to the west of the Champney Falls Trail. The trail follows a lumber road, crosses the Champney Brook and the site of a logging camp. The trail crosses the brook twice after this, and where the ascent begins proceeds by easy grades, but with a steady rise, so that fine views may be obtained to the north. From the forest the trail enters burned-over areas and beyond the ledges enters a series of zigzags on a horse trail which replaced the somewhat precipitous old one.

From the summit Chocorua seems to lose the isolation which distinguishes it when seen from other peaks, or even from its own base. Though logical enough, this is not usually true of mountains whose remoteness seems greater when the climber at last becomes a part of it. For Chocorua affords such a charming and intimate view of its surrounding country, presents such agreeable prospects of the distant peaks and altogether makes its forbidding eminence a pretty place of observation that it quite beguiles the visitor into dawdling.

Its immediate scene naturally lends itself to this feeling of summit hospitality. Other mountains look solemnly out upon their too-near neighbors—but Chocorua, by its serene apartness, arranges its views with more suavity, lends contrasts between the near meadows and far horizons, looks down upon adjacent spurs and decently removed summits with a geniality that is unique and unforgettable, belying utterly the gruff sides that give access to this vantage point. In this it has a quality which neither Moosilauke nor Washington can lay claim to.

The Albany Intervale, which extends into the wilderness, lies at the base of Chocorua to the north, and separates the peak from the central system. To the east the eye languishes upon comparatively open country, takes in the southern spurs of the Moats, and discovers North Conway village nestling at the foot of Pequaket (Kearsarge) which mounds bulkily up against the horizon line. Farmhouses and sparkling lakes dot the country away to the southward, while to the west Paugus and Passaconaway stretch out in the great buttress of the Sandwich Range. All satisfied climbers testify to the fact that no other eminence embraces so much in so small a compass.

As Mr. O'Kane points out, the view from the top is "essentially twofold" since to the west and north it embraces typical mountain scenery, while to the east and south it is made up of fairly level country.

If the observer will take orientation by Mount Washington, the "constant star" of all such observations, that vast peak will be found almost due north of Chocorua, rising between Bear and Table Mountains, topping "the ermine of the Presidential Range like a magical iceberg." Through Pinkham Notch, to the right of Table Mountain on the horizon, a glimpse may be had of Mount Madison. The Moats lie closer at hand to the northeast, rising in a long hummock, and over Moat can be seen the more distant outlines of the

Baldfaces. To the right of the Moats, Kearsarge lifts its solitary cone.

From this point the view passes into the first segment of a more map-like picture, while far off the mass of Pleasant Mountain hems in the vista. Several lakes lie due east, the nearest being Knowles Pond. Some observers, specially privileged by the weather, report having seen the ocean far off to the southeast.

A little more to the right, but far off, are the Ossipees, and nearer by the eye follows a pretty chain of water—Silver Lake, Ossipee Lake, and nearer still, almost under the bulging shoulder of Chocorua, is Chocorua Lake. To the right of the Ossipees may be seen parts of Lake Winnipesaukee and Squam Lake.

Now the scene changes again as it returns to its turbulent mountain scenery. To the westward is the ridge of Paugus, thickly wooded in part rising "like a blue-black toppling wave." Over the shoulder of Paugus Passaconaway peers, flanked by Tripyramid and Whiteface, which, from this angle, bares to the world the reasons for its christening. Still farther off, beyond Tripyramid, Osceola and Tecumseh may be seen, and on very clear days the unmistakable outline of Moosilauke and the Franconia Range are visible.

Three subsidiary peaks, known as "The Three Sisters" stretch away from Chocorua to the northeast, while below this ridge lies the valley of Swift River. Across the head of the valley in a northwesterly direction is Carrigain Notch, guarded on its left by the huge bulk of Mount Carrigain, flanked by Hancock (to the left, or southwest of Carrigain).

© *Hunting Studio*

Moat Range and Ledges, Intervale

The Peak of Chocorua

To the right of Carrigain rises Mount Lowell, flanked on the right by Anderson and Nancy. This completes the circuit of a fascinating panorama.

Any account of Chocorua must include mention of an Indian legend which, in many forms, is attached to this peak, and which lends it greater interest in Indian lore than any of its neighbors. It has to do with the death upon this splendid summit of the Indian whose name stands as a memorial to, from one account, a piece of awful redskin treachery, and a white man's revenge, and from the other to the even more horrible greed of the invading settlers.

The second of these, which is the shorter, contains fewer of the elements which perpetuate legends in the hearts of men, and since it is by far the more unpleasant of the two, it has been shrugged off by a consensus of later prejudice, not overly anxious to give the red man his due in any particular.

It is the version included in Drake's "History of the North American Indians," and repeated, years later, to Mr. Sweetser by an ancient resident of Tamworth who was, at least, in a position to get the facts at first hand. The two accounts differ only in detail, and take up the story after the battle at Lovewell's Pond, where, on May 8, 1725, Captain Lovewell and Paugus, at the head of a band of Indians greatly outnumbering the whites, fought a desperate fight. Though in modern warfare the number of men engaged would be considered ridiculously small, the fighting was so sanguinary that both commanders and three-fourths of their men were killed. Afterwards the Indians, belonging to the

Pequaket tribe, migrated to Canada, but one of them, Chocorua, a chieftain and a prophet, having made friends with the white men, remained behind.

"Chocorua," according to Sweetser's version, "refused to leave the ancient home of his people and the graves of his forefathers. . . . On one occasion he was obliged to go to Canada to consult with his people at Saint Francis, and, wishing to spare his son the labors of the long journey, he left him with Campbell (a settler living near what is now Tamworth)." What happened as the bloody climax of this version will be narrated in detail from early accounts.

The other version is taken indirectly from Drake, and reprinted in Mr. Willey's "Incidents in White Mountain History."

"To this [peak] Chocorua had retreated pursued by a miserable white hunter. To the highest point he had climbed, and there he stood, unarmed, while below, and within gunshot, stood his pursuer. Chocorua besought the hunter not to kill him. He pled his friendliness to the whites, and the harmless, scattered condition of his few followers. But the hardened hunter was unmoved; the price of his scalp was too tempting. [About that time the Province of Massachusetts gave a bounty of about $500 for every scalp brought into Boston. Eds.] Gold pled stronger than the poor Indian. Seeing that he should avail nothing, the noble chieftain, raising himself up stretched forth his arms and called upon the Gods of his fathers to curse the land. Then, casting a defiant glance at his pursuer, he leaped from the brink of the precipice on the south side to the rocks below. And to this day (1856) say the inhabitants, a malignant disease has carried off the cattle that they have attempted rearing around this mountain."

The story in its other form is taken in its entirety from "Chocorua's Curse" published in 1830 in The Token, an annual popular at that time, and printed in Boston. The copy in the hands of the present authors credits the tale simply to "The Author of Hobomok," and is accompanied by George W. Hatch's engraving of Cole's painting. The author of "Hobomok" was Mrs. Lydia Maria Child.

Her account, redolent of its time, follows:

"The rocky county of Stafford, New Hampshire, is remarkable for its wild and broken scenery. Ranges of hills towering one above another, as if eager to look upon the beautiful country, which afar off lies sleeping in the embrace of heaven; precipices, from which the young eagles take their flight to the sun; dells rugged and tangled as the dominions of Roderick Vich Alpine, and ravines dark and deep enough for the death scene of a bandit, form the magnificent characteristics of this picturesque region.

"A high precipice, called Chocorua's Cliff, is rendered peculiarly interesting by a legend which tradition has scarcely saved from utter oblivion. Had it been in Scotland, perhaps the genius of Sir Walter would have hallowed it, and Americans would have crowded there to kindle fancy on the altar of memory. Being in the midst of our romantic scenery, it is little known and less visited; for the vicinity is as yet untraversed by rail-roads or canals, and no 'Mountain House,' perched on these tremendous battlements, allures the traveler hither to mock the majesty of nature with the insipidities of fashion. Our distinguished artist, Mr. Cole, found the sunshine and the winds sleeping upon it in solitude and secrecy; and his pencil has brought it before us in its stern repose.

"In olden time, when Goffe and Whalley passed for wizards and mountain spirits among the superstitious, the vicinity of the spot we have been describing was occupied by a very small colony, which, either from discontent or enterprise, had retired into this remote part of New Hampshire. Most of them were ordinary men, led to this independent mode of life from an impatience of restraint, which as frequently accompanies vulgar obstinacy as generous pride. But there was one master spirit among them, who was capable of a higher destiny than he ever fulfilled. The consciousness of this had stamped something of proud humility on the face of Cornelius Campbell; something of a haughty spirit strongly curbed by circumstances he could not control, and at which he scorned to murmur.

"He assumed no superiority; but unconsciously he threw around him the spell of intellect, and his companions felt, they knew not why, that he was 'among them, but not of them.' His stature was gigantic, and he had the bold, quick tread of one who had wandered frequently and fearlessly among the terrible hiding-places of nature. His voice was harsh, but his whole countenance possessed singular capabilities for tenderness of expression; and sometimes, under the gentle influence of domestic excitement, his hard features would be rapidly lighted up, seeming like the sunshine flying over the shaded fields in an April day.

"His companion was one peculiarly calculated to excite

and retain the deep, strong energies of manly love. She had possessed extraordinary beauty; and had, in the full maturity of an excellent judgment, relinquished several splendid alliances, and incurred her father's displeasure, for the sake of Cornelius Campbell. Had political circumstances proved favorable, his talents and ambition would unquestionably have worked out a path to emolument and fame; but he had been a zealous and active enemy of the Stuarts, and the restoration of Charles the Second was the death-warrant of his hopes. Immediate flight became necessary. America was the chosen place of refuge. His adherence to Cromwell's party was not occasioned by religious sympathy, but by political views, too liberal and philosophical for the state of the people; therefore Cornelius Campbell was no favorite with our forefathers, and being of a proud nature, he withdrew with his family to the solitary place we have mentioned.

"It seemed a hard fate for one who had from childhood been accustomed to indulgence and admiration, yet Mrs. Campbell enjoyed more than she had done in the days of her splendor; so much deeper are the sources of happiness than those of gaiety. Even her face had suffered little from time and hardship.

"The bloom on her cheek, which in youth had been like the sweet-pea blossom, that most feminine of all flowers, had, it is true, somewhat faded; but her rich, intellectual expression, did but receive additional majesty from years; and the exercise of quiet domestic love, which, where it is suffered to exist, always deepens and brightens with time, had given a bland and placid expression, which might well have atoned

for the absence of more striking beauty. To such a woman as
Caroline Campbell, of what use would have been some modern doctrines of equality and independence?

"With a mind sufficiently cultivated to appreciate and enjoy her husband's intellectual energies, she had a heart that
could not have found another home. The bird will drop into
its nest though the treasures of earth and sky are open. To
have proved marriage a tyranny, and the cares of domestic
life a thraldom, would have affected Caroline Campbell as
little, as to be told that the pure, sweet atmosphere she
breathed, was pressing upon her so many pounds to every
square inch! Over such a heart, and such a soul, external
circumstances have little power; all worldly interest was
concentrated in her husband and babes, and her spirit was
satisfied with that inexhaustible fountain of joy which nature
gives, and God has blessed.

"A very small settlement, in such a remote place, was of
course subject to inconvenience and occasional suffering.
From the Indians they received neither injury nor insult. No
cause of quarrel had ever arisen; and, although their frequent
visits were sometimes troublesome, they never had given indications of jealousy or malice. Chocorua was a prophet
among them, and as such an object of peculiar respect. He
had a mind which education and motive would have nerved
with giant strength; but growing up in savage freedom, it
wasted itself in dark, fierce, ungovernable passions. There was
something fearful in the quiet haughtiness of his lip—it
seemed so like slumbering power, too proud to be lightly
roused, and too implacable to sleep again. In his small, black

fiery eye, expression lay coiled up like a beautiful snake. The white people knew that his hatred would be terrible; but they had never provoked it, and even the children became too much accustomed to him to fear him.

"Chocorua had a son, about nine or ten years old, to whom Caroline Campbell had occasionally made such gaudy presents as were likely to attract his savage fancy. This won the child's affections, so that he became a familiar visitant, almost an inmate of their dwelling; and being unrestrained by the courtesies of civilized life, he would inspect everything, and taste of everything which came in his way. Some poison, prepared for a mischievous fox, which had long troubled the little settlement, was discovered and drunk by the Indian boy; and he went home to his father to sicken and die. From that moment jealousy and hatred took possession of Chocorua's soul. He never told his suspicions—he brooded over them in secret, to nourish the deadly revenge he contemplated against Cornelius Campbell.

"The story of Indian animosity is always the same. Cornelius Campbell left his hut for the fields early one bright, balmy morning in June. Still a lover, though ten years a husband, his last look was turned towards his wife, answering her parting smile—his last action a kiss for each of his children. When he returned to dinner, they were dead—all dead! and their disfigured bodies too cruelly showed that an Indian's hand had done the work!

"In such a mind grief, like all other emotions, was tempestuous. Home had been to him the only verdant spot in the wide desert of life. In his wife and children he had garnered up all his heart; and now they were torn from him, the remembrance of their love clung to him like the death-grapple of a drowning man, sinking him down, down, into darkness and death. This was followed by a calm a thousand times more terrible—the creeping agony of despair, that brings with it no power of resistance.

> 'It was as if the dead could feel
> The icy worm around him steal.'

"Such, for many days, was the state of Cornelius Campbell. Those who knew and reverenced him, feared that the spark of reason was forever extinguished. But it rekindled again, and with it came a wild, demoniac spirit of revenge. The death-groan of Chocorua would make him smile in his dreams; and when he waked, death seemed too pitiful a vengeance for the anguish that was eating into his very soul.

"Chocorua's brethren were absent on a hunting expedition at the time he committed the murder; and those who watched his movements observed that he frequently ascended the high precipice, which afterward took his name, probably looking out for indications of their return.

"Here Cornelius Campbell resolved to effect his deadly purpose. A party was formed under his guidance, to cut off all chance of retreat, and the dark-minded prophet was to be hunted like a wild beast to his lair.

"The morning sun had scarce cleared away the fogs when Chocorua started at a loud voice from beneath the precipice, commanding him to throw himself into the deep abyss be-

Swift River and Mount Chocorua

© *George F. Slade*

Kearsarge and Bartlett Mountains and Saco River, North Conway low. He knew the voice of his enemy, and replied with an Indian's calmness, 'The Great Spirit gave life to Chocorua; and Chocorua will not throw it away at the command of a white man.'

" 'Then hear the Great Spirit speak in the white man's thunder!' exclaimed Cornelius Campbell, as he pointed his gun to the precipice. Chocorua, though fierce and fearless as a panther, had never overcome his dread of fire-arms. He placed his hand upon his ears to shut out the stunning report; the next moment the blood bubbled from his neck, and he reeled fearfully on the edge of the precipice. But he recovered himself, and raising himself on his hands, he spoke in a loud voice, that grew more terrific as its huskiness increased. 'A curse upon ye, white men! May the Great Spirit curse ye when he speaks in the clouds, and his words are fire! Chocorua had a son—and ye killed him while the sky looked bright. Lightning blast your crops! Wind and fire destroy your dwellings! The Evil Spirit breathe death upon your cattle! Your graves lies in the war path of the Indian! Panthers howl, and wolves fatten over your bones! Chocorua goes to the Great Spirit—his curse stays with the white men!'

"The prophet sank upon the ground, still uttering inaudible curses—and they left his bones to whiten in the sun. But his curse rested on the settlement. The tomahawk and scalping knife were busy among them, the winds tore up trees and hurled them at their dwellings, their crops were blasted, their cattle died, and sickness came upon their strongest men. At last the remnant of them departed from the fatal spot to mingle with more populous and prosperous colonies.

Cornelius Campbell became a hermit, seldom seeking or seeing his fellow men; and two years after he was found dead in his hut.

"To this day the town of Burton, in New Hampshire, is remarkable for a pestilence which infects its cattle; and the superstitious think that Chocorua's spirit still sits enthroned upon his precipice, breathing a curse upon them."

Burton is now Albany, and as a matter of scientific record there was, at one time, a serious disease among the cattle which the superstitious naturally attributed to the curse of Chocorua. So widespread was the interest in the case that in 1821 Professor Dana of Dartmouth College was appointed to visit the place and to ascertain, if possible, the causes of the disease.

"After much investigation," says Mr. Willey, "he found the difficulty to be in the water. It was a weak solution of muriate of lime. He recommended as a remedy or preventive weak lye, or ashes, or soap-suds. A certain kind of mud, however, had been discovered by the citizens which was used with great benefit. This mud is found on a meadow and during the summer it is collected for use." From his own tests Mr. Willey found the mud to contain carbonate of lime, so that Chocorua's Curse has at long last, yielded to science, or one witchcraft to another.

If the exigent motorists will pause a moment in their palpitant automobiles, or better still leave them in their garages and take this part of the journey on Shank's Mare, they will enjoy on an agreeable and plausible scale the rare delights of climbing. For the peaks which file off from Chocorua to the westward offer engaging possibilities. They can be reached by roads from the south and east, centering on Wonalancet, or by necessarily longer trails from the other side of the range from Albany Intervale, on the road from North Conway.

From the summit of Chocorua we have seen Passaconaway beyond the crest of Paugus, with Whiteface behind and to the left, or, if you believe in compasses, over the south flank of Passaconaway. Wherefore Paugus, which used to be called Old Shag until Lucy Larcom rechristened the mountain in honor of the Indian chieftain, may be seen to lie between Chocorua and Passaconaway, dominated by both, but presenting, or perhaps, therefore, presenting, from the bare eminence to the south of the main peak, a superb view of both its neighbors.

Well, if you hanker to explore Paugus, and happen at this typographical juncture to be on the summit of Chocorua you may proceed over the Bee Line Trail directly between the two mountains, which crosses the Bolles Trail just north of a ruined camp, jumps a stream, takes a narrow bridge, and then joins the Old Paugus Trail near the top of the ridge. All junctions of the trails as the indefatigable and indispensable A.M.C. Guide points out, are marked by the yellow signs of the Chocorua Mountain Club. There is a fine view of Chocorua, which comes to be a specialist's hobby, from the point just below the meeting of the Old Paugus and Bee Line Trails.

The Old Paugus Trail, thus joined, has naturally started somewhere below for the benefit of those who approach from the southerly side instead of from the peak of Chocorua. It

begins at Paugus Mill and branches to the left from the Bolles
Trail through the valley, and follows the main road, carefully
marked, beyond Whitin Brook where it again diverges at a
log cabin, turns north up the valley side and meets the Bick-
ford Path from Big Rock Cave and Wonalancet. After crossing a steep slope, graveled over by loose débris, it joins the
Bee Line Trail to the summit. Old Shag camp is on a short
branch to the north, about a fifth of a mile below the summit. Southwest of Paugus is the Carrigain outlook, much
favored as a vantage point, which may be reached over the
Old Paugus Trail, descending by the Lawrence Trail to its
junction with the Cabin Trail. Though these trails can be
reached from the north by the Bolles Trail, originally a logging road between Tamworth and Albany, the difference in
length, and the fact that the Bolles Trail runs through desolate country, make this approach more difficult and not particularly rewarding.

Mount Passaconaway, named for a chieftain of the Pena-
cooks and loftiest of the Sandwich Range, lifts its steeply
symmetrical dome to a height of 4,116 feet, and although its
flanks are densely wooded, there are extended views from its
summit. It may be reached from the north by the Oliverian
Brook Trail, which leaves the highway near the Oliverian
Brook, about three-quarters of a mile east of Swift River Inn,
or from the south from Wonalancet, named, incidentally,
for the son of Passaconaway, who succeeded his father when
the old chief abdicated in 1660.

Since Dicey's Mill Trail was the first blazed up the mountain and is still perhaps the most popular, it may be outlined

briefly, though the climber cannot be too often reminded that for all but the simplest ventures in climbing, the A.M.C. Guide is not only advised but necessary. This trail follows the highway from Ferncroft, beyond the point where it becomes a wood road, turns to the right, and begins to rise steeply. There are two tributary trails near the site of an old mill, but the main trail crosses to the west bank of the stream, and begins its steepest climb, following an old logging road on the east side of a ridge to the virgin spruce woods on the upper slopes. The main trail turns left, and in about a quarter of a mile reaches the Wonalancet Out Door Club's camp, Passaconaway Lodge, an open log shelter with an iron roof. The trail leaves the camp and climbs steadily to the summit, which it reaches by the west outlook.

To the southwest of Passaconaway and connected with it by a ridge lies Whiteface, deriving its name from the bare face left by a great landslide in 1820. While it is seldom visited even by experienced climbers in this region, though it is readily accessible, and its height, 4,057 feet, is topped in this range only by Passaconaway. Since the peak of the mountain is heavily wooded the best views are obtained from the precipices some distance south of the actual summit.

Approach is made usually from the south, although the trail along the Downes Brook, from the Albany Intervale side renders it accessible from the north. The southerly approach is over the Blueberry Trail, marked with the blue paint of the Wonalancet Out Door Club, and begins beyond Ferncroft, crosses the "Squirrel Bridge" over the Swift River (not to be confused with the larger stream of the same name which almost parallels the highway to the north) and turns sharply to the right. There is a fork in the trail opposite a cottage, but since the right branch joins the main trail on the ledges, after traveling through the "Gorge" we follow to the left. The ledges have a gentle declivity, and on the upper edge the trail enters thick woods, where it begins a steady ascent. Beyond the ledges the path rises to Wonalancet Outlook over a series of cut-out steps and then over a difficult rocky ridge for which the wary climber will need utmost caution, to the summit.

This last section of the climb looks across the precipitous wall exposed by the great slide, on which a few bushes and small trees cling tenaciously, but which, for the most part, is bare. "The effect," says Mr. O'Kane, one of the Whiteface enthusiasts, "as you look across this wide area and down the almost sheer drop is one that will not soon be forgotten."

About forty yards north of the ledge, which on account of its outlook is called the summit, is Camp Heermance, named for the Rev. Edgar L. Heermance, one of those enthusiastic mountaineering ministers to which the mountains of this whole section owe so much of their history and popularity. Another camp about a quarter of a mile from the top of Whiteface, and known as Shehadi, though frequently shown on trail maps, is now in ruins.

The other mountains of this range, Flat Mountain, Sandwich, and Tripyramid, present their special allurements to the relentless climbers. Their specifications are readily obtainable by those who wish to explore their trails and summits.

Since the hypothetical motors of these jaunters are purring hopefully in some adjacent garage or roadside, we may return to them and continue the gradual explorations through Crawford Notch to our final objective, Mount Washington.

CHAPTER VIII

CRAWFORD NOTCH

WE HAVE left the Chocorua region behind, and the distant view of Washington across the Conway Intervale is summoning us onward to the final conquest of the peak; but instead of retracing the way northwest up into Jackson, Pinkham Notch and the Glen, our spiraling progress leads us westward to Bartlett and Crawford Notch. At Bartlett the nearer and lower mountains have already cut us off from view of the higher mountains of the Range and we become aware as we climb steadily beside the meandering Saco into the shadows of the mountains that we are approaching the famous pass, the White Mountain Notch, most historic of all the mountain notches.

There are legends to the effect that this pass was known to the Indians and that through it they occasionally led their captives from raids upon the seaboard colonists up into Canada, but there is no record of its being known to the white settlers before 1771. In that year, as noted in the chapter on Jefferson, Timothy Nash, hunting moose on the slopes of Cherry Mountain, climbed a tree and spied this defile in the apparently impassable mountain wall to the southeast. He made haste to investigate and, following the Saco down through it, appeared before Governor Wentworth at Ports-

Crawford Notch

Carter Notch from Jackson

mouth with the news that he had discovered a nearer way of access from the sea to the regions behind the mountains. The delighted governor made him a grant of a large tract of land on the northwestern side of the pass in recognition of his discovery, cannily making this grant contingent, however, on his successfully getting a horse down through it to Portsmouth.

This feat was by no means easy but, setting out from Lancaster with another Nimrod named Sawyer, Nash succeeded in accomplishing it by lowering the poor beast with rope and tackle over the precipices in the notch and triumphantly presented himself, horse, Sawyer and all before the surprised governor. Being a man of his word the governor awarded them the Nash and Sawyer Location.

It was some years, however, before traffic up through the White Mountain Notch became very heavy, although before the close of the Revolution a road was constructed up through to the Coös country, with, according to Kilbourne, the proceeds of a confiscated Tory estate. This was the route used, as we have seen, by Colonel Whipple and the early settlers of Jefferson. According to accounts it must have been a rather fearful piece of engineering. It was so steep in places, Mr. Kilbourne says, that horses and wagons had to be drawn up with ropes, and it crossed the Saco no less than thirty-two times.

Travel over this primitive road was made by "horse and car" the car in this instance being an extremely simple vehicle without wheels made by fastening two long poles together with two bars of wood near the center. The heavier ends of the poles dragged on the ground, the lighter ends served as the thills into which the horse was harnessed. The bars of wood carried the load to be transported.

This transportation system was first tested out by the offer on the part of some Portland merchants of a barrel of rum to the man who would get it through the notch. The challenge was accepted by Captain Rosebrook, Ethan Allen Crawford's grandfather, and gloriously won. At any rate, the Crawford "History" records that Rosebrook built a raft to transport it across the Saco at Bartlett and then "put it upon his car and carried it up through the Notch, at least as much of it as was left through the politeness of those who helped manage the affair." Well, what did he expect? we wonder.

The hinterland returned the compliment by sending down to Portland a barrel of tobacco raised in Lancaster. This, says Spaulding in his "Relics" of 1855, was the first produce to be carried down through the Notch. He further moralizes: "Thus, we see, *rum* and *tobacco* ranked here, where, among many good people of olden times, they were considered absolutely necessary, as first. But, thanks be to reformers, may the day not be far distant when an intemperate use of either shall be looked upon by the public, under the influence of moral persuasion, as an evil to be ranked in the same light with the follies of witchcraft!" The Notch, at any rate, is still open.

The settlers could not long be satisfied with so precarious a road for such precious freight and in 1803 forty thousand dollars was raised by a lottery and a turnpike incorporated. The next year the turnpike—the tenth in New Hampshire—

was constructed from the west line of Bartlett twenty miles up through the Notch to Captain Rosebrook's (where Fabyan now is). This greatly facilitated traffic. "We can now go to Portland and back with a team," says Crawford, forty years later, "in from six to eight days; in old times it has taken twenty-two days to go from Lancaster to Portland, and back." Let the tourist of a summer afternoon ponder that for a moment.

From Bartlett, then, (whither, as the Crawford "History" quaintly puts it, Abel Crawford and his wife went one Saturday night to spend the sabbath "among the christians,") the Theodore Roosevelt Highway proceeds up into the fastness of the Notch which now bears the name of this illustrious mountain family.

A mile or so out of Bartlett the road passes a high rock, on the left. This is Sawyer's Rock, so named because Sawyer smashed upon it his empty rum bottle to honor it as the last precipice over which he and Nash lowered their nag on their historic journey. Further on Sawyer's River comes down from the left into the Saco. Here the hiker who has a hankering for a wilderness trail may follow the lumber railroad to the trail for Carrigain and the Waterville region.

The tourist, however, will stick to his car and climb on up into the Notch. Two miles or so beyond Sawyer River he will come to a brook plunging down a little water fall. This is Nancy's Brook, where Nancy's body was found, "with her head resting upon her hand and cane," with her clothes, wet from fording the brook, frozen about her after her tragic and futile thirty mile pursuit of her faithless lover.

Just beyond Nancy's Brook is Bemis. Hither, in the last years of the eighteenth century, came Abel Crawford, with his family, to escape the congested civilization of his father-in-law, Eleazar Rosebrook, twelve miles up through the Notch, and here he established, in subsequent years, the Mount Crawford House which, in his declining years, he turned over to his son-in-law, N. T. P. Davis. Later the property came into the possession of Dr. Samuel A. Bemis (hence the name), a wealthy dentist of Boston. The Mount Crawford House, Mr. Kilbourne tells us, was torn down in 1900 but the stone cottage Dr. Bemis built for himself and lived in until his death in 1881 is still standing and as "Notchland" is open for the entertainment of the public. Nearby are the graves of Abel Crawford, "the Patriarch of the Mountains," and his wife.

Just beyond Bemis the Davis Path over the Montalban Ridge to the summit of Mount Washington leads off to the right. We shall explore this path later in the chapter on the Mount Washington trails but the tramper who has been for some time now deprived of a sight of the principal mountain may wish to diverge for a while from the state highway and follow us along the path over Mount Crawford to the Giant Stairs for a glimpse of the great Range.

Leaving the highway, the trail crosses the Saco, follows old roads for half a mile or so, then begins the ascent of the Mount Crawford ridge. Two and a third miles from Bemis is a branch trail to the left which leads after a quarter of a mile to the top of Mount Crawford and the view. It is a view worth climbing for. To the southeast lies the Conway Intervale; to the south the Ossipee Mountains; to the southwest across the Notch are the peaks of Mounts Bemis, Nancy, Anderson and Lowell, culminating in the rugged summit of Carrigain (4,647 feet). Northwest are Willey and Webster on either side of the narrow valley of the Notch; across the upper valley of the Mount Washington River, rising in Oakes Gulf, stretches the ridge along which lies the Crawford Path to Mount Washington; almost due north is the sharp peak of Mount Monroe, just beyond at a distance of ten miles airline is Washington, our final goal. From Washington south, beginning at Boott Spur, stretches the Montalban Ridge over which leads the Davis Path. Just to the north of Mount Crawford are the two sharp cliffs of Giant Stairs. The tramper will be strongly tempted to go on following the Davis Path to the west of Mount Resolution, past the Resolution Shelter of the A.M.C., to the head of the Giant Stairs, four and a half miles from Bemis, where there is another splendid view. But having done that the temptation to go on for the remaining ten and a half miles to Washington may be too great to overcome. We had better, therefore, return down into the Notch.

Three miles or so beyond Bemis one enters the State Forest Reservation, acquired by purchase in 1912. Three miles beyond the boundary line is the camp of the State Forest Ranger, from whom permission to camp in the Reservation should be obtained. One half mile further on are the Willey Log Cabins, a public camp ground. Here the Notch is merely a narrow valley with scarcely room enough, one would think, for a clearing.

Night descends early, here in the Notch for Mount Willey to the left and Mount Willard straight ahead rise abruptly to shut out the later afternoon sun. The tourist or tramper, spending the night, will notice the premature cool of the evening. After darkness comes he will be impressed by the ominous mountain walls all about him—for Mount Webster covered with slides rises as precipitously on the eastern side of the valley as Mount Willey does on the west. He will be aware of unearthly stillness: all the sounds of the world seem to be shut out; only the Saco just below the cabins rushes on unceasingly down the valley, only the night wind stirs the leaves of the trees.

Then perhaps in the depth of the stillness the deep-throated whistle of a freight locomotive high up on its shelf will reverberate awesomely from mountain wall to mountain wall and the laborious panting of the engine as it toils up the steep grade will fill the narrow valley with multitudinous sound. But after the train has passed beyond the Gateway of the Notch the impressive and peaceful silence again descends. And in the silence the imagination of the tourist will inevitably go back to the historic tragedy of over a hundred years ago. . . .

Spaulding says in his "Relics" that the Willey House, the first house in the Notch, was built by one Davis in 1793 "to accommodate the unfortunate storm-bound traveler, who, from curiosity, or on business, might dare the dangers of this wild pass. Then a little grassy meadow stretched along the bank of the Saco; tall rock-maples, and a towering mountain barrier, rose in the background from this little home of the pilgrim. How like a cool shadow of a great rock was this retreat among the frowning crags!" This story and a half house was kept for several years as an inn and then abandoned. In the winter of 1824 Ethan Allen Crawford hauled hay from Jefferson down to the "Notch House," as he called it (not to be confused with the Notch House built at the head of the Notch some years later by his brother).

It was evidently his intention to open a hostelry there but for one reason or another he gave up the idea and it was not until the fall of 1825 that Samuel Willey, Jr., moved into it with his family. The fall was spent in renovating the abandoned dwelling and enlarging the stable, and that winter, his brother says, he and his shelter were "greeted with as much warmth by the traveler in those mountain passes, as the monks of St. Bernard by the wanderers upon the Alps."

Starr King records a conversation with a man who had little use for poetic descriptions of mountain scenery (Starr King's among them, we suppose). "Now," said this man, "what can be honestly said of this Willey Notch, but, 'Good Heavens, what a rough hole!'" Samuel Willey and his family, however, seem to have had no such uncomplimentary opinion of their dwelling place nor any particular premonition of their fate until one day in June, 1826. A sudden rain came up, so heavy that Abel Crawford and some men who were at work near at hand on the turnpike were obliged to take refuge in the Willey's house. The Crawford *History* records the episode: "While there they saw on the west side of the road a small movement of rocks and earth coming down the hill, and it took all before it. They saw, likewise, whole trees coming down, standing upright, for ten rods together, before they would tip over,—the whole still moving slowly on, making its way until it had crossed the road, and then on a level surface some distance before it stopped. This grand and awful sight frightened the timid family very much."

Upon second thoughts, however, they decided not to leave the place. Mr. Willey took the precaution to place a tight cart body away from the house in such a manner that they could take refuge in it if a similar disturbance occurred and they comforted themselves with the assurance that such another cataclysm was unlikely.

An unusually hot dry summer succeeded but on Monday, August 28th, it began to rain. At nightfall it was raining in torrents and it kept on raining for several hours into the night. The clearing skies of the next morning revealed more devastation upon the flanks of the Presidential Range than had been made in the region in the whole time since the country was settled. At Abel Crawford's, six miles below, the Saco River tore away a saw-mill and a large pile of lumber, drowned twenty-eight sheep, rose two feet on the lower floors of the house, sweeping the coals and ashes from the fireplace, and would doubtless have swept the house away had not Mrs. Crawford in her husband's absence kept watch with a pole at a corner window to ward off the débris that swirled down upon them. While taking stock of their losses the friends and relatives of the Willeys in the intervales below had little time to worry about their fate.

The next day—Tuesday—the Willey dog appeared at the

house of Mrs. Willey's mother and "by moanings and other expressions of deep inward anguish around the persons of the family," to quote the account by Mr. Benjamin Willey, "tried to make them understand what had taken place; but, not succeeding, he left, and after being seen frequently on the road between the Notch House and the residence of the family just referred to, sometimes heading north, and then south, running almost at the top of his speed, as though bent on some most absorbing errand, he soon disappeared from the region, and has never since been seen."

On the same day a certain John Barker, having urgent business down the Notch, left Ethan Allen Crawford's house at four in the afternoon, and though the road was almost completely destroyed, arrived at the Willey House just before dark. But the house appeared to have been hastily deserted: the doors were open, the beds disturbed, upon the bar Mr. Willey's money and papers, upon the table an open Bible. He prepared himself a supper and lay down on one of the beds to sleep, supposing that the family had fled to Abel Crawford's house below. Sleep was prevented by the sound of low groans coming from somewhere near the house. It was so dark that he was unable to investigate but in the morning he discovered that the sounds came from an ox which had been crushed beneath the stable. Freeing the animal he proceeded down the Notch only to discover that no one had seen anything of the missing family. A searching party was quickly organized and set out for the lonely house. A messenger was dispatched to Bartlett to inform Samuel Willey, Sr., of the disappearance of his son's family. At midnight the old gentleman was awakened by a loud trumpet call from across the river (during the freshet the Saco had risen sixteen feet and spread to thrice its ordinary width and the flood had not yet subsided). The messenger, having succeeded in waking the family, gave them the news that their relatives were missing.

Early Thursday morning the rescue party had made its way to the house over the badly washed highway. They saw that a large slide had come tearing down the mountain, burying the road to the depth of thirty feet in places. The avalanche had split on a large flat rock behind the house and had gone completely around it. Whether the frightened family, hearing the rising flood of the Saco and escaping to the refuge Mr. Willey had prepared for emergencies higher up the hill, had been there overwhelmed by the descending landslide or whether, hearing the crash of the mountain-side behind them and rushing out into the storm in their panic they were thus caught and crushed beneath the mass of rocks and trees was never established. By diligent digging in the débris six bodies were found: those of the father and mother, two children, and the two hired men. The bodies of three other children were never discovered.

Those who are familiar with the effect of catastrophes of this sort in quiet country districts will not be surprised at the profound impression the sudden destruction of these nine people in this lonely mountain fastness has made upon future generations. It is out of all proportion to the magnitude of the accident: the episode has been related at length in all the White Mountain chronicles; poems have been written about it; Hawthorne gave an imaginary account of it in "The

Ambitious Guest"; for years afterwards the Willey House was a Mecca for the curious, the sentimental, the romantic. In 1844, Horace Fabyan repaired the old house and built a large addition. In 1898 both houses burned. But even today this solitary spot is shadowed with the gloom of that August catastrophe of over a hundred years ago.

The devastation wrought by the flood of 1826 has been equalled in New England, perhaps, only by the flood of November, 1927. "The road in many places," says Crawford, "was almost entirely gone; the bridges, the whole length of the turnpike, excepting two, a distance of seventeen miles, gone." The good people of Portland "to encourage us" raised fifteen hundred dollars; the directors voted an assessment on the shares to make up the balance. Under the direction of Nathan Kinsman, Esq., the new road was laid out. "We all went to work," says Crawford, "and, as it was said, the sun shone so short a time in this Notch, that the hardy New Hampshire boys made up their hours by moonlight."

The tourist of today goes over approximately the line of that highway. Indeed, with the narrowing valley there is nowhere else to go. From the Willey House site to the Gateway the Notch becomes increasingly impressive. The road rises steadily, and though one has only occasional glimpses of the mountain walls through the trees one has the sense of their imminence. About a mile below the Gateway one passes on the right "the windings and leapings of the Silver Cascade, whose downward path for more than a mile is in view" on the ledgy slope of Mount Webster. (Starr King continues its description with a quotation from Shelley.) Then the road

172 BOOK OF THE WHITE MOUNTAINS

rises sharply to the Gateway, where road, railway, and the Saco River crowd through between two high ledges.

"This," says Ethan Allen Crawford of the early travelers and their "cars," "was a trying place to get through. To go where they now do, was then utterly impossible. They then turned out at the top of the Notch and went over the edge and so managed to get to the top, and by taking a zigzag course, as much as possible, got down; but in doing this there was danger of the horse tipping over, the hill was so steep. And when they returned, they would tie a rope around the horse's neck, to keep him from falling backwards. At one time, however, one horse did so fall; but he was helped up without receiving much injury. At length a committee was chosen to search and look out the best road. They agreed in all places until they came to the Notch. There they held a council. One half was for making the road on one side of the stream, and the other half, on the other side; but after considerable consultation on the subject, one of them turned and voted to make the road on the side of the Saco, where it is now. Reader, when you pass this place, now spoken of, please to look and judge for yourself, if you would devise a way to make a road on the other side of the stream, and then imagine what courage and perseverance our forefathers possessed. They never seemed to take hold of the plow and look back, but drove on."

Now that we are on the subject of transportation a word must be said about the railroad through the Notch. The Portland and Ogdensburg (now the Maine Central) was chartered in 1867; by 1871 it had reached North Conway;

by 1875 Fabyan's. That it was no mean engineering feat the Frankenstein trestle and the Willey Brook Bridge attest; the grade overcome is considerable; in the thirty miles from North Conway to Crawford's the rise is 1,369 feet, between Bemis and Crawford's 116 feet to the mile for nine consecutive miles. And here is one place where the railroad ought not to feel the competition of the automobile. As between going through the Notch by car and by train there is no comparison. Only in the latter way can the full extent of its beauty and impressiveness be appreciated.

But if one has to travel by car a couple of hours or more spent at the Gateway will be well repaid. Issuing from the Notch one faces the Crawford House on the plateau with its altitude of nearly 1,900 feet. Just this side is Saco Lake, whence the Saco—here a tiny stream—takes its source. Turning back one sees Elephant's Head sloping down into the Notch, the road and river, side by side, the railroad right of way riven out of the granite. The road pitches down into the floor of the Notch, the railroad curves away to the right along the side of the western mountain wall.

The tramper with half a day to spend may profitably take the Willey Range trail at the Crawford House, going back over Mounts Avalon, Field and Willey and down into the Notch to the Willey House Station. The distance is not quite seven miles.

But even so long an expedition is hardly necessary. Years ago, in 1846, Thomas Crawford, Ethan Allen's brother, built a carriage road up Mount Willard, the low mountain (2,786 feet) with the ledgy summit, which seems to the traveler coming up the Notch to block all egress from it. The distance is only a mile and a half from Crawford's. The A.M.C. Guide is seldom superlative in its language: what it has to say about this mountain may well be heeded: "There is perhaps no point in the mountains where so grand a view can be obtained with so little effort." The summit which one is on is about eight hundred feet higher than the road at the Gateway. To the right is Mount Willey (4,260 feet); across the Notch, beyond Elephant's Head, is Mount Webster (3,875 feet); along the steep eastern slope is the line of the railroad; the mountain sides and the floor are clothed thickly with woods—one is thankful for the public spirit which has preserved their beauty. Looking down into the deep wilderness one also, perhaps, has a thought for the hardy pioneers hoisting their horses over the ledges and for the little family far down at the bottom of the wooded defile which heard the rumbling mountain behind them and rushed out into the summer night to be crushed beneath it.

CHAPTER IX

BRETTON WOODS

EMERGING from the shadows of Crawford Notch one comes out into the sunlight of the great basin formed by the southern peaks of the Presidential Range on the south, by Washington and Jefferson and Clay on the east, and by Dartmouth Range and Mount Deception on the north. The view of the Range here is an essentially public one: by which we mean that if the Founding Fathers had not forever forbidden heraldic pageants in this Republic one would be almost forced to conceive of Washington from this point as holding a royal levee. Other views of Washington reveal it as an integral part of the range or, as in the Glen, scarred by the ravines which an iconoclastic fancy may interpret as an un-dress view of the Father of his Country. But here the mountain is indisputably the focal point; it is beyond the peradventure of a doubt the highest of all the peaks: this is the Washington of the Stuart portrait or better yet of the noble Houdon statue. Not of Parson Weems, we hasten to add, for there is nothing of pompous perfection or of hollow pretentiousness about it (in spite of the convictions of the early explorers that the peak *was* hollow, "as may be guessed by the resounding of the rain upon the level on the top.")

But long saturation in the Ruskinian vocabulary of our

predecessors has threatened to infect us with their metaphorical nimbleness. Without taking back anything our patriotic fervor may have led us to say let us get on to other matters.

The interest of this region lies not only in its dominance by the principal mountain but also in its historical preëminence. For in 1817 Ethan Allen Crawford came hither from New York State to brighten and support the last years of his maternal grandparents, Eleazar and Hannah Rosebrook. Ethan Allen Crawford is, by all odds, the most striking figure in White Mountain chronicles, as his story, "The History of the White Mountains," told by his wife, Lucy, and first published in 1845, is by all odds the best book, our own, may we modestly say, included. Crawford was no clergyman—there are signs, in fact, to indicate, that the picturesqueness of his private language was quite other than ministerial; he fortunately antedated Ruskin; he was, thank God, practically a pioneer in White Mountain literature, as he was in mountain history, and he had, therefore, no temptation to match metaphors with poetic enthusiasts. The tempo of his life was good sober prose, but a prose, after all, which has more genuine poetry than all the later flights. We should like to have known him; we should have been a little abashed in the presence of Starr King or Mr. Ward, but Ethan Allen Crawford, we are sure, would have made us feel at home: with him we should not feel as if we were committing an indiscretion in taking in deep breaths of this rarefied mountain air.

Crawford's bailiwick was, roughly, what is now the town of Carroll. Cherry (or Pondicherry, as it was first called) Mountain stretches down through the town, just east of its

Crystal Cascade, Pinkham Notch

© *Hunting Studio*

Mount Webster, Crawford Notch

center. The Dartmouth Range, Mount Washington, and the mountains of Crawford's Notch lie in various grants, purchases, and locations—the tip of Mount Washington, for instance, is in Sargent Purchase; we have already narrated how a strip of land was granted by Governor Wentworth to Nash and Sawyer on condition that they would get a horse up through the White Mountain Notch. (Nash and Sawyer's Location is now a part of Carroll.) Carroll was originally granted in 1772 as "Britton Woods" to Sir Thomas Wentworth, Rev. Samuel Langdon and eighty-one others. It got its name from Bretton Hall, Sir Thomas's country seat at Bretton, England. In 1832 the town was incorporated as Carroll. Recently the name Bretton Woods has been fittingly revived and applied to the locality of the Mount Pleasant and Mount Washington Hotels. Ethan Allen Crawford's dominion was the elongated triangle of land whose apex is Mount Washington, the base angles being what is now the Crawford House at the head of the Notch and Fabyan's.

In the early years there was at the site of the present Fabyan House a curious mound which, from its tumulus shape, received the name "Giant's Grave." "There is a strange tradition extant," says Spaulding, "of an Indian, who, long years ago, stood on that mound, with a blazing pine torch, lighted at a tree struck by lightning, and, swinging it wildly around in the darkness, he said, 'No pale-face shall take deep root here; this the Great Spirit whispered in my ear.'" True or not, this was just the sort of challenge to appeal to the Crawford family, and shortly after the Revolution Abel Crawford, "the Patriarch of the Hills," built a log cabin near this spot, where now, as a later historian bears witness, "all the railways of the White Mountain region concentrate, and, during the season, the crowd of people coming and going is almost innumerable." Abel Crawford was followed, in 1792, by his father-in-law, Eleazar Rosebrook and his wife Hannah. We have already given an indication of the quality of this couple in relating, in our account of Jefferson, the vigorous action Hannah Rosebrook took on one occasion, when her husband was absent fighting for the Colonies, in clearing her house of an intoxicated squaw. The Rosebrooks had come up into the Coos wilderness from Grafton, Massachusetts. Her admiring grandson relates how many a time, in the absence of her husband, she would shut one child in their lone cabin and taking her infant in her arms would go out into the forest in search of their cow and, bringing it home, milk it, her infant still in her arms.

Soon after his father-in-law's arrival, Abel, "rather than to be crowded by neighbors"—did he foresee, we wonder, the present "innumerable" crowds?—moved down the Saco into the White Mountain Notch where he established himself in the Mount Crawford House in Hart's Location, near the present site of Bemis station. Meanwhile, with the incorporation of the turnpike through the Notch in 1803, Eleazar Rosebrook built the first White Mountain tavern, a large two story dwelling on the west end of the Giant's Grave. "From the chamber in the second story, was an outside door, which opened so that one could walk out on the hill, which was beautiful, and gave a view of all the flat country around it." He also built a large barn, sheds and outbuildings, a sawmill and grist mill. "Thus he prospered and lived well." . . . But his children, in the manner of all younger generations, "were not satisfied with their situation; married, and left him, one after another."

Young Ethan, with his brother, down in the Notch, helped their father clear the land, having never "a hat, a mitten, or a pair of shoes" of his own, that were made for him, till he was nearly thirteen years old; went to school until he could read, write and cipher; in 1811 at the age of nineteen, enlisting, went to Plattsburg; finally got dissatisfied with army life and was discharged; settled for a time in northern New York; in March, 1817, returned to the Giant's Grave, with two hundred and eighty dollars he had earned, to take care of his old grandparents, giving notes for from two to three thousand dollars to pay off his grandfather's debts and receiving in return a deed to the farm; and in May of that year brought back his cousin Lucy to nurse the old gentleman who was suffering from a cancer of the lip. "He would converse upon death with as much freedom as though he was going to take a long journey into a far country, and never expected to return." In the fall he took the long journey. A month later Ethan and Lucy, fulfilling their grandfather's wish that she should stay there to "rock the cradle for the declining years of grandmother, as she did for him," were married.

It was by no means a sinecure that Ethan and his young bride had come into. In the morning of a day in the next July their child was born. At noon the mother lay in bed resting and talking with a Mrs. Boardman, a transient guest on her way home to Lancaster from the Saco Valley with her husband. Grandmother Rosebrook and the hired girls were getting dinner for the Boardmans. Ethan had gone to carry the dinner to the men-folks working on the Cherry Mountain road. As she lay talking to Mrs. Boardman Lucy noticed smoke and leaves blowing by the window. They were silver leaves from the poplar tree outside Grandmother Rosebrook's bedroom but why the smoke? The wind shifted and the exhausted mother ceased to speculate. A little later one of the girls heard crackling flames and opened the door of Grandmother Rosebrook's room. It was in flames. (A candle which old Mrs. Rosebrook had accidentally left lighted on a chair in the tightly ceiled room had burned down and set fire to it.) The girl closed the door and gave the alarm.

When Ethan returned he found the house in flames and his wife and baby lying on a feather bed behind the blacksmith shop. (Three times sparks from the burning building set fire to this bed.) Lucy, her grandmother, the hired girls and the Boardmans had saved all they could—but that was little. The mother and new-born child had been fortunate to escape with their lives. Six miles from the nearest neighbor to the west, twelve miles from Abel Crawford's in the Notch, the family was in desperate case. All the wagons were burned. Mrs. Boardman, being an invalid, could not give up her chaise to them, even if it had been large enough. At last "as though directed by the hand of Providence," a tin peddler happened along, emptied his cart, put into it the feather bed with Lucy, her baby, and four-year old brother (who lived with them) upon it, and drove them to the nearest neighbor's.

All the year's provisions against the winter were gone: salt and salt fish; forty dollars' worth of wheat and forty of pork; two-thirds of a barrel of maple sugar. Only some new cheese was saved. All the farming tools, except those the men on the road were working with, were burned. The passage with which Ethan Allen Crawford closes his account of this catastrophe is Scriptural in its simplicity: "In the morning we had enough and to spare; in the evening, nothing left but this new cheese, and the milk of the cows."

The swallows, losing their nests, followed the family to their neighbor's whose barns seemed to be alive with them. "They were actually partakers of our trouble," says Crawford.

> "One had to be versed in country things
> Not to believe the phoebes wept."

The loss was three thousand dollars; there was no insurance; he was heavily in debt. No wonder, as he says, that the shock of the misfortune almost overcame him. But Ethan Allen Crawford had not been made tough and healthy in his childhood by unharnessing horses in the winter, with head, hands and feet nearly bare, for nothing. With the help of relatives, neighbors, and oxen he immediately set about moving a small twenty-four foot house a mile and a half away on to the site of the ruins and there, in the most primitive circumstances, he and his wife Lucy were ready when winter came to take care of the steady train of farmers and drovers who passed down through the Notch from northern New Hampshire and Vermont to Portland and the markets.

"Lucy would many times have to make a large bed on the floor for them to lie upon, with their clothes on, and I would build a large fire in a large rock or stone chimney, that would keep them warm through the night. It was no uncommon thing to burn in that fireplace a cord of wood in twenty-four hours, and sometimes more."

The "White Mountain Giant" became more famous and popular as a landlord and guide with the years. In 1819, he and his father blazed out the first trail up Mount Washington, over the southern peaks from the Gate of the Notch. "It was advertised in the newspapers, and we soon began to have a few visitors." Thus the avalanche was begun: hundreds of trampers traverse this trail every summer, each with a prayer, we hope, for the tranquil rest in the Elysian Fields of the shades of Ethan Allen Crawford and his father. In 1821, he blazed, with Esquire Stuart, another trail: a rough roadway to the present Base and a path which scaled the mountain approximately where the railroad goes up now. In 1824 he built a larger house.

In 1826 flood followed fire. In August, after a day and night of deluge, they were awakened by their little boy coming into the room and saying, "Father, the earth is nearly covered with water, and the hogs are swimming for life."

"I arose immediately and went to their rescue. I waded into the water and pulled away the fence, and they swam to land. What a sight! The sun rose clear; not a cloud nor a vapor was to be seen; all was still and silent, excepting the rushing sound of the water, as it poured down the hills. The whole interval was covered with water a distance of over two hundred acres of land, to be seen when standing on the little hill which has been named and called Giant's Grave, just back of the stable, where the house used to stand that was burnt. After standing here a short time, I saw the fog arise in different places on the water, and it formed a beautiful sight. The bridge which had so lately been crossed, had come down and taken with it ninety feet of shed which was attached to the barn that escaped the fire in 1818. Fourteen sheep that were under it were drowned, and those which escaped looked as though they had been washed in a mud puddle. The water came within eighteen inches of the door in the house and a strong current was running between the house and stable. It came up under the shed and underneath the new stable, and carried away timber and wood, passed by the west corner of the house and moved a wagon which stood in its course."

The next three or four days were full of anxiety. The Notch road was gutted by the freshet; the Crawfords were concerned for the fate of their father and the Willey family down in the Notch. Well they might be. Two days later the destruction of the entire Willey family was definitely established with the discovery of their bodies underneath the avalanche. "This was the second time," says Crawford, "my eyes were wet with tears since grown to manhood."

In 1832 a rival landlord established himself at the White Mountain House, a mile away from the Crawford hostelry at the Giant's Grave. He acquired control of the property in a clandestine fashion, made free use of Crawford's mountain road, and attempted by misrepresentations to the Post Office Department to have the White Mountain Post Office

—that post office which, in Hawthorne's words, distributed "letters and newspapers to perhaps a score of persons, comprising the population of two or three townships among the hills"—moved from Crawford's hotel to his. Moreover, the Crawfords were being overrun with guests so that, sometimes, Lucy would have to sleep on the floor. Therefore, a large addition was built, sixty feet by forty, two stories high, with a two-story piazza on the front facing Mount Washington. He had already installed on the top of Giant's Grave a piece of artillery which, when fired, would echo from hill to hill and which "was really grand and delightful, and all who heard it were well pleased, and some used to call it Crawford's home-made thunder." With the new addition and his home-made thunder, the house became even more popular than before, in spite of the nefarious competition of the man who wished "to dip into the same business."

But in 1837, broken down in health, heavily in debt, Ethan Allen Crawford was forced to retire from the place he had made famous and moved to his birthplace in Guildhall where he lived on one farm or another until 1843. In that year the old war horse returned to the scene of his activities and renting the three-story dwelling which had been abandoned by his former rival he opened the White Mountain House. (This is now, according to Mr. Kilbourne, the oldest hotel in the mountains.) There he died in 1846 at the premature age of fifty-four years. His father Abel, "the Patriarch of the Mountains," survived him by several years, dying around 1850 at the age of eighty-five.

Ethan Allen Crawford is now a legend. Hawthorne de-

Silver Cascade, Crawford Notch

© Hunting Studio

A Birch Road, Intervale

scribes him as "a sturdy mountaineer of six feet two and corresponding bulk, with a heavy set of features such as might be molded on his own blacksmith's anvil, but yet indicative of mother-wit and rough humor." Many tales are told of his giant strength. He himself tells us how, when he was a young man in New York, he used to be able to put a barrel of potash weighing five hundred pounds into a boat, hoisting it two feet: "there was but one other man in the boat that could lift more than one end of a barrel." He was a lover of animals, alive or dead—it being always against his principles to keep them in misery. Spaulding records that "the first bear kept at the White Mountains for a show" was caught by Ethan in 1829. He thereby started a tradition that is still lively, as the tourist may discover. Ethan's run-ins with bears (to say nothing of deer and wild-cats) were nothing short of stupendous. Once he found a good-sized yearling bear in a trap, "sitting in an humble and ashamed-looking position," and decided to take him home alive. He cut a ten foot stick to lead him with, divested his horse of throat-latch, stirrup leather and the mail straps from the saddle, got hold of Bruin's hind feet and tied him to a tree. Then he secured his mouth, "but not so tight but that he could lap water." Though the bear with his front foot ripped out a piece of his captor's pantaloons, he would not give in. He tried to lead him but the bear played his part so well that Ethan could do nothing with him. He would come to a tree and hold on—and Ethan could not move both bear and tree. At last he tied the bear's fore and hind feet together so that he couldn't scratch and then "placing him on my shoulder, with one hand hold of his ear, to keep his head from coming too near mine, in case he wished to make a little closer friendship, I trudged on; but he was so heavy and ugly to manage that it made me sweat, and I was obliged to lay him down often and rest, and whenever I came to water, I would let him lap it. I made out to get two miles, he all the while growing worse and worse. At last he actually turned upon me and entered into an engagement with me by scratching and trying to bite, and after tearing my vest, I concluded I would once more lay him down,—and the way was not easy,—lifting him up as high as I could, I let him fall, and the ground being hard, the breath left his body."

It is nowadays by no means uncommon for motorists traveling the lonely road from the Profile to Bretton Woods to surprise a bear ambling across the highway. But there is no Ethan Allen Crawford. (One wonders if he did not perhaps suspect the decline of the race. At any rate he records, in 1845, that "as in the providence of God, everything changes in this world, the weather now is not so cold as it formerly was. . . . We now seldom have over two feet of snow at a time, and in years past it was no uncommon thing to have from six to nine feet." What about the men? Are they now what they were?) No, there is no Ethan Allen Crawford. His irascibility, his humor, his independence, his adventurousness; his menagerie, his long tin trumpet, his cannon and his rugged physique have long since gone the way of mortal things. But his Homeric spirit, we trust, still thunders about the mountains. Truly, there were giants on the earth in those days. . . .

In 1837 the hotel at the Giant's Grave, after Crawford's

twenty-year reign, came into the possession of Horace Fabyan, a provision merchant of Portland. Mr. Fabyan seems to have been an enterprising man, operating a chain of hotels which included besides the Mount Washington House, as he named the Crawford hostelry, a hotel at the Willey House and the Conway House at North Conway. Mr. Fabyan either inherited Ethan's tin horn or brought a new one for the delectation of his guests; in the forties he converted the short trail up the Ammonoosuc ravine into a bridle path, remodeled his establishment thoroughly and added fifty rooms. In 1837 the rate was $1.50 a day; for $3.00 Mr. Fabyan provided a guide and horses to within three miles of the Summit: these charges seem reasonable enough. But in the spring of 1853 the curse of the mad Indian operated for a second time and the hotel was destroyed by fire.

Twenty years later, in 1873, a new hotel was opened on the site of the Giant's Grave (which was leveled to the ground, for the purpose, doubtless, of evading the Indian's maledictions). This is the present Fabyan House, with accommodations for four hundred guests. In 1874 the White Mountains Railroad penetrated to this point from the west. The next year the Portland and Ogdensburg, so-called, according to a sharp mountain wit, because it started out from Portland and never reached Ogdensburg, reached Fabyan's. These railroads are now respectively the Boston and Maine and the Maine Central—until, that is, the long-threatened consolidation of New England transportation systems shall take place. From 1878 until 1913 the Fabyan House was under the management of Colonel Oscar G. Barron, perhaps the most famous of modern White Mountain hotel landlords. It was largely owing to his advocacy that the Crawford Notch was made a state reservation in 1912.

This leads us naturally to the other Crawford stronghold in this vicinity—the Crawford House at the Gate of the Notch, five miles from Fabyan's. Shortly after the famous freshet of 1826, the redoubtable Ethan "having a disposition to accommodate the public, and feeling a little self-pride to have another Crawford settled here, to make up a road" consulted with his father and agreed to have his brother established there in another hotel. In January, 1829, the Notch House was opened under the management of Thomas J. Crawford, who remained its proprietor until 1852. The Notch House stood on the left of the road between the present Crawford House and the Gateway of the Notch: old sketches show it to be a picturesque building, two and a half stories in height, the upper story extending at the lower end out over two of the beautifully arched shed doorways that are distinctive of this period of northern New Hampshire farmhouses. In 1852, under another management, a new hotel was opened on the site of the present house. Mr. Eastman, in his guide book of 1858, gives us a pleasant picture of life at this hostelry in that gay age:

"The Crawford House is a large and new edifice, very commodious and agreeable for a summer hotel. There are pleasant piazzas on the outside, and five halls, much used in the evening for promenading, run the entire length of the house within. The parlor is large and well furnished, the dining-room ample in its proportions, and its table always supplied with the delicacies of the metropolitan markets, as well as such substantial articles of mountain production, as delicious berries, and the richest milk and cream. The Office is situated in the central part of the house, and generally presents as busy a scene as the great square in a city. Hither every one comes to talk over his plans, and to make arrangements for various excursions, or for continuing his journey to other points of interest. You should be careful *as soon as* you arrive, to book your name at this place for a horse to Mt. Washington, if you intend to make the ascent within a few days, as often all the ponies are engaged for a day or two beforehand. . . . Here also is the Post Office of this wild region. Portraits of two of the Crawfords, patriarchs of these mountains, adorn the wall. The lodging rooms of the house are well furnished, and pleasant. . . . Connected with the hotel are a bowling-alley for rainy-day and evening amusement, and extensive stables. . . . Last summer two tame bears, in the edge of the forest at the southwest of the house afforded the guests much amusement. . . . The price of board here, as at all the first class houses among the mountains, is $2.50 per day."

But alas! the next spring this hotel, without the shadow of a red-man's curse upon it, was burned. (The old Notch House had succumbed to the flames in 1854.) American efficiency, however, in the person of Colonel Eastman, one of the proprietors, rebuilt and opened it for business within two months of its destruction. This house is the one, substantially, which exists today, white, broad-verandahed, many gabled, dignified but unpretentious, stretching across the Gateway as one comes up the Notch. Its atmosphere is in the best Bostonian manner. We are sure the Crawford family would quite approve.

Bretton Woods, four miles back, represents, rather, the New York idea. Bretton Woods consists, primarily, of the Mount Pleasant, situated at the railroad station, and the Mount Washington about a mile away under a combined management. The Mount Pleasant is the older of the two. Built in 1876, it was remodelled in 1881 by Joseph Stickney, and again in 1895. It is a large and distinguished hostelry. The Mount Washington, which was opened in 1902, is the largest and most elaborate of all the White Mountain hotels. It was conceived by Joseph Stickney, a New York capitalist of New Hampshire birth. "As the result of this gentleman's enterprise and command of large means," says Mr. Kilbourne, "one of the most magnificent summer hotels in the world stands about a mile from Fabyan upon a little plateau seventy or eighty feet above the Ammonoosuc River, with its eastern outlook toward Mount Washington and the Presidential Range. The architect was Charles Alling Gifford, of New York, and the style of the architecture is of the Spanish Renaissance. The general shape is that of a capital letter Y, and prominent features are two octagonal towers, five stories in height, between which is the main portion of the structure. The foundation is of granite, the blocks where exposed being left in a rough finish, and the superstructure is of wood, covered with light-colored cement, laid upon a steel net-work, the whole building being as nearly fireproof as possible. The kitchen is in a detached building. . ."

There is a great ball-room, a swimming pool; there are

dining-rooms and tea-rooms for all the occasions the books of etiquette prescribe; there is a grill; the smartest New York shops, the leading brokerage houses, are represented, the stock tape ripples excitedly under the ticker; one of its confirmed habitués, until very recently at least, has been the silent powerful dean of American high finance. The grounds are elaborately landscaped: there is a splendid golf course and miles of beautiful walks, bridle paths, and drives. A mile or two away, toward Crawford's, is a small field-stone chapel erected to the memory of Joseph Stickney. A mile away in the westerly direction is the little cemetery where lie the bodies of Eleazar and Hannah Rosebrook, Ethan Allen and Lucy Crawford. There they lie, blissfully unmindful of this august present of the region in which they were hardy pioneers, oblivious alike of its splendors and its dooms.

CHAPTER X

MOUNT WASHINGTON—BASE AND SUMMIT

THE story of Mount Washington is a story of its apparent capitulation to the white race. We have related how the Indians shunned Agiochook or Waumbekketmethna or Kan Ran Vugarty (said to be Indian for "The Continued Likeness of a Gull," sounding to us, however, suspiciously Celtic). But ever since the first sailors spotted them off the New England coast the White Hills piqued the curiosity of the English, and it was only twelve years after Governor Winthrop had established himself in Boston that the first ascent was made by Darby Field in 1642. The pale-faces far from being frightened away by the Great Spirit, were fired with a passion to visit his abode above the clouds. Before long we find them taking the particularly characteristic English tone towards His handiwork. In 1803 we find the Rev. Timothy Dwight expressing the qualified approval of Yale. Speaking of the Notch he observed how "the rocks, rude and rugged in a manner hardly paralleled, were fashioned and piled on each other, by a hand operating only in the boldest and most irregular manner." But Boston was not to be outdone. Starr King, though on the whole laudatory as we have seen, does nevertheless seem gently to chide the Creator for

Lakes-of-the-Clouds from Mount Washington

Mount Washington from Pinkham Notch U. S. Forest Station

the "extent and lawlessness of the spectacle" from the summit of Mount Washington.

Ourselves, we are inclined to think it rather too bad to take quite that tone toward the—undoubted—lawlessness of the Creator or the bold irregularity in the working out of His designs. It is indeed true that a cursory glance at a contour map of the Presidential Range might warrant the conclusion that the mountains were the finger prints of God, but living in a scientific age we think it unlikely. Somewhere there must be a geological explanation. Geological origins, however, or thumb prints of God, early ascents, views, later trails—all these concerns we shall postpone to later chapters. Here we have to do mainly with man's mechanical attempts to conquer the mountainside and his endeavors to wrest a shelter from the tornadoes of its summit.

However magnificent the Mount Washington Hotel may be, its existence without the dome of the mountain behind it would be—as Mr. Drake would have suggested if the hotel had been built in his day—a little like Boston without its State House, perhaps even worse. At any rate, there the mountain rises, reached by a lovely and steadily ascending road, some six miles behind the hotel. There is the Base Station of the Mount Washington Railway, with its cluster of buildings erected severely for utility rather than with any notion of beautifying the mountain. Normally we should now proceed with this most interesting of all the human embellishments of the peak, but this railroad without its upper terminus would be worse than useless. Therefore, with even more celerity than the railroad itself can exhibit, we shall leap to the summit to find some shelter for the arriving train-loads.

And, on second thought, it seems fitting, even before the shelter is provided, to see that the peak is properly and officially named. The Americanization—or better, perhaps, canonization—of the mountain must have occurred before Washington's first administration and was therefore, we hope, not the deed of an office-seeker. In his description of the mountain in his history of New Hampshire, first published in 1792, the Rev. Dr. Jeremy Belknap records: "It has lately been distinguished by the name of *Mount* WASHINGTON." This is the first appearance of the name in print, but its existence in letters dates back at least to 1784. Indeed, it is likely that the party, of which Dr. Belknap himself was a member, which made an ascent in this year, named the mountain. It is pleasant to record that, so far as we have been able to discover, the name met with unanimous approval. Here and there one finds strong partisans among our authors hinting that the names of the other peaks might better have been something else (the presence of so many Southern Democrats in a normally Republican state is indeed somewhat of a miracle) but the highest peak, all seem agreed—even in spite of a lingering romantic fondness on the part of Starr King for its aboriginal appellation—could not have been more nobly christened.

The christening of the other peaks of the Range was the occasion for a happy party recorded by Crawford in his "History." This event occurred on July 31st, 1820, and the participants besides Crawford, who acted as a guide and pack horse, were seven other gentlemen. One of them was Philip

Carrigain, "author of the New Hampshire map" of 1816, a former Secretary of State of New Hampshire, the first man (if not the last) to have the happy inspiration of applying to the White Mountains the term Switzerland of America, and the dignitary for whom the rugged Mount Carrigain in the wilderness behind the Notch was named. The other six gentlemen were from Lancaster; one of them, John W. Weeks, was of the well-known North Country family which later gave Massachusetts the congressman, senator, and Secretary of War to whom this region owes, perhaps more than to any other one man, the legislation that has saved what is left of the White Mountains from the lumberman's axe and made of it a National Forest. This gay and illustrious occasion occurred, as would be indicated by the date and the names of the peaks, in the first administration of James Monroe. This is a period known to contemporaries and to historians as the Era of Good Feeling. It would seem that the christening party was in complete harmony with the Zeitgeist.

After a dinner of trout at the Giant's Grave the party set out on horseback for the Gate of the Notch. There they loaded Ethan down with cloaks and food for two nights, "with a plenty of what some call 'Black Betts,' or 'O-be-joyful,' as it was the fashion in those days, to make use of this kind of stuff, and especially upon such occasions." (The A.M.C. Guide informs us, superfluously of course, that alcohol or liquor for internal use cannot now legally be carried in the mountains. Fortunate mountains, to have been christened a hundred years ago!) They made camp for the first night about three miles up the ridge, eating supper and spreading their blankets. After some interesting stories he *believes* they all fell asleep. The next morning they started on with only provisions enough for the day and "a sufficient quantity of 'O-be-joyful.'" (Unlike Congress, Ethan does not define "sufficient" for us, but the context indicates rather well the 1820 point of view as to this much debated matter.) They stopped at what is now the Lakes-of-the-Clouds, not, we should guess, for water. (Though the A.M.C. Guide informs us that mountain water is practically sterile.) They proceeded to the summit. "There they gave names to several peaks, and then drank healths to them in honor to the great men whose names they bore, and gave toasts to them; and after they had all got through, they put it upon me to do the same; but as this was a new thing to me, and not being prepared, I could only express my feelings by saying I hoped all of us might have good success and return to our respective families in safety, and find them in health; which was answered by a cheer from all, as they had cheered at other times before, when any one had drank a toast. The day was fine, and our feelings seemed to correspond with the beauties of the day, and after some hours had swiftly passed away in this manner, we concluded to leave this grand and magnificent place and return to a lower situation on earth."

We doubt if the mountain has ever been grander or more magnificent. But all things must end. They went down again to the pond. There they lingered, this time "partaking of its waters, until some of us became quite blue, and from this circumstance we agreed to give it the name of Blue Pond. . . This water so much troubled one of our party, or the elevated situation on which we traveled, fatigue, or some other cause, had such an effect upon him that he could not get along without my assistance; and he being a man of two hundred weight, caused me to make use of all my strength, at times." But at last they got down and Ethan, being "tired to the very bone," told them they must fend for themselves. This they did, after a fashion. But in the morning they all felt better and arrived home in good spirits. How much of the "Black Betts" or "O-be-joyful" was left we are not told. But it really would take a great deal for such an important christening.

We have elected to give the story of this ascent out of its proper place but we did so because we felt that such an occasion should be signalized in some special way. The Presidential peaks have been named only once: how fortunate that it was done so worthily. The names the distinguished gentlemen gave are of course well known: Madison, Adams, Jefferson, Monroe. There, of course, the presidents came to an end, though the mountains did not. But they still had Franklin in their bag. Surely his name is in every way deserving of a place in the distinguished company. Pleasant seems a name entirely devoid of inspiration, unless one recalls the quality of the occasion. Coming to the last mountain of the southern peak, their inspiration seems to have completely failed. They appear to have left it unnamed. Later it was named Clinton, when and by whom we have failed to discover. Doubtless it was for De Witt Clinton, the famous New York governor who flourished at this time. The New Hampshire legislature in 1913 re-named this peak "in honor of Franklin Pierce, fourteenth president of the United States, and the only citi-

zen or resident of New Hampshire who has been the incum-
bent of that exalted office" ("he's your one chance to score
against the state") but no one has paid much attention in this
law-breaking age. Mount Jackson, beyond Clinton on the
eastern spur of the ridge, was named by Oakes at the same
time he named Mount Clay. Mount Webster, at the tip—well,
New Hampshire never doubted that he was of presidential
timber, whatever politicians may have thought.

But we have promised some account of the housing situation on the mountain.

One could easily guess that the enterprising Ethan Allen
Crawford would be the first person to build a shelter on the
summit. In July, 1823, he built three small stone cabins near
the top, providing them with dry moss beds. "The ruined
walls of one," says Mr. Kilbourne, "may still be seen near the
Gulf Tank on the railroad." The cabins proving to be too
damp for comfort, the next year he bought a marquee in
Portland, large enough for eighteen persons, at a cost of
twenty-two dollars, and a sheet iron stove for six dollars. The
tent with its tackling weighed over eighty pounds but Ethan
toted it to the top and set it up near the spring just below the
summit. A waste of effort—as we could have told him—the
winds which frolic about the cone made short work of it. He
was slightly more successful with the first mountain register
(a sheet of lead seven inches wide, eight or ten feet long, the
progenitor of the present A.M.C. copper cylinders.) With
this he provided an iron pencil. In 1825 a party of vandals
from Jackson celebrated the Independence Day of their country by appropriating the lead (which they made into musket

balls, Crawford says he was informed) and "the spirit which we had left there in bottles,—which I justified them in doing, but did not justify them in carrying away the bottles, which belonged to mother." These experiences with the elements and depraved human nature seem to have discouraged Crawford who made no further attempt to provide shelter on the summit. Shortly after the opening of the Crawford Bridle Path by his father and brother in 1840, a small wooden shelter was erected which lasted three or four years and then was scattered by the winds.

The first Summit House was built in 1852 by the enterprise of three men, Perkins of Jefferson, Rosebrook and Hall of Lancaster. All the lumber had to be taken up by horses from the mill at Jefferson Highlands. Mr. Spaulding describes it thus: "This structure is of heavy stones, blasted with powder from the mighty pyramid on which it stands; and it it is twenty-four feet by sixty-four feet, firmly secured to its everlasting foundation by cement, heavy iron bolts; and over the roof are tightened four strong cables."

In the summer of 1853 the Tip-Top House was built. (there *is* a subtle distinction between these two names, despite the fact that the houses were built by rival entrepreneurs. The Tip-Top House, as its name suggests, has always been the higher.) This house was built by Samuel F. Spaulding, an uncle of one of our historians. It is not surprising, then, to find his description of the Tip-Top House more heartfelt than that of the Summit House: "Cement and iron rods hold this monument of daring enterprise, in proud defiance of wind and storm, to the most bleak top crag of Mount Washington.

This house is twenty-eight feet wide by eighty-four feet long; and has a deck-roof, whereon the visitor may stand and look down six thousand two hundred and eighty-five feet, on to the vast map spread on every side at his feet." In his book there is an engraving of this house "with a telescope, and three visitors on its roof, under a flag of our country." It may be noted here that the flag still waves.

In 1853 the two houses entered upon a combination in restraint of trade under the Spaulding managership which lasted until 1862. Mr. Eastman, in his Guide of 1858, enlightens us as to the functions of each building. The Tip-Top House is used as a dining-room. The Summit House is divided into two principal rooms with stoves around which the shivering guests crowd. "In the rear of the main rooms are narrow dormitories, with berths arranged along the wall, like those in the cabin of a steam-boat." There are also sleeping rooms above. Tallying up the expense of this enterprise, Mr. Eastman asks us not to be surprised "at the charge of $4 a day for our board, if we choose to stay awhile."

Mr. Eastman is for himself satisfied that the project for building a road up the mountain and a first-class hotel on the summit has been abandoned. "Perhaps then the accommodations would be better, and the price lower, but there would be little to satisfy the love of adventure in ascending Mr. Washington over a macadamized road, in a cushioned omnibus!" Thus early did the rift develop between the hardy trampers and the effete who have to be carried to the summit by car or train. Looking at a picture of the dream, however, with the massive masonry hotel and observatory, not unlike the Einstein Observatory, one is inclined to agree with Mr. Eastman. Not, by any means, that we object to the Einstein Tower. But it seems to us better adapted to Potsdam than to Mount Washington. Among the distinguished guests who, in these years, consumed bacon, tripe, pancakes, johnnycake, and doughnuts are recorded the names of Jefferson Davis, Charles Sumner, Horace Greeley, and William H. Seward.

For the next ten years (1862-1872) the house was under the management of Colonel John R. Hitchcock, of the Alpine House in Gorham, who paid a yearly rental of two thousand dollars for the season. In 1854, an observatory was built at a cost of six hundred dollars but though it boasted a species of elevator, capable of elevating eight persons at a time, it seems to have been a failure as an observatory and was torn down two summers later. Meanwhile, the carriage road had been completed in 1861 and the cog railroad in 1869. This necessitated an expansion of facilities and in 1873 the second Summit House, a building with accommodations for one hundred and fifty guests, was opened. In 1874, a "Signal Station" was erected for the use of the Government's weather-bureau service. In 1880 the railroad built a pyramidal observatory of wood behind the Summit House. This unsightly object was torn down in 1902. Other buildings about the summit have been three train sheds—with the destruction of the third one the railroad gave it up; a little house where the summer daily *Among the Clouds* was published from 1884 until 1908; a stage office; and barns under the lee of the summit.

On the evening of June 18, 1908, after the employees who had spent all day getting the house ready for the season had reached the Base, a fire broke out in the Summit House. The flames were soon spectacularly visible in the clear night sky from the whole country-side. By telephone from Fabyan's the alarm was given (the Summit House being invisible from the Base) and a train despatched up the mountain; rounding the curve by the Gulf Tank the men saw the flames. The train was unable to get closer than the water tank just below the top. And nothing could be done to save the buildings: by morning nothing was left on the Summit except the Tip-Top House (for the wind happened to be blowing away from it), and only the high wind which blew the burning embers off the roofs as soon as they had lighted saved the barns belonging to the Stage Company below. Except for the smoking ruins and the tall chimney that remained standing the mountain had resumed about the appearance it had in 1855.

A new Summit House was projected at once, but construction was delayed for several years while another prodigious scheme for the improvement of Mount Washington was being mooted. (This scheme, by the grace of that God who reputedly watches over drunkards and the United States, came to naught as we shall soon see.) Finally, in 1915 the third and present Summit House was built. This structure rests on the site of the burned hotel. It is a modest story and a half low-gabled building with long dormers reaching from end to end in which are the bedrooms. Instead of being cabled down in the approved mountain manner, the sills have been sunk into the concrete of the foundation and securely bolted to it and the framework securely bound together at all points with wrought-iron straps. The first floor is devoted to the large living-room with its huge welcoming fireplace, and the restaurant. Above are the twenty-two comfortable guest-rooms, heated by steam and provided with running water—to such an altitude has modern plumbing reached. With its low simple lines and weatherbeaten shingles the Summit House harmonizes well with the gray rocks of the mountain. The opening was signalized on August 21, 1915, by a flag-raising, a dinner, an address, and bombs bursting in air.

But life on a mountain top is hard. No sooner was the new house open than Tip-Top House celebrated the event with a fire, supposedly started by a defective chimney and fed by paints and oils stored there. The wind was again amenable, having chosen this time to blow in the other direction and the new hotel was therefore saved. Luckily, too, the Tip-Top House was largely of stone and the walls were consequently spared. The undaunted railway company proceeded to replace the wooden roof upon the walls. It is now provided with a few bed-rooms and two large rooms, male and female, with tiers of bunks for trampers. This house, also, is steam-heated. By a happy thought on the part of someone it has been connected to the Summit House below by a long passage-way built of stone and cement. The tramper rocked to sleep by the wind in this building has the satisfaction of knowing that he is not only in the highest building on the mountain but also in the oldest one—the Tip-Top House dates, as we have said, from 1853.

There is still another building on the mountain (besides the Stage Office across the track which we have mentioned) which by some people would be considered most important of all. This is Camden Cottage, the little emergency hut for winter climbers which is situated to the southwest of the passage-way between the Summit House and the Tip-Top House. It is built on the approximate site of the printing office occupied from 1884 to 1908 by *Among the Clouds* and is named for the veteran roadmaster of the railway, who celebrated the opening of the Summit House in 1915 by tearing down the railroad to the Base on a slide board with red lights gleaming to port and starboard.

And this brings us to what is, perhaps, the most famous of all the human activities connected with the mountains—the Mount Washington Railway. The railway was the project, as every one who knows anything about the White Mountains knows, of Sylvester Marsh, a native of Littleton. Marsh was one of those ingenious and sometimes irritating tinkers who always know a better way of doing things. Not content with life in staid New Hampshire, he had taken Horace Greeley's advice—doubtless, as a matter of fact, long before it was given —and gone westward in 1833, when he was thirty years old, and assisted in the founding of Chicago. There he turned his talents to the infant meat-packing industry and invented many of those processes which have made fortunes, facilitated life from a delicatessen, and lightened the burdens of tramp-ers. ("The dried-meal process," says Mr. Kilbourne, "was an-other of his inventions." This, we suppose, was primarily of interest to cows.)

In 1852 he returned to his native haunts, and with a friend took a strenuous tramp up Mount Washington. "This is not the way we would do in Chicago," he thought. Forthwith the idea of the cog railway sprang to life in his brain. He made a model of his proposed line and exhibited it to the State Legislature, asking for a charter. The request was met by the typical crusty conservatism of Yankee folk-ways. "Why doesn't he ask us to let him build a railroad to the moon?" one Solon asked in the course of the debate. Nevertheless, the charter was granted, in 1858. At any rate, the contraption couldn't do much harm. Skepticism and financial difficulties, increased by the Civil War, prevented operations for several years but at last, in 1866, the road was begun. The nearest railroad was still at Littleton, twenty-five miles away. Before progress could be made a highway had to be cut through the woods from Fabyan's to the base, following the trail cut out by Ethan Allen Crawford and Esquire Stuart forty-five years before. Over this road all the supplies had to be carted by ox teams. Colonel Orville E. Freeman, a son-in-law of Ethan Allen Crawford surveyed and located the route which took in general the path that Crawford had long ago blazed out.

After crossing the infant Ammonoosuc—a more or less husky infant, at that—the railroad ascends for about a mile the first pitch, which is known as Cold Spring Hill. At the crest the train stops at Waumbek Tank for water. Now the trees begin to shrink, the moss on their trunks grows thicker and thicker, the tree line is reached. Alongside the trestle one may see discarded ties and stringers—mute witnesses to the ravages winter-weather commits on mountain railroads. At Jacob's Ladder—so named from the crag which the old path surmounted, not from the trestle, in some places thirty feet high—the steepest gradient is reached nearly 1,980 feet to the mile. Here the trainmen take great delight in suspending their watches to emphasize the steepness of the grade. The view from the right of the Ladder is of the Lakes-of-the-Clouds, Ethan Crawford's Blue Pond. On the left Clay, Jefferson, Sam Adams and Madison curve away to the northeast. At the Gulf Tank, passengers are allowed to step to the edge of the Great Gulf on the eastern side of the Range. Ten minutes or so later the summit is reached. The distance from base to summit is about three miles and a third; the time taken about an hour and ten minutes (depending on head-winds or the lack of them!); the altitude of the Base Station is twenty-six hundred feet, the distance climbed about thirty-seven hundred.

But in spite of the steepness the journey can be made in absolute safety. For Sylvester Marsh's slogan was "Safety First, Second, and Third." The first device is the third rail—not a third rail, strictly speaking, but a rack over which the large pinion wheel under the engine revolves, propelling the locomotive. The second device is a tooth and ratchet mechanism on both car and engine which prevents the wheels from turning backward on the ascent. The third device is the separate brakes on the car and engine axles. The engine is a dinky little contraption with a miniature cab and tender. The smokestack has the old-fashioned bell-shaped funnel; the boiler is tipped up sharply behind so that it may be as nearly horizontal as possible on the steepest grades. Each engine pushes one car in front of it (on a fine day three or four trains are often run up the mountain). With a fine belching of smoke, hissing of steam, and a jolly clanking of gears and gadgets the flotilla starts gallantly off up the hill. On the return journey the engine backs down against compression. The car is not fastened to the engine—gravity governs its journey. The brakeman sits with his eye on the buffers: when the engine hauls away from the car he relaxes the brakes; the measure of his skill is the gentleness with which he allows it to come back to the engine. But his skill is often wasted—the passengers are too busy with the view and the decided sharpness of the drop in front of them. But there is no need for worry. It is the proud boast of the railroad (which has served, incidentally, as a model for several other mountain railroads, notably those up the Rigi and Mount Pilatus in Switzerland) that during the entire period of its operation from 1869 to the present the life of no passenger has been lost. It is not likely that one ever will be lost.

This does not mean, however, that lives have not been lost on this daring transportation system. We have already mentioned the descent of Roadmaster Patrick Camden on a slide-board at the dedication of the new Summit House. The slide-board is a simple plank, fitted over the central rail by grooves. There is a braking arrangement by which the flange of the rail may be gripped tightly at the will of the rider. The trip to the Base could be made by the skillful in three minutes. On one such occasion an employee was killed; a few years ago two amateurs with more courage than wisdom attempted the feat with fatal results. Since then this sort of mountain sport has been strictly forbidden by the Boston and Maine Railroad (which now controls and operates the Mount Washington Railway).

And there still remains to be told the exciting and tragic story of Old Peppersass. Old Peppersass was the curious little bottle-shaped contrivance that Marsh himself designed for the first flight, which accomplished it gloriously and operated thereafter for twelve years, when it was succeeded by the present type of locomotive (designed by Walter Aiken, who supervised the construction of the road). Becoming outmoded it was side-tracked as a curiosity. In 1893 it was sent to the World's Fair at Chicago. After wandering around the country to numerous expositions it finally came to rest in the Field Museum at Chicago. In 1927 it was acquired by the Baltimore and Ohio Railroad to be exhibited at its Fair of the Iron Horse. In 1929 it was presented by Mr. Daniel Willard, President of the B. & O., to the Boston and Maine, and brought back to the base of its parent mountain. It was surprisingly discovered that the boiler was still sound. After careful testing, it was refurbished and re-conditioned; minor parts were restored; wood was split and piled into the woodbox perched jauntily on behind; steam was made; a veteran of the Railway was put in charge of the throttle. Everything was ready for Old Peppersass's last triumphant ascent. For that occasion—its fiftieth birthday—a distinguished party had been gathered together by the railroad, including several governors who were only too glad to flee their solemn conference and exchange the political rigors of a debate on Prohibition for the ascent of New England's highest mountain. The train loads of celebrities were dispatched to the Summit. There was a hiss of steam, an eager treble rattle—Old Peppersass was off. Wheezing mightily it surmounted Cold Spring

© Boston and Maine Railroad

"Old Peppersass"

© *Hunting Studio*

Hermit Lake, Tuckerman's Ravine

Hill—on, up the steeper and steeper grade. It stopped for rest and water. Pictures were taken. Can she do it? Sure, she can do it! I should say! Life in the old dog yet! But on Jacob's Ladder something happened, something slipped. Back she started down the track, gathering more and more momentum. She left the rails, she ripped up ties, with a wild leap she cleared the trestle and smashed on the rocks below. With her, alas, were her engineer, who was severely injured, and a gallant photographer, who was killed. Otherwise what a romantic and triumphant end! For hours the governors were marooned on the summit (while the affairs of their states went on without a ripple). At last they were rescued, the next day the track was restored. When the tumult and the shouting died and the souvenir hunters had been driven away, it was found that Old Peppersass, after all, had not been completely demolished. Gradually she was reassembled: she is now on exhibition at Bretton Woods in all her ancient glory. But the photographer could not be put together again. . . .

Mountain atmosphere is rarefied atmosphere, though that of Washington, of course, is not the rarest in the country. It is rare enough, however, to produce some queer fantasies. One of the gaudiest of these was the project for the scenic railway around the mountain which we have already hinted at as being still discussed after the burning of the Summit House in 1915. For this scheme in the years 1911-12 elaborate surveys were actually made. An electric railway twenty miles long was to start out from the Base, go up Jefferson to the edge of the Castellated Ridge, cross the west slopes of Jefferson and Clay, wind around the cone of Washington two and one half times, taking in the Tuckerman Head-wall, Boott Spur, and the Lakes-of-the-Clouds, and landing with a final swoop upon a massive hotel of stone, concrete, steel, and glass with its center on the very apex of the summit. But the two railroads involved failed to merge; New England business depression caused the million dollars needed to fade away; the War, also, had its minor compensations. . . . The railroad was never built, trampers hope they will never have to clamber over it in its coilings. It would, of course, be nice to sit at one's ease and take in all the points of interest on the Range. But if one wants to ramble thus about it, for many years to come, apparently, one will still have to do it on foot.

CHAPTER XI

THE PRESIDENTIAL RANGE

GEOLOGICALLY speaking, the Presidential Range, the White Mountain region itself, may be said to be a giant monadnock in the New Hampshire peneplain. That is to say, the mountains are composed of the sterner stuffs—the gneisses, crystalline schists, and hard granites—that have defied the torrents and freshets of the hundreds of thousands of winters and springs that succeeded to the great Ice Age of North America. What cosmic convulsions, what siesmic contortions far down in the bowels of the earth occurred, during the millions of years before this event, to cause this major upheaval of the earth crust in this particular place we, being no geologists but mere idle singers of an empty day, dare not speculate. Professor J. W. Goldthwait in his monograph, "The Geology of New Hampshire," assures us that once the White Mountains were perhaps thousands of feet higher than they are now. Erosion and weathering brought them to approximately their present height. Then came the Glacial Age and small local glaciers, like those on the Alps, gouged out the great ravines in the flanks of the Range that are so distinctive a part of their topography. For centuries the region was buried under the great ice sheet moving southward from Canada. Even Mount Washington itself was covered, Professor Goldthwait tells us. The "striae" or scratches of the advancing and retreating ice sheet are visible to the trained eye upon the summit itself and deposits of boulders carried from Randolph and Jefferson and dropped by the glacier in its retreat may be seen along the Gulfside Trail. . . . The sun shone more brightly—or whatever it is that causes the changes of climates happened—and the glacier fled back into the north. The White Mountains were safe for tourists.

In a competitive age it is perhaps galling to have to admit that there are higher mountains even in the east than the White Mountains, especially when Mother Nature originally made them much higher than they are. But, we shall find, they are high enough for tourists and if they have not the supreme height there are, as we shall see, other compensations. There is nothing like the mountains for putting one into a hyperbolical frame of mind. For that reason, therefore, and for the additional reason that we live in the age of Einstein we hesitate to assign heights to the Presidential peaks. For, if one didn't know better, one would guess from the record that Mount Washington had wavered from time to time. Belknap, New Hampshire's first historian, did his best to preserve the historian's proper detachment. He urges us to conservatism: "When amazement is excited by the grandeur and sublimity of the scenes presented to view, it is necessary to curb the imagination, and exercise judgment with mathematical precision; or the temptation to romance will be invincible." But, alas, in a footnote several pages later (in regard to a computation which places the top of the mountain at 10,000 feet above sea-level) he proceeds to inform us that "subsequent observations and calculations have induced the author to believe the computation of his ingenious friend too moderate, and he is persuaded, that whenever the mountain can be measured with the requisite precision, it will be found to *exceed* ten thousand feet of perpendicular altitude, above the level of the ocean."

Subsequent figures for the height of the mountain obtained by barometric observations and spirit leveling have ranged from 6,284 feet (obtained by Cavis and Ricker, engineers of the carriage road in 1854) to 7,055 feet, with the best opinion hovering around 6,290-6,293 feet. One's guess seems as good as another's in such a predicament. The government maps have given the figure 6,290 (until recently, at least); the railroad votes for 6,293. But the U. S. Geological Survey's permanent bench mark on the summit rocks behind the Summit House—a brass plate set in concrete—confirms the modest estimate of Cavis and Ricker—6,284 feet. But, alas, in this slippery age what things are true? There are higher points on the mountain than this bench mark: the water tank, for instance and the ridge poles of both the Summit and Tip-Top Houses. A happy thought, however, occurs to us. In the march of time these buildings can scarcely be called permanent—fire and wind may do much. But the bench mark will doubtless, perhaps for centuries still to come, defy the forces even of erosion. Let us take it, then, and its figure of 6,284 feet, as our final goal. . . .

In the middle of the century, when Starr King flourished, there were, he says, three ascents of the mountain. These were the two Crawford trails on the western side whose histories we have already given and the road and bridle path from the Glen House on the east. Progress! Progress! Nowadays the A.M.C. map shows a region dotted with trails. We know of no better way of spending a week or two's outing than to explore, with the A.M.C. Guide for Bible, the various windings, dippings, and aspirings of these trails. What two weeks of this sort may do for the human organism may be gathered by reading such a book as Mr. Atkinson's "Skyline Promenades." In the pages that follow we can do no more than suggest a few of the pleasantest ways of taking the Range in one's stride.

For convenience one may divide the trails into two main groups: Ridge Trails and Ravine Trails. Tastes differ, of course, some prefer one kind, some another, others (the more discriminating, perhaps) a combination of both. The Ridge Trails provide the best views; the Ravine Trails are shorter. We shall try to give a brief and by no means complete description of the Ridge Trails first.

For ourselves, if (along with the ten best books and a desert-island library) we had to choose the one route up and down the mountain to take and then die (fortunately no such alternative has been presented to us) we should vote for the Gulfside-Crawford route over the northern and southern peaks from Appalachia on the north to Crawford's on the south. This is, naturally, a reversible route but let us for convenience's sake go from north to south. Anyone wishing to reverse the direction may read this backward in Oriental fashion. (First let us say for the benefit of those wits which may have wandered or been lulled to slumber by the monotonous chanting of the guides that the Range proper extends from Madison on the north, Pine Mountain being, as we said earlier, really the remote northern outpost, in a curve bulging to the west at Jefferson back to the east at Washington thence almost due southwest in a fairly straight line over the southern peaks to the Gateway of the Notch. The Range is crossed from west to east by the railroad from the base to the top and by the carriage road from the top to the Glen. These two distinct landmarks serve as valuable guides in case one is lost on the cone.)

The distance over this route is approximately nineteen miles: ten miles on the north to Washington and eight or nine miles thence to Crawford's. At least twelve miles of the middle section is above the timber line at an elevation of four thousand feet on the south, of five thousand and upwards on the north. It may, of course, be done by an athletic person who wants to do that sort of thing in a day's hike but people who are not obsessed with the American mania for merely getting somewhere will want to take at least two days. It is nowhere excessively steep; the northern portion especially is clearly marked and in normal weather conditions or for an experienced mountaineer there is no danger. The fact that the earliest explorers had no maps is no excuse for a modern explorer being without one: a map, in fact, is the sine qua non for an adequate comprehension and enjoyment of this route. A compass is a good thing to have along, too. For in stormy weather this trail can be exceedingly ugly—particularly the southern portion which is not quite so easy to follow. Mount

Washington, though it may not be an Alp, is no mountain to take liberties with. Once we have made this fact clearly understood we can then continue the rest of our journey in amity.

The route starts, then, at the Ravine House on the highway just north of the Moose River. It follows a nicely graded path, the Valley Way, for three and a half miles to the Madison Spring Huts of the Appalachian Mountain Club, at an altitude of 4,825 feet. These are stone huts in the shelter of the mountain; they have a caretaker in season and provide sleeping quarters and simple mountain meals. From this point a side trip east for half a mile to the summit of Mount Madison (5,380) and return can easily be negotiated in an hour's time and in clear weather is easily worth it for the views of the Range and the North Country. A quarter of a mile south of the Huts are the Parapet and Star Lake, a tiny mountain tarn.

From the Madison Spring Huts the Gulfside Trail leads over the cols of the principal peaks but loop trails lead over the summits if the tramper desires to climb them. It goes to the north of John Quincy Adams and of Adams (5,805 feet high, the highest peak outside of Mount Washington in the mountains); to the south of Sam Adams (5,585) and not far from its summit (here the trail reaches an altitude of 5,520 feet); dips downward, skirts Adams 5, a small peak, follows along the edge of Jefferson Ravine to the Edmands col; turns south, passing Mount Jefferson (5,725) on the east; crosses Monticello Lawn; skirts the western ridge of the three peaks called Mount Clay (more properly the col between Jefferson and Washington); approaches and parallels the railroad for about half a mile; finally joins the carriage road at an altitude of about 6,000 feet half a mile below the summit of Mount Washington.

This path was largely laid out by Professor J. Rayner Edmands, of the Harvard Observatory, who began the work in 1892 and continued it until his death in 1910. For large portions of the way (the half mile along the edge of Jefferson Ravine where the path is marked by cairns is an exception) it is graded with carefully placed stones (though the trail has somewhat deteriorated in late years). For this reason it is sometimes called Edmands Boulevard. It is now maintained by the U. S. Forest Service and the A.M.C. The views are magnificent. From the early portion of the trail one may look back upon Madison in its comparative solitariness. Between Clay and Jefferson and from the slopes of Clay (especially if one chooses to go over the summits of Clay instead of to the west) one can look down into the Great Gulf, the largest of the glacial cirques, and catch glimpses of the West Branch of the Peabody River glittering far away among the green of the trees on the floor of the ravine. The nearer one comes to Washington the more impressively do the peaks of the northern range loom up behind.

The descent by the Crawford Bridle Path is no less impressive. From the top of Washington one may see in the col between the cone and the peaks of Monroe the Lakes-of-the-Clouds gleaming in the sunlight or shining like polished steel against the darker rock-gray of mountains in shadow. These are the first objective. The route begins at the end of the railroad trestle, goes through the stone corral in which the saddle horses used to be stabled nearly a hundred years ago, and proceeds abruptly down through a well-worn path that lies in a trench in the rocks for over a mile until it levels out upon the plateau of the Lakes-of-the-Clouds. Here is located, providentially in time of storm, the Lakes-of-the-Clouds Hut of the Appalachian Mountain Club. It is perched on a shelf overlooking the Ammonoosuc Ravine west of the larger of the two Lakes at the foot of Mount Monroe. Its elevation is about 5,000 feet. It is built of stone; one of its unusual features is large plate glass windows through which the tramper, if beleaguered, may observe the storm in comparative comfort. Thence the path proceeds to the east of the two peaks of Monroe (the higher one being 5,390 feet high) which may be reached by a loop; over the shoulder of Franklin (5,028); to the east of Pleasant (4,775), a loop to which in fair weather affords a splendid view; enters the woods near the top of Mount Clinton and descends, not far from Gibbs Brook, to the Crawford House.

The portion of the trail up Clinton was the trail blazed up the mountain by Ethan Allen Crawford and his father in 1819. Thence, as the A.M.C. Guide says, it proceeds to Washington being entirely exposed and none too clearly marked "by sparse cairns and the marks of many feet on the moss and rocks." It is a beautiful trail: one may sometimes see ladies, from the hotels below, strolling in light dresses there of a summer afternoon. In all politeness, it is no place for them to stroll. For all its balmy delightfulness this is a treacherous trail. Storms come up quickly and sweep down across it from the northwest with extraordinary violence, even in summer. Of the lives lost on the mountain four of them have been lost on this trail. Because of this fact the Edmands Path, north of Mount Pleasant, and the Ammonoosuc Ravine Trail at the Lakes-of-the-Clouds Hut have been provided as means of escape on the western slope below the timber-line. If caught in a storm the tramper should by no means attempt to take shelter on the eastern side of the trail. Here lie the precipitous cliffs of Oakes Gulf and an uncharted wilderness. A word about the cone of Washington from the Lakes-of-the-Clouds: it rises impressively before one and seems but a short distance: the impatient tramper is eager to conquer it. But the distance is a mile and a half, the height climbed in that distance twelve hundred feet. The cone is a mass of long rectangular stones piled helter-skelter, grayed and ravaged by centuries of Mount Washington weather. The trail zigzags amongst these rocks, higher and higher; for the first time in the White Mountains the altitude begins to tell, even the more or less seasoned tramper finds himself pausing for breath. If the weather is fine and it is not too near sunset there need be no fear. But if it is growing dark, above all, if it is stormy and if the storm has given previous trouble let the climber possess his soul in patience and return to the Lakes-of-the-Clouds Hut, thanking his stars that a benevolent A.M.C. has provided a shelter there. A night's sleep in the hut will do him no harm. Buffeting the wind and weather on the exposed ridge or on the summit cone of Washington is not for human beings, as we shall subsequently see. But with common sense and a map and compass to fall back on, the

Crawford trail is one of the most exhilarating in the mountains.

This long trail over the northern and southern peaks may be made with several variations. On the southern end the Edmands Path, branching off north of Mount Pleasant to the highway from Crawford's to the Base will save some distance. From the top of Clinton there is a trail—the Webster Cliff Trail—leading southeast by the Mizpah Spring Shelter (A.M.C.) over Jackson and Webster down into Crawford Notch a half mile or so below the New Hampshire State Camp.

On the north there are all sorts of possibilities. Instead of the Valley Way one may take the Snyder Path which coincides with the Valley Way for perhaps a third of the distance then branches to the left a short distance beyond the junction of the Valley Way and the Randolph Path and follows the Snyder brook nearly to the Madison Spring Huts where it rejoins the Valley Way again. Or, going still further east one of the Howker Ridge trails up Madison may be taken. There are at least three of these which start from the Dolly Copp Road from Randolph to the Pinkham Notch. The easternmost one of these, the Pine Link, is a continuation of the trail up Pine Mountain from Gorham, previously described. This is a recent trail. The distance from Gorham to the Huts over this trail is about eight miles (there is a loop over Mount Madison). From the Dolly Copp road, however, it is not quite four miles to the Huts, and the advantage of this path is that the altitude of the starting point on the Dolly Copp road is already 1,700 feet so that the ascent is an easy one, with many fine views; the distance along the highway from the starting point to the Public Camp Ground at the Dolly Copp Farm is about two and a half miles. Going still further around into the Glen one may take the Great Gulf Trail at the Dolly Copp Farm, follow the West Branch of the Peabody River for two miles or so to its junction with the Osgood Trail from the Glen House, and take the Osgood Trail over the Osgood Ridge to the summit of Mount Madison four miles further. Most of these trails, obviously (especially the latter), will take more time than the trip up the Valley Way.

West of the Valley Way the principal Ridge Paths are the Air Line over Durand Ridge to Mount Adams; the Israel Ridge Path from Bowman to the Gulfside Trail; and the Castle Trail over the Castellated Ridge. The Air Line starts from Appalachia, crosses the Short Way to King's Ravine and the Randolph Path in the early part of its ascent; makes a steep ascent to the crest of Durand Ridge; skirts the edge of King's Ravine along the famous Knife Edge, where the drop into the ravine is almost perpendicular; comes to the Gateway of King's Ravine at an altitude of 5,080 feet; joins the Gulfside Trail and diverges from the latter shortly afterward to scale the peak of Adams, about four miles from Appalachia.

The Israel Ridge Trail starts from Bowman (toward Jefferson on the Randolph-Jefferson road); coincides with the Castle Trail for a mile and a quarter; uses logging roads through a lumbered region for a mile or so; continues on, with some backing and filling, over the ridge between the

Ravine of the Castles and the Ravine of the Cascades, through virgin woods to the Randolph Path and the tree line, nearly four miles from Bowman. There one may turn south for the Gulfside Trail to Washington, or east for the Gulfside Trail back to Adams and Madison.

The Castle Trail, about four and three-quarters miles from Bowman to Mount Jefferson, for about half its distance follows old logging roads along Israel River, diverging from the river to the south along the east flank of Mount Bowman; enters upon a steep trail and finally comes out upon the Castellated Ridge. The Castellated Ridge is a northern spur of Jefferson and consists of a series of sharp, rough, precipitous crags that are unique upon the Range. The trail here is steep but in the open and the views of the Presidential Range, the Dartmouth Range to the west, and the Jefferson plateau and Crescent Range to the north are magnificent. One can continue on this trail to the top of Jefferson or, turning east about half a mile below the summit on the so-called Cornice, pass on to the Gulfside Trail on the Edmands Col.

It was in the region traversed by these two last paths that the wild and uncanny events having to do with the candlesticks and golden image of St. Francis occurred. Therefore, it will be well for the superstitious tramper to take these expeditions only on the fairest of days. There is a more practical reason for this course: the views are better then and there is less likelihood of getting lost in a fog and plunging over a precipice, for this could be done, although there is no record of anyone having done so that we know of. It was also in the

Castellated Ridge, as the reader may remember from the chapter on Jefferson, that Mr. Drake nearly lost his eye.

Aside from these various Ridge Trails on the northern slopes of the range there are three other Ridge Trails worth noticing. The first is the Caps Ridge Trail from the height of land in Jefferson Notch. The Jefferson Notch Road is one of the most interesting of White Mountain projects. It was planned, at the beginning of this century, to connect Crawford's with Jefferson by a route running along the edge of Mount Clinton, across the road from Fabyan to the Base, and on between the Dartmouth Range and the great Range. The road from Crawford's to the Base Road was completed and is now a state highway. From there on, the way was much more difficult but, largely owing to the initiative and enterprise of the third Ethan Allen Crawford (blood will tell!) of Jefferson Highlands, the road was actually put through to Jefferson Highlands in 1902, mainly by private subscription. Because of the wildness and steepness of the region through which it goes it has had a somewhat precarious existence, being sensitive to flood conditions. The great flood of November, 1927, played havoc with it, but it has been repaired and is supposedly open to automobile traffic in the summer season. It would be well, however, for the tourist to make local inquiries before proceeding over it: these may be prosecuted on the south at Crawford's and on the north at Jefferson, or even further into the notch, at the Israel River Guard Quarters of the U. S. Forest Service. Providing the road is passable to cars the Caps Ridge Trail has the distinction of being the shortest and easiest approach to the northern peaks.

From the height of land at Jefferson Notch (3,000 feet) over the Ridge of the Caps to the top of Jefferson is only about two miles and a half, to Washington not quite six miles.

The second Ridge Trail is the Davis Path from Bemis, in Crawford Notch direct to the summit along the Montalban Ridge. In the chapter on Crawford Notch we have described the portion of this trail to the Giant Stairs. This trail is named for N. P. T. Davis, the son-in-law of Abel Crawford, who succeeded to the management of the Mount Crawford House, as we have said, and constructed this as a bridle path in 1845 to compete with the Crawford and Fabyan Bridle Paths. Long since discontinued as a bridle path it was re-opened by the A.M.C. in 1910 and has since become popular with hikers, especially those coming across country from the Sandwich Range. After the Giant Stairs the trail winds up and down the ridge, passing Mount Davis (3,800 feet) which may be reached by a spur trail in a few minutes and which affords a splendid view, especially of Oakes Gulf and the Range; goes on over Mount Isolation; passes near the Isolation shelter on the right; and comes out above the tree line about twelve miles from Bemis; thence proceeds slightly to the west of Boott Spur (5,520 feet) a bold protuberance of the Mount Washington mass. About a half mile further on the Boott Spur ridge toward the summit a path to the right is the most direct and also the steepest route to the summit. To the left a path leads to the Lakes-of-the-Clouds. The Davis Path leads straight ahead across the Bigelow Lawn to the Crawford Trail where one turns right for the summit, or proceeds straight ahead by the Westside trail under the railroad

Mount Adams and Mount Madison

Cathedral Pines, Intervale

track to the Gulfside Trail, if one wishes to reach the northern peaks without going to the summit. This is the longest ridge trail: from Bemis to Washington the distance is about fifteen miles. Ordinarily it will prove of more interest to confirmed trampers than to the neophyte.

The third Ridge Trail is, of course, the carriage road passing up Chandler Ridge from the Glen. This route, which we have spoken of before, is naturally the easiest of all to follow, though it is eight miles long. The views from it are superb. From the upper part of it especially one looks across to the northern peaks. Backward one looks down into the Great Gulf, the symmetrical pyramid of Adams rising grandly from its floor. The traveler, stopping on this ridge to look at it, will agree with us, we hope, in thinking that Adams is easily the most imposing mountain of the Range, not excluding the father peak itself.

One disadvantage of some of the ridge trails we have mentioned—and especially of the Gulfside-Crawford journey— will have occurred to the intelligent reader. A trip over them often leaves the tramper rather far from his base. If that base happens to be a car and if he has no obliging chauffeur or relative to meet him, he is left somewhat stranded. To be sure there are always railroads but these are of little use in getting from one side of the range to the other in a particular hurry. An hour or so spent with time tables figuring out how to get from Crawford's back to Gorham by train will soon convince one of the sombre truth of this fact. Let us draw a curtain on the scene.

This obstacle however is generally overcome by making

use of the Ravine Trails. They are usually shorter; excellent combinations of Ravine and Ridge Trails can be worked out so that a tramper may get back reasonably near his base without too much re-duplication of his route. There are six important Ravine Trails, going around the mountain from the railroad from west to east: Ammonoosuc, on the Bretton Woods side; the Ravine of the Castles and King Ravine on the north; the Great Gulf, Huntington and Tuckerman's on the east.

The Ammonoosuc Ravine Trail is, next to Tuckerman's, the shortest trail up Mount Washington. (The railroad—three miles in length—is, of course, the shortest way of all, but this, except in winter, is not for pedestrians.) From the Base Station to the summit the distance by this trail is four miles and a half. It is also one of the newest trails, having been built in 1915 by the A.M.C. to provide a graceful retreat from storms on the Crawford path. It starts just behind the restaurant at the Ammonoosuc station of the Mount Washington Railway (this is the place where motorists board the train for the top) and goes to the Lakes-of-the-Clouds hut (three miles) along the brook to which the Ammonoosuc has here dwindled. Most of the way is reasonably steep but there are in the upper part of the trail spectacular views of a gorge and cascades down which the brook plunges. We have called the stream a brook: it is a very healthy brook and in wet weather which is Ammonoosuc and which is trail is sometimes difficult to distinguish. From the Lakes-of-the-Clouds hut to the summit (one and a half miles) the usual route is the Crawford Path. This trail may profitably be worked in combination with the Crawford Path. From the Base back along the road to Crawford's where the Edmands path emerges from the woods is about three miles, to the foot of the Crawford Path, seven.

For the next ravine—the Ravine of the Castles—we must swing far around to Bowman on the northern side of the range. If one's objective is Washington this trail is considerably longer than the Ammonoosuc Ravine Trail. From Bowman to the Edmands Col on Mount Jefferson it is four and a quarter miles, to Washington thence about four. From Bowman it coincides with the Castle and Israel Ridge trails, branching off right from the latter at about one and a half miles, to follow Castle Brook. It follows this brook, largely by logging roads, to the head wall of the ravine, Castellated Ridge being on the right ascending. It climbs the head wall of the ravine steeply, the trail being marked by cairns and white paint. In the flood of 1927 this trail was much damaged but since then it has been repaired. (The Cascade Ravine Trail in the next ravine—the lower end at least—was largely destroyed by the flood. Whether restored or not we cannot say.) The Castle Ravine Trail can be used to advantage with the Castle Trail or Israel Ridge Trail, whether or not the tramper wishes to go on up Washington.

King Ravine, in the side of Mount Adams ("to the very heart, and up to the throat of the noble mountain") is the most spectacular ravine on the northern range. It is a true glacial ravine, gouged out, undoubtedly, before the last ice age by a local glacier. Starr King, for whom it is named, like Abel Crawford, was unenamored of crowds. Already in 1859 he complained that not less than five thousand persons made the ascent of Mount Washington every summer. Therefore he began the exploration of the northern side. Here, he thought, no " 'carriage roads' and hurrying feet and 'Tip-Top Houses' " could disturb him. Though the head wall was generally believed unscalable, with a guide who had the instinct of a bee for compass, Mr. King and four companions attempted it. What he did the first time we may do now. King Ravine may be reached by the Lowe Path and King Ravine Path from Bowman or by the Short Line from Appalachia—the latter, being shorter as the name implies, is probably the more usual approach. To the Gateway of the ravine from the Ravine House by this trail is four miles, to the top of Mount Adams four and a half. For best enjoyment it should be worked in combination with a returning route —Valley Way, or still better, the Air Line down Durand Ridge. The trail, after it has reached the lower floor of the ravine, follows the Cold Brook. (This is the beautiful brook, with beautiful cascades below this point, which Starr King rhapsodized about for two pages, not relying, as in another case, upon Tennyson's "Brook," quoted liberally, to convey the impression of wetness.) At nearly three miles from the Ravine House one comes to Mossy Falls, above which the brook loses itself under giant rocks which the retreating ice sheet stripped away from the ridges above and then debonairly, without a backward glance, strewed in reckless profusion over the floor of the ravine. The route over and under these boulders may be avoided by taking the path dubbed by some emancipated strap-hanger "Elevated Road for rapid transit." But the "Subway" route is more fun. The head wall rises straight ahead, with the Knife Edge and Nowell Ridge to left and right. The path slabs the wall steeply to the east, coming to the Gateway where one is surprised by a gorgeous solitary view of Madison to the east. The A.M.C. Guide estimates the time from Mossy Falls to the Gateway at about two hours. The same distance, approximately, took Starr King, his guide, and his four cronies about six hours. But we, must remember that this route, before them, had probably never been trodden by foot of man. They had to find their own way among the boulders (which the metropolitan trails find for us now) and their route was blocked by tough thick-growing scrubs. Moreover, they had to stop to poetize. Therefore, all hail to Starr King! This ravine proves him to have been a mountaineer as well as a poet.

In 1823, while guiding a party up and down the mountain, the redoubtable Ethan Allen Crawford himself got lost for a short time. He started east instead of west and "wandered about until we came near the edge of a great gulf. Here we staid and amused ourselves by rolling such large stones as we could find loose, and these being started, went with such force that they would take others with them, and then rest only in the valley beneath." Thus was the Great Gulf accidentally named. Ethan's game of ducks and drakes, though, is not to be recommended, for so thick have trampers become that the chances are not bad for one of them getting hit by a rolling stone. Not that the Great Gulf is any small affair. It is the largest of the glacial cirques and, though not so steep nor so spectacular, to our way of thinking fully as satisfactory to the eye, as the others. From the edge of the floor to the top of the wall the distance is three and a half miles. The wall is fifteen hundred feet high; for sides it has Chandler Ridge on the south, Clay and Jefferson on the north. The Great Gulf Trail proper starts at the Dolly Copp Farm but travelers from the south will save some distance by starting from the Glen House. From the Dolly Copp Farm to Washington the distance is eight miles and a half, from the Glen about eight. It will be seen, then, that this trail is only for those who have plenty of time as well as muscle. It follows the West Branch of the Peabody River to the Great Gulf Shelter (altitude 3,250 feet), an open camp with accommodations for twenty-two persons. From here the distance is about three miles to the summit: the trail rises steadily beside beautiful cascades (with superb views of Adams and Madison) to Spaulding Lake which, says its godfather in his "Relics," with the Gulf of Mexico—that is the Great Gulf—"are at least worth a trip from the Atlantic, from all who would look with proud satisfaction upon nature in her sublimest mood." The distance from here to Washington is a mile and a half up the head wall and cone, the altitude gained in this distance over two thousand feet. If one has grown weary of ravines he may return over the Gulfside Trail and down the Osgood Trail or down the carriage road back to the Glen.

As we make the circuit of the Range in our search for Ravine Trails the next ravine is Huntington and the trail up this ravine is the steepest and most exciting of all. It may be reached by the Tuckerman Ravine Trail from Pinkham

Notch or by the Raymond Path which leads off the carriage road just below the two mile post. We have felt its shadow from that path shortly before dark and at that hour of the twilight this ravine is indeed an ominous affair. The description of the climb in the A.M.C. Guide begins as follows: *"The head-wall should not be ascended by the inexperienced, nor descended by anyone who is not familiar with the ravine."* Perhaps we had better let it go at that.

After all, the Great Gulf, because of its size, and Huntington, because of its steepness, are primarily for connoisseurs. One can always look at them from below, or from above, with perfect safety (provided one does not go too near the edge or start rolling rocks down). But our last ravine, the most famous of all, Tuckerman Ravine, named for an Amherst botanist, can be negotiated by any enthusiastic mountaineer. The trail up this ravine, as we have said, is the shortest trail up the mountain—the distance from the Pinkham Notch Camp of the A.M.C. being not quite four miles. (From the Glen House by carriage road and the Raymond Path it is about six and a half miles.) The altitude gained from Pinkham Notch (2,000) is about four thousand feet— a little more than a thousand feet to the mile. Most of the steepness comes in the latter half. Shortly after leaving the Camp one passes the Crystal Cascade, one of the early sights of the region (Mr. Drake devotes three pages to a description of it—let that suffice). Hermit Lake Shelter—an open A.M.C. shelter—is situated about half way along the trail and just beyond is Hermit Lake from which one gets, straight ahead, a view of the imposing head wall; to the right, of the precipitous Lion's Head; to the left, of gnarled Boott Spur. One somehow has the impression of an early sunset. Beyond the lake a short distance is the foot of the wall and the famous snow arch. This is made by the piling up of the winter's snows from off the mountain. With the coming of spring the snow melts behind and tunnels its way out from beneath leaving an icy cave which sometimes lasts until August. The temptation on a hot day to penetrate the cool recesses is great but it had better be resisted. It is true that on July 16, 1854, Mr. Spaulding and some functionaries of the Mount Washington Carriage Road dined under it (it then measured 266 feet long, 84 feet wide, 40 feet high) and gathered Alpine flowers at its base. But in 1886 it fell and killed a young boy; eight years later one hundred feet of it fell just after fifty Appalachians had passed through. Keeping a safe distance from it, then, one climbs the head-wall over the loose débris to the top. Thence, at the second right-hand turn, the direct route to the Summit House is less than a mile. (The first right-hand trail leads across the Alpine Gardens; the route straight ahead at the Tuckerman Junction leads across Bigelow Lawn to the Westside Trail.) Returning, the trail over Lion's Head on the north side of the Ravine, or over the crags of Boott Spur to the south give imposing views of this startling relic of the Age of Ice.

There are, of course, several trails which are, strictly speaking, neither ridge nor ravine trails. Two of these may be mentioned. One of them is the Alpine Gardens-Six Husbands Trail. This leads from the Tuckerman head wall across the more or less level plateau to the carriage road. (All moun-

tain streams are excellent as drinking water but the A.M.C.
Guide warns us that the stream encountered upon this trail
should not be drunk since it is largely drainage water from
the Summit House. So much for civilization.) From this trail
there is an excellent view down into Huntington Ravine.
Crossing the carriage road it becomes the Six Husbands Trail
(so named for the six-successive-happily—husbands of Queen
Weetamoo, for whom a waterfall in the Great Gulf is
named), dips sharply down into the Gulf, up and out on the
other side to the summit of Jefferson.

The other trail to be mentioned is the Randolph Path—
a graded path built by Mr. Edmands—which extends from
the Randolph Post Office to the Edmands Col and Jefferson
across the northern slopes of the Range. This path is maintained by the Randolph Mountain Club. We have already
spoken of Randolph and the view from Randolph Hill. The
Ravine House, as we have said, has long been a center for
trampers, as well as a hostelry of distinction for those who do
not care to tramp. The whole township, from the days of
Starr King, has been a rallying point for mountaineers, as
the number of criss-crossing paths within its purlieus would
indicate. There is nothing, apparently, which Randolphians
from J. Rayner Edmands to the present had rather do than
locate, blaze and then grade a path. This is a streak in human
nature unaccounted for by either Behaviorism or Freudian
psychology. (Probably it is atavism.) At any rate, we can
think of no more altruistic enterprise than the activities of
these mountain organizations like the Randolph Mountain
Club or the Dartmouth Outing Club, with its trails and

cabins in the Moosilauke region, or the A.M.C. (founded in 1876, incorporated in 1878). Many of the paths on the Range, it is true, now that the Presidential peaks are a part of the National Forest, have been taken over and are maintained by the U. S. Forest Service. But for the numerous trails (a few of which we have tried to indicate) for the huts and shelters, the guide-posts, cairns, maps, and descriptions of trails all mountaineers owe a deep debt to these amateur pioneers and their successors. Surely, like the children of a virtuous woman, generations of trampers will rise up and call them blessed.

CHAPTER XII

MOUNT WASHINGTON: EVENTFUL ASCENTS AND BOUTS WITH THE WEATHER

Four score miles (upon a direct line), to the Northwest of *Scarborow,* a ridge of Mountains run Northwest and Northeast an hundred Leagues, known by the name of the *White Mountains,* upon which lieth Snow all the year, and is a Landmark twenty miles off at Sea. It is a rising ground from the Sea shore to these Hills, and they are inaccessible, but by the Gullies which the dissolved Snow hath made; in these Gullies grow Saven Bushes, which being taken hold of are a good help to the climbing Discoverer; upon the top of the highest of these Mountains is a large Level or Plain of a day's journey over, whereon nothing grows but Moss; at the farther end of this Plain is another Hill called the *Sugar Loaf,* to outward appearance a rude heap of massive stones piled one upon another, and you may as you ascend step from one stone to another, as if you were going up a pair of stairs, but winding still about the Hill till you come to the top, which will require half a days time, and yet it is not above a Mile, where there is also a Level of about an Acre of ground, with a pond of clear water in the midst of it; which you may hear run down, but how it ascends is a mystery. From this rocky Hill you may see the whole country round about it; it is far above the lower Clouds, and from hence we beheld a Vapour (like a great Pillar), drawn up by the Sun Beams out of a great Lake or Pond into the Air, where it was formed into a Cloud. The Country beyond these Hills Northward is daunting terrible, being full of rocky Hills, as thick as Mole-hills in a Meadow, and cloathed with infinite thick Woods.

JOHN JOSSELYN: *New England's Rarities Discovered*

(1672)

MOUNT WASHINGTON, being the highest mountain on the North Atlantic seaboard was, as we have said, from the very earliest days a focal point for sailors and the curious. It was apparently first mentioned by the Florentine sailor Verrazano, who sailed up the coast

235

in 1524, visiting the site of Portsmouth, New Hampshire, departing from thence "keeping our course Northeast along the coast, which we found more pleasant champion and without woods, with high mountains within the land." In 1605 Samuel de Champlain descried them, sailing along the coast of Maine. And in June, 1642, twenty-two years after the founding of the "Plimouth Plantation," Mount Washington surrendered, for the first time, probably, to the insistence of Darby Field.

In our first chapter we have mentioned Field's historic ascent, the account of which is given in the Journal of Governor John Winthrop. Starting from what is now Saco, Maine, with two Indian guides he made the journey "to the top of the white hill" in eighteen days. "Within 10 miles of the top," Winthrop says, "was neither tree nor grass, but low savins, which they went upon the top of sometimes, but a continual ascent upon rocks, on a ridge between two valleys filled with snow, out of which came two branches of the Saco River, which meet at the foot of the hill." Some of the Indians in the Indian town at the junction of the two rivers accompanied him within eight miles of the top 'but durst go no further, telling him that no Indian ever dared go higher, and that he would die if he went.' But he persevered, and his two Indians with him. Here is the description of the ascent and the view he saw:

"They went divers times through the thick clouds for a good space, and within 4 miles of the top they had no clouds but very cold. By the way, among the rocks, there were two ponds, one a blackish water and the other reddish. The top of all was plain about 60 feet square. On the north side there was such a precipice, as they could scarcely discern to the bottom. They had neither cloud nor wind on the top, and moderate heat. All the country about him seemed a level, except here and there a hill rising above the rest, but far beneath them. He saw to the north a great water which he judged to be 100 miles broad, but could see no land beyond it. The sea by Saco seemed as if it had been within 20 miles. He saw also a sea to the eastward, which he judged to be the Gulf of Canada. He saw some great waters in parts to the westward which he judged to be the great lake which Canada River comes out of. He found there much Muscovy glass; they could rive out pieces of 40 feet long and 7 or 8 broad. When he came back to the Indians, he found them drying themselves by the fire, for they had had a great tempest of wind and rain. About a month after he went again, with five or six of his company, then they had some wind on the top, and some clouds above them which hid the sun. They brought some stones which they supposed had been diamonds, but they were most crystal."

It is impossible to say precisely which of the routes we have described was the one by which Darby Field made his ascent but from the general direction he took and from the fact that for a long distance they were above the tree-line it seems likely that he followed, more or less, the Montalban ridge over Boott Spur—what is now the upper end, at any rate, of the Davis Path. It is obvious, too, that he saw the Lakes-of-the-Clouds, though they seem to have lost color since. As for the view Field saw—well, we must not be too hard on him; his was the first chance to describe the view from Waumbekketmethna: who can blame him for wanting to do his best? The gulfs and great waters he espied have since disappeared, alas! But clouds at a distance sometimes have the look of water—and why shouldn't they if chemically that is what they are?—and the imagination (especially in a rare altitude) is powerful. It seems likely that Field, in addition to making the first ascent, had the first view "above the clouds." At any rate, he peered down into the Great Gulf. No one else, perhaps, has ever since seen such sheets of mica as he saw then, but erosion may do much; and Darby Field was neither the first nor the last man, probably, to mistake quartz crystals for diamonds.

The next ascent of historical interest was apparently Josselyn's, with whose account we have headed our chapter. On a second ascent he found, instead of the snow, black flies "so numerous . . . that a man cannot draw his breath, but he will suck of them in" and remarks, as we have elsewhere noted, that the mountains are hollow "as may be guessed by the resounding of the rain upon the level of the top."

Dr. Jeremy Belknap, in his "History of New Hampshire," published in 1792, records several ascents in the eighteenth century, describes various features of the mountain with considerable accuracy (except the height!) and concludes with an account of the celebrated ascent in 1784 which we have already referred to as the probable occasion for the baptism of the central peak. This expedition consisted of a party of nine men among whom were the historian himself, the Rev. Manasseh Cutler of Ipswich, Massachusetts, the botanist of the trip, and our friend Colonel Whipple of Jefferson (then Dartmouth) acting as one of the two guides.

Their camping base was in Pinkham Notch, just beyond Glen Ellis Falls. Dr. Belknap and another member of the party gave out before reaching the summit and returned to the camp to wait for the others. Dr. Cutler, the leader of the party to the summit, has been immortalized—at his own request, apparently—by the name of the stream along which they took their course, their route evidently being up into Tuckerman's Ravine and thence to the top over Boott Spur. "Their exercise in ascending the mountain," says Belknap, "was so violent, that when Doctor Cutler, who carried the thermometer, took it out of his bosom, the mercury stood at fever heat, but it soon fell to 44°, and by the time that he had adjusted his barometer and thermometer, the cold had nearly deprived him of the use of his fingers." Clouds coming up, they were unable to make adequate use of the various instruments they had carried laboriously up the mountain. One of their pilots, on the descent, slipped "in one of the long deep gullies" and Dr. Belknap therefore concludes "that it is more practicable and safe, to ascend or descend on the ridges, than in the gullies of the mountain." (Later history does not bear out this conclusion of the good doctor, as we shall shortly see.) Belknap, as we have said, did not himself reach the top. We have also quoted his warning about "the temptation to romance" in these altitudes. But surely some poetry should be allowed even a historian. Therefore let us forgive him his peroration: "A poetic fancy may find full gratification amidst these wild and rugged scenes, if its ardor be not checked by the fatigue of the approach. Almost every thing in nature, which can be supposed capable of inspiring ideas of the sublime and beautiful, is here realized. Aged mountains, stupendous elevations, rolling clouds, impending rocks, verdant woods, crystal streams, the gentle rill, and the roaring torrent, all conspire to amaze, to soothe and to enrapture." This was his consolation while waiting for the others in camp near Glen Ellis Falls.

From the time of Ethan Allen Crawford, some thirty years later, the ascent of the mountain became more and more fashionable. Starr King's more than five thousand each summer in 1859 has grown to what proportions we dare not say. The 1930 census will doubtless reveal them. It is not surprising that during the years many celebrities have honored the mountain with their presence. Irving, Hawthorne, Sir Charles Lyell, the geologist, Dr. Charles T. Jackson, the discoverer of ether, Francis Parkman, Anthony Trollope, Phillips Brooks, Ambassador Bryce are among the eminent who have gone up a-foot or horseback. Thoreau went up twice. The second time he celebrated by discovering the leaves of the *arnica mollis* in Tuckerman's Ravine and spraining his ankle there the next day. In 1831 Daniel Webster went up the Crawford Trail with Ethan Allen Crawford as guide. When they arrived at the summit Webster, as was fitting, made an oration which has been preserved by Crawford: "Mount Washington, I have come a long distance, have toiled hard to arrive at your summit, and now you seem to give me a cold reception, for which I am extremely sorry, as I shall not have time enough to view this grand prospect

The Summit of Mount Washington: As Imagined by the Projectors of the Carriage Road

which now lies before me, and nothing prevents but the uncomfortable atmosphere in which you reside!"

Our annals, however, are not concerned with the expeditions of the illustrious but with the ascents of those humbler travelers whose names would hardly have been remembered had it not been for their arduous—and in some cases, alas, fatal—buffetings with this mountain and the uncomfortable atmosphere about which Webster chided it in his apostrophe.

During Ethan Allen Crawford's suzerainty of the Range —and probably, as Mr. Kilbourne suggests, largely owing to it—things went comparatively well. The first of September, 1821, under his guidance, the Misses Austin had the honor to be the first females to place "their feet on this high, and now celebrated, place." It was their presence, perhaps, which inspired Crawford to the most eloquent description of the view from the summit which he gives in his history. It is pleasant to record that this expedition was conducted with so much prudence and modesty on the part of the young ladies as to leave not "a trace or even a chance for a reproach or slander excepting by those who thought themselves outdone by these young ladies." The next summer he conducted up the mountain a party of theological students whom he endeavored to divert with little stories but these not coinciding with their feelings—what can the little stories have been?—he remained silent most of the way. It appears that the young gentlemen must have been busy composing the prayers which they delivered on arriving at the summit—the first prayers, Ethan says, he had heard on the mountain. We should guess that he preferred the society of the young ladies.

Some time after the opening of his more direct route in 1821 Ethan built him a camp which must have been located somewhere near the present location of the Base Station. He provided it with an iron chest for blankets and there he used to entertain his parties with the chest for a table: with tea, plenty of salt pork, and a "dish of trout" caught near the camp he enjoyed many a good meal with his friends (and they with him, we imagine). He built two shelters, one for men, one for women. Between them a fire of six and eight foot logs kept both sexes warm on the coldest of nights; spruce and hemlock boughs made comfortable beds—except that, after all this was done, "now the untiring mosquito would sing to us constantly and every now and then would stop and taste a little." But in the flood of 1826, which destroyed the Willey family, the camp, the furniture, even the iron chest was carried away.

People were lost on the mountain, even in Crawford's day. Once a sea-captain, having gained the summit with his party, became impatient and set out alone for the base. He eventually arrived in Jackson, the other side of the mountain; Ethan, meanwhile, spent the better part of two days looking for him. On another occasion, an intrepid Vermonter, not wishing to be balked by a heavy rain, insisted on going to the summit without his friends. He, however, had the good sense to lay up piles of stones so that he could retrace his way. "Such," says Ethan, "was the spirit of a Vermonter." To the Green Mountain State, then, should go the credit for the first cairns on Mount Washington.

In October, 1851, occurred the first of a series of fatalities

on the Presidential Range. Frederick Strickland, a Canta-
brigian, the eldest son of a member of Parliament, an heir to
large estates, started up the Crawford Path with another
Englishman and a guide. Encountering wind and snow on
Mount Clinton, the guide and the other Englishman returned; Strickland pressed on, planning to return by the
Fabyan Trail to Fabyan's, whither Landlord Thomas Crawford had sent his baggage. When it was discovered that he
had returned to neither place, however, a searching party
was formed. They traced him to the summit and down into
the Ammonoosuc Ravine. The next day they found his dead
body lying in the river.

Beside the railroad track about five hundred feet below
the summit is a pile of stones and a weather-beaten monument to the memory of the second of the mountain's known
victims, Lizzie Bourne, who "perished" at ten o'clock on the
evening of September 14th, 1855, from exhaustion and heart
failure. In the blackness her uncle had endeavored to build
her and his daughter a rough rock shelter against the high
wind but in her case it had been useless. They had started at
two o'clock from the Glen House to go to the summit by
the half-finished road and the bridle path. Lizzie Bourne is
the most famous and the only woman of the mountain's
victims.

In August, 1856, Benjamin Chandler, an old gentleman
of Wilmington, Delaware, for whom Chandler Ridge was
subsequently named, started up from the Glen late in the
afternoon, was lost in a storm, and disappeared. It was not
until the next July that his skeleton was found half a mile

east of the top. In 1874 another lone climber, Harry W. Hunter, twenty-two years old, was lost on the Crawford Bridle Path. Not till 1880 was his body discovered half a mile south of the summit. He had evidently become lost in the dark and fallen a victim to severe weather conditions. In August, 1890, Ewald Weiss, a violinist at the Summit House, set off to climb Mount Adams, was lost in a severe storm, and disappeared from sight forever. "That, bewildered by the storm," says Mr. Kilbourne, "he wandered from the path and went or fell down into one of the ravines and there perished, or that one of the large jagged rocks with which the cone of Adams is largely covered rolled from its place and crushed him . . . are two plausible guesses which have been made as to the mystery of his fate."

Perhaps the most dramatic of the Mount Washington tragedies was the fate of William B. Curtis, a well-known New York amateur athlete, sixty-three years old, and his companion Allan Ormsbee, an athletic young man, not quite thirty, on the 30th of June, 1900. These two started out on the Crawford Path, Saturday afternoon, to meet fellow members of the Appalachian Mountain Club who had gone up by train for a field meeting on the summit. Up on the ridge a storm which had been threatening finally broke. That morning at the Summit House the thermometer had dropped to 25°. There was a rising wind that reached a rate of one hundred miles an hour, driving rain, then sleet, then snow before it. Late in the afternoon, two trampers, a father and son, staggered into the Summit House after an exhausting struggle up the cone. Coming out upon the exposed crest of Boott

Spur at eleven o'clock in the morning they had been met by the full force of the rising wind and storm. It was impossible to make any headway against it except by crouching down and waiting for the lulls in the blast. It took them two hours to cross the mile or so of practically level Bigelow Lawn to the base of the cone. The cone itself was covered with ice and the wind-driven sleet struck them with terrific force. They were obliged to take shelter from it behind the large rocks every hundred feet or so in order to get their breaths. At last they reached the summit. They were unable to give the anxious Appalachians any information about Curtis and Ormsbee. Night came; the storm continued unabated.

All Sunday it raged violently. (During the course of it over forty panes of glass were broken in the Summit House.) The helpless Appalachians were completely marooned in the hotel: they could do nothing. (Anyone who has thrust his head out of warm shelter into a hundred-mile-an-hour gale of sleet and snow will readily understand why.) At last came Monday with fair weather, and searching parties went out. About noon, Curtis's body was found lying on the rocks near the Lakes-of-the-Clouds by Louis F. Cutter, the Appalachian Mountain Club cartographer. Ormsbee's body was found late in the afternoon within five minute's walk of the summit but somewhat off the path.

One can only guess the fearful last hours of the two men. They had been warned back by two trailmen on the south side of Mount Pleasant. Curtis was familiar with the path and they had apparently paid no heed. They signed the A.M.C. cylinder roll on Mount Pleasant and gave a weather record: "Rain clouds and wind sixty miles—Cold." They were last seen and urged to turn back by two men on the north slope of Mount Pleasant. For two miles more they struggled on against the increasingly violent storm, with the temperature below freezing. In the lee of the northern Monroe peak they had evidently attempted to make a shelter. Giving that up, they had decided to press on. Then Curtis evidently slipped on the icy rocks and was struck unconscious by a severe blow on the head. Ormsbee, knowing that the only hope of help was at the summit, by an almost superhuman expenditure of energy struggled on up over the mile and a half of the cone. The wind, the storm, the altitude, the steep pitch were all against him. Yet he crawled and dragged himself on over the sharp icy rocks, his hands and arms torn, his body covered with bruises. Against the overwhelming odds his heart could not stand out: it failed him when he had almost reached the top and safety. Bronze tablets mark the spots where these men perished. The Lakes-of-the-Clouds hut is indirectly also a monument to their memory.

The psychical as well as the physical effect of being lost in a storm on the lonely wastes of Mount Washington is shown by the curious case of eighteen-year-old John M. Keenan, a surveyor's helper, attached to the party of engineers who were engaged in surveying the proposed route for the scenic railway in 1912. On Wednesday, September 18th, they were sighting around the summit and Keenan was posted by his chief at a point below the Ormsbee monument and told to remain there until summoned, or, if it clouded up, till someone came for him. About ten in the forenoon a heavy cloud, the forerunner of a three-day storm, settled down over the mountain and work was discontinued. They went down to get Keenan; he was not there. They scoured the cone until noon, with no success. They telephoned to the Base; he had not arrived. Search was continued until dark; all night the bell at the Summit House was rung out over the mountain; at the Base the steam whistle was blown. For the next two days, in the clouds and increasing cold the search was continued fruitlessly.

Late Friday morning, two county officials, making an inspection of the roads passed down through Pinkham Notch in their car and observed a man standing by the roadside and pointing in a wild manner at the mountain. Not knowing a man had been lost they went on. At Fabyan, they heard the news and gave their information. The railroad officials, guessing that the lost youth had traveled with the wind down over the precipice into Tuckerman's ordered guides into the Notch to conduct the search from the Glen. A fire warden, learning of the affair, informed the searchers that on Friday morning he, also, had come upon a bedraggled stranger on a lonely logging road who inquired incoherently for the Keenan farm, and, on learning that there was no such farm in the region, passed up the road toward the Glen House. Through Saturday and Sunday the hunt was continued, a hundred men combing the country-side about the Glen. A few days later it transpired that a chauffeur, on the same Friday, had taken in a dishevelled and evidently demented stranger and carried him two miles down the Notch, letting him out at his own request into the pouring rain. Again a search was made. But the hatless and coatless stranger, getting aimlessly out of the car into the driving rain was the last anyone ever saw of young Keenan.

These casualties might lead one to credit the Indian belief that no footmarks are ever seen returning from the home of the Great Spirit in the clouds. But after all, when one thinks of the thousands of uneventful ascents one's apprehensions are quickly allayed. It will be noted that all of these fatalities, except those of Lizzie Bourne and Curtis and Ormsbee, occurred to lone and inexperienced travelers. And the storm in which the experienced Curtis and Ormsbee perished was one of the worst summer storms known on the mountain. It will also be noticed that none of them occurred in winter ascents. That, of course, may largely be due to the fact that it is only recently that winter ascents of Mount Washington have become popular.

Not that winter ascents have been confined to recent years by any means. The first one was achieved in 1858 by Lucius Hartshorn of Lancaster and Benjamin Osgood of the Glen House, the noted guide. Hartshorn was a deputy sheriff who went up to serve a legal process upon the property on the summit in connection with a litigation as to its title. They went up the carriage road and bridle path from the Glen, performed their legal function and had luckily reached the timber line before a bad storm which they had noticed approaching on the summit hit them. A second ascent was made by a party of several men in February, 1862. They started by moonlight from the Glen, arrived at the Half-way House, where they spent the remainder of the night, made the rest of the journey to the top the next morning without untoward adventure but were marooned in the Summit House for two days and nights by a ferocious snowstorm.

In the winter of 1870-71 occurred the famous occupation of Mount Washington by the expedition of the State Geologist, C. H. Hitchcock, and his colleague Professor J. H. Huntington, an indefatigable White Mountain explorer for whom the steepest ravine on the mountain has been fittingly named. We shall have a word or two to say about this affair a little later but we may anticipate to describe briefly one of the most exciting winter ascents, that of Nov. 30, 1870, made by the two photographers, Clough and Kimball, who were to winter on the summit, and their two adventurous companions. Driving to the base of the mountain they started up the railroad in apparently clear weather at half-past two in the afternoon. Somewhat wearied by the arduous effort of picking their way over the ties they stopped for rest at the end of the first mile only to observe the black threat of storm approaching from the Green Mountains. Deciding, nevertheless, to go on they had reached the foot of Jacob's Ladder when the storm struck, wrapping them in clouds of frozen vapor, with suffocating force. Retreat to the Waumbek shelter seemed inadvisable; they determined to climb on. Two of them kept on up the track; the other three left it and found themselves buried to their waists in snow. Kimball, completely exhausted, begged to be left behind. His two companions refused; fastening a cord about him, they pulled and dragged him on up the mountain, reaching at last the Lizzie Bourne monument thirty rods from the summit. (The wind was blowing seventy miles an hour—a wind of forty-five miles an hour at sea-level will blow down buildings and uproot trees, says the narrator—the temperature at the top registered 7° above zero.) There, almost mad with exhaustion, the despairing photographer begged them again to leave him, muttering remarks about the removal of his corpse from the mountain, the probability of another monument, and the likelihood of his fate proving a remunerative attraction to the railroad and hotel the coming summer. But he was not thus to serve a bait for the morbid curious. After half an hour's effort, during which the two others half pushed, half carried the almost unconscious man, they reached the shelter of the Observatory building at which the two other members of their party, who had kept on up the railroad, had already arrived. It had taken them five hours to do the three miles from the base. Nevertheless, over a hundred other ascents without accident were made during the ensuing season. Numerous ascents were also made in the following years of observation by the U. S. Signal Service, many of them hazardous, none of them fatal. But in 1887 the government observations were discontinued and after that date winter ascents declined.

Enthusiastic Mount Washingtonians expressed the opinion at the time of the Hitchcock-Huntington occupation of the mountain that the time would come when the Summit House would be kept open in winter. The optimistic Mr. Marsh affirmed that he would live to see his little toy run at all seasons of the year. Such a millennium has not yet arrived but if winter ascents keep on increasing in number more com-

modious accommodations than Camden Cottage may be required. The Dartmouth Outing Club parties alone, during
the winter months, number around a hundred men. The first
official D.O.C. attempt was made in 1911 by F. C. Harris,
founder of the Club, and eleven others but was unsuccessful. In 1913 Harris, Cheney, and Shumway climbed up on
skis; coming down, they covered the four miles from the
Half-way House to the foot in sixteen and a half minutes.
Since then yearly trips have been regularly run. Several years
ago an unfortunate accident occurred when a man slipped in
descending Tuckerman's and broke his back. By the most
heroic efforts his companions succeeded in getting him out
to Pinkham Notch Camp and thence to civilization.

These mountain expeditions are always in charge of experienced men; they are undertaken with a full equipment
of skis, snowshoes, wind-proof parkas, and ice crampons. In
spite of these precautions, however, a tragic experience occurred on the winter expedition of 1929. The party had gone
up Tuckerman's, and were going down the Ammonoosuc
Ravine on the other side of the mountain. It was extremely
cold, with a high wind. At last, one of the party, a freshman
named Young, sank exhausted and with a rapidly failing
heart beside the railroad track. Despite unbelievable exertions
on the part of his companions he had frozen to death
before they could bring up assistance from the base below.
Since then the Outing Club has adopted the additional precaution of requiring a careful medical examination of each
prospective member of an expedition and a stiff conditioning
trip. For the last few years, moreover, the A.M.C. Hut in

Pinkham Notch has been kept open with a caretaker in charge and a radio for communication with the outside world.

This brief catalog by no means exhausts the adventurous and exciting experiences of trampers on the mountain which, however imposing, rather belies the reputation for integrity and reliability earned by its distinguished godfather. There was, for instance, the ascent of John Ball, a Dartmouth student, in 1819, an interesting account of which is preserved. He set out with three others in May, after a clearing rain storm, up the Crawford trail, much against the advice and without the guidance of Landlord Crawford. They camped out over night; the next morning they attempted the ascent in a thick fog; a storm came up; they had the good sense to turn back and, plunging down the route Strickland took, so fatally, they at last, by the grace of God, followed the raging Ammonoosuc to quiet weather below and safety. And there was the rough experience of Sylvester Marsh and his friend in 1852 when, caught in night and storm, they barely made their way to the Tip-Top House, Marsh then and there resolving that what the mountain needed most of all was a railroad. But we must not leave the summit without some mention of that dauntless explorer, Dr. B. L. Ball, who should go down in history as the man with the blue umbrella (for it must have been blue). His adventures are recorded in his book: "Three Days on the White Mountains" for here, at last, is a tale with a happy ending; wonder of wonders, he endured to tell the story himself.

B. L. Ball, a stalwart young physician, a globe-trotter,

insofar as that phenomenon existed in the fifties (he had climbed around in the Alps, had been in Java and the Philippines and was already, at thirty-five, the author of "Rambles in Eastern Asia") having heard much of the fascinations of the White Mountains from Starr King and other enthusiasts, suddenly decided in late October of 1855 that nothing would suit him better than an expedition to Mount Washington. Failing to make connections with fellow-explorers, he set out one bright afternoon from Boston, by himself, reached Portland, where he spent the night, awoke to a rainy morning, in spite of that, took train to Gorham, looked dismayed at the mass of clouds in the direction of the Range, was, nevertheless, undaunted, and set out on horseback in a pouring rain holding his valise and reins in one hand, his trusty umbrella over his head in the other, for the Glen House.

At that hostelry there ensued a colloquy with Landlord Thompson about the weather and the likelihood of the mountain's unveiling itself. The landlord suggested a stroll up the new carriage road, built by a New York company, to the Camp House at the end of the road, halfway up the mountain —"but don't go beyond!" With his umbrella he set out. He reached the Camp House four miles up in an hour or two and decided to go on up over the Ledge. Surmounting the Ledge he encountered a foot of snow; it began to rain, icily; darkness fell. He decided to retrace his steps. With some difficulty, he reached the Camp House, much exhausted, covered with ice and completely chilled. Mr. Myers, in charge of the Camp, took him in. Food, coffee, a warm fire, the cheer of Mr. Myers' conversation, a night's rest re-invigorated him. In the morning a glance up the bridle path, cleared of its snow by softening weather, spurred him on to conquer the peak. Mr. Myers expostulated: "You have heard of the lady who lost her way one day last month on the summit, and died there?"—"Miss Bourne, you refer to, I presume?" —"Yes, Miss Bourne, from Kennebunk. She was a beautiful lady. . . ."

Dr. Ball had heard of Miss Bourne and her blighted beauty. It did not deter him—she had some difficulty of the chest. . . . After a hurried breakfast he exchanged his shoes for a pair of Mr. Myers' stout boots and fared forth—with his inseparable umbrella. There would be four mountains, said Mr. Myers. He passed the FIRST MOUNTAIN successfully. After that, the snow crust through which he broke cut his ankles badly, the way was rough, icy, steep, rocky. He pressed on, over the SECOND MOUNTAIN, neared the THIRD. The air was cold; the drizzle had become sleet, snow. It swarmed about him in clouds. Only a squall? Surely the summit was just ahead. But the squall continued, the summit failed to appear. Still he persisted, on the summit was shelter, he would not admit himself beaten. There were the Bernese Alps, the lofty group of mountains near Bains de Loeuk, the volcanic cone of Marapee in Java—had he been faint-hearted he would have missed those sights. To be beaten by Mount Washington—never!

The way became rougher and his feet and hands began to freeze (he had long ago furled his umbrella and tied it to him with a cord so that he could pocket his hands). It was

the hardest storm he had ever known and the cold was severe
—not less than 10°-12° below zero, Fahrenheit. (He had no
thermometer—but let us leave him this satisfaction.) Ice had
completely congealed his whiskers—perhaps the ice mask
formed by his whiskers, even more than his umbrella, saved
his life. Icicles two inches long hung from his cap. But—*"I
will still try for the Summit House!"* He had always accomplished what he had undertaken. Surely he must now be on
the FOURTH MOUNTAIN. The fury of the wind would indicate
it. (More than once it hurled him to the ground, immersing
his hands in the icy snow.) At last, level ground! *Mount
Washington at last—and here is the Summit!* But the storm!
"If ten hurricanes had been in deadly strife with each other,
it could have been no worse." Still he called it a squall. Where
was the Summit House? Over there. After several falls he
reached it—only a large rock. Again he explored the plateau
of the summit for the house—again he failed. The wind buf-
feted him, threw him to the ground. He must find the house
or perish. But still he failed. In the shelter of a rock he took
counsel: perhaps he had miscalculated, this might be the
third mountain.

Well, here was comparative comfort; he felt drowsy; he
could go to sleep. But—*once lost in sleep would be to wake no
more!* Again the search; again no Summit House. There was
nothing for it—it was now the middle of the afternoon—but
to start back. He followed his wandering foot-tracks; he was
losing valuable time; he gave that up; he plunged straight
down the mountain. Suddenly he came upon a line of stakes
—the line for the rest of the carriage road! He followed them

excitedly down into the scrub with increasing difficulty—he lost them altogether.

And now night suddenly fell, the wind and storm still raged, it was suddenly borne in upon him that he was destined to spend the night out in this terrible weather! Then thank God for the umbrella! In the shelter of a rock he spread it, fastened the handle to a root with his benumbed fingers, banked it as best he could with snow crusts, rocks, and bushes. He crawled beneath. He tried to kindle a fire with damp wet wood, he used some ten dollar bills (for which the Northboro' bank would be no loser) for kindling. In vain. He coiled up in his rocky bed but he knew that it was death to go to sleep. . .

It was the longest night he ever knew. He took constrained positions, leaning on one elbow then on another, drawing up his legs, stretching them out again, leaning against the icy rock. He thought of comfortable beds at home, with friends, at the Camp House, even, at the Glen; he thought of Sir John Franklin in the polar seas, of soldiers, maimed and mangled in the Crimea. At last the first light of morning came.

The second day was a more intense repetition of the first. The storm had ceased but the wind still blew and heavy clouds still hung down upon the mountain. His hands and feet were more or less frozen, his body was stiff, he was hungry and his mouth was parched with thirst. He tried melting snow in his mouth—by the time he had thawed enough to get a little water his mouth was numb with cold. He could get glimpses only through the clouds of the mountain he had climbed the day before (and which he had no wish to climb again) and a valley below with no sign of civilization. He traveled toward what he thought might be a path, breaking through the crust at every step. Toward noon he found himself at the edge of a great ravine (it was the Great Gulf). Once, the clouds lifted and he thought he saw two men on the bluff across the valley. He hallooed to them as loudly as his parched mouth would permit: there was no response or movement. He decided to go back over his track and perhaps circle the mountain with a view to catching a glimpse of the Glen House below. Toward night he approached his shelter again and the terrible truth forced itself upon him that he was doomed to still another night of exposure without sleep and that this night would be the last.

Still consumed with intolerable thirst, frozen and numbed in every limb, he crawled into his humble shelter: "and, if ever I had in my heart anything like vain pride, I am sure there was none now remaining." So this was to be the abrupt culmination of "Rambles in Eastern Asia." He examined his pulse, he took up again his cramped positions of the night before. He speculated on the comments of his friends as to his fate: loss in the fog, insanity, suicide? He thought of his friends at home and abroad, his remissness in acknowledging their hospitalities. He mused on the strange chance of his taking his umbrella along. He experimented with himself to see how far he could get toward sleep without going under. He got very far, flirting with death, then his elbow upon which he had propped himself gave way and recalled him to consciousness.

At last the third day dawned, still cold and cloudy. And suddenly a lifting cloud disclosed, far off down in the valley, a view of the Glen House. After two hours spent in limbering up his numbed limbs he started painfully along the ridge. For two days now he had had nothing to eat, little to drink, he was in a fearfully weakened state. But he hobbled on indefatigably. About noon he paused on a flat rock to take an observation. All at once, around a bluff appeared a party of men. With all his strength he shouted. They stared at him: they had come up to look for his body.

On the first day, Dr. Ball had circled the Great Gulf in the cloud, going too far to the north, and gone up Jefferson instead of Washington and thus had wandered about lost for two more days on the Range. At the Camp House they put him on horseback and carried him below to the Glen. Mr. Thompson greeted him: "You have been through what no other person has, or probably will again, in a thousand years." At the Glen House he was confined to his bed for a week, suffering excruciating pain. Then he was put on a sofa and carried to Gorham, thence by train to Boston. For three months he was in a helpless condition but gradually his health was restored. . . Four years later, Mr. Kilbourne tells us, he died at Chiriqui, Panama, and all the buffetings with the weather on Mount Washington had come to naught.

But what, meanwhile, we hear our readers asking, exhausted and with heart panting from the stupendous exertions of Dr. Ball and other mad mountaineers, what, good sirs, of the view? To which we calmly reply,—be it *lese majesté* or whatever—the view? we should ourselves never climb Mount

Washington for the view alone. For that, it is really too high, if we must be critical. For the views several other mountains are, we think, much superior: Moosilauke, Lafayette, Chocorua. Not that the view from Washington is to be by any means despised. We have quoted Darby Field's imaginative description. Belknap in his History, indicates its extent: "On the S.E. side, there is a view of the Atlantic ocean, the nearest part of which, is sixty-five miles, in a direct line. On the W. and N. the prospect is bounded by the high lands, which separate the waters of Connecticut and Amariscoggin rivers, from those of Lake Champlain and St. Lawrence. On the south, it extends to the southernmost mountains of New Hampshire, comprehending a view of the Lake Winipiseogee. On every side of these mountains, are long winding gullies, beginning at the precipice below the plain, and deepening in the descent."

Starr King and his successors have all given eloquent descriptions to which we refer the reader: the Atlantic, the Catskills, the Adirondacks, Katahdin—cheerful liars! Only on a very clear day and then more conveniently with a telescope can all these geographical features be easily seen; Katahdin, it has recently been established, never. Of course, the nearer mountains are visible. On the platform east of the Summit House is a range-finder for the more minutely curious.

But there are better sights than the panoramic one of six hundred miles circumference which all the travelers brag about. The view on a clear night, for instance, when the wilderness of northern New Hampshire suddenly springs up

populous with towns: Lancaster to the northwest; Gorham
and Berlin to the northeast; Jackson, Bartlett, and the Con-
ways to the southeast; the great gloom of the southern ridge,
Crawford Notch and the wilderness behind it, Bethlehem. . .
Littleton. . . Sugar Hill; at the very base of the mountain
the glittering electrical display of the Mount Washington
Hotel, reminiscent of Broadway. One immediately begins to
think, like the older guides, in terms of carbuncles, sparkling
gems, necklaces, and other gew-gaws.

Or there is the famous view from above the clouds: There
has been a storm, perhaps, the wind has at last subsided, sunrise comes (or moonrise). The clouds sink below the tip of
the cone, a vast white rolling expanse, only here and there a
peak, like Lafayette, thrusting its tip out of the billowy sea.
The cloud spray, struck by a sudden gust, boils up out of
Tuckerman's, the heat of the sun disperses it until it becomes
invisible in the blue emptiness above from which we turn to
look upon the white emptiness below hiding almost every
vestige of the black earth. This is indeed something to come
even hundreds of miles to see. . . .

But on the whole it is not the view which is the unique and
exciting thing about Mount Washington, it is the weather. It
seems strange, one may think, to go to all these efforts of
tramping, motoring, or cog railways just for the weather
which, like the poor, is always with us. Not at all. From the
accounts of the various ascents we have given more than a hint
as to the versatility of its antics. A perusal of the records of
the Hitchcock-Huntington expedition in the winter of 1870-
71 and the weather observations of the U. S. Signal Service

Boott Spur and Head of Tuckerman's Ravine from Mount Washington

© *Shorey Studio*

Mounts Adams and Madison from Mount Washington Road

during the winters for several years on until 1887 enlightens one further.

The first, an expedition supported by the Smithsonian Institution and private subscribers, occupied a building especially made for them, securely anchored to the mountain and thoroughly insulated, the room where the party stayed occupying one corner, about a third of the edifice. This little room was their laboratory, kitchen, dining, living, and sleeping room. The large outer vestibule served as an admirable refrigerator for their food. They reported their observations daily by telegraph to Washington—that is, except when their telegraph line to the base was disrupted by the elements. On Christmas Eve it was 15° below zero outside, in the room with their two stoves 42° above. The most frolicsome weather was that recorded in their Journal for Saturday and Sunday, February 4th and 5th. At no time was the wind below seventy-five miles an hour, at seven in the evening the thermometer was 40° below. In the room, five feet from the stove, they managed to push the thermometer up to 65° above; on the floor ten feet from the stove it was 12° above zero. One of the party froze his fingers while sawing off the pork in the vestibule for their "Sunday baked beans." No one dared to stick his head outdoors. In the evening the wind rose so that they had to shout to be heard; the timbers creaked and groaned, the windows rattled, the walls bent inward. At three of the next morning the mercury had sunk to — 59°. At two Sunday afternoon the anemometer recorded a velocity of eighty-eight miles an hour. . . They stayed indoors; they cut their butter with hammer and chisel.

During observations in later years by the Signal Service the anemometer recorded frequent velocities of one hundred and eighty miles an hour; once it reached its highest record of one hundred and eighty-eight miles. In that gale an engine shed and the board walk from the hotel to the Signal Station were scattered helter-skelter over the mountain. In the rocking and creaking Station the observers wrapped themselves in quilts and blankets held down by iron bars and waited to be whipped off, building and all, into Tuckerman's Ravine.

But enough. The weather of New England is notorious. Mark Twain among others has immortalized it. As for winds —even in the comparative seclusion of Crawford Notch it often takes—Ethan Allen Crawford is our authority—two men to hold one man's hair on. The weather of Mount Washington,—we have given enough evidence to convince any skeptic,—is more notorious yet. We have said that, because of its height, it is the focal point for tourists from all over the North Atlantic states. It is our theory (being no meteorologists) that its height makes it the focal point for all the storms of the same region. Mount Mitchell in North Carolina, though higher, is three hundred miles inland, is wooded nearly to the top and is situated at a much lower latitude. It knows nothing of the extreme storms that visit Washington. Even the Sierras and Rockies, though they are twice as high and many of them are snow-covered all the year round—from a difference in latitude, greater dryness of air, distance from the seacoast or whatever—have no such capricious weather conditions, in spite of sudden showers and squalls. The government weather reports reveal that Mount Washington has a much higher average wind velocity than any other mountain in the United States. We have seen what it can do at a maximum and sixty miles an hour is by no means an unusual blow, even in summer. Its climate, therefore, may be said to be unique in the United States. Not even the other peaks of the White Mountains (except Jefferson and Adams of the Presidential Range) can boast anything like it. The change from the Lakes-of-the-Clouds to the summit is noticeable in vegetation and insect life even to the casual observer. "It is a few square miles of Labrador or Greenland," says Professor Goldthwait, "rising out of an inhospitable sea of New Hampshire hills."

We do not wish to create the impression that there are nothing but storms in summer on the Range. Far from it. There are many fair, even mild, days. But if there is a storm anywhere around, it will hit Mount Washington before it gets through. The tramper, or the tourist coming up by rail or car will look about him in complacency before going into the Summit House. Clear skies, a rosy sunset, a balmy breeze: over there in the northwest a cloud no bigger than a man's hand. And in an hour's time he finds himself in a swirling fog with the wind tearing along like an airplane, in desperate haste for some reason to get out on the open Atlantic. What was a calm Olympus has become the most entirely adequate setting for *King Lear* we have ever known.

At such a time a night spent in the shelter of the Summit House or Tip-Top House will give one a peculiarly cosy sensation. It is exactly as Starr King said: one has a sensation of the planet's motion as it scuds at twelve hundred miles a minute, over the star-islanded immensity.

Let us take leave of it in this cosmic mood with an *ave atque vale* for it and that gallant company of our predecessors, those lost adventurers, our peers. We have not always treated them and their lucubrations altogether reverently, not even the mountains themselves as reverently as they would have wished us to. Well, let us make this gesture of propitiation to the spirit of Agiochook. But other times, other customs. The mountains at any rate seem serene. "They are so patient!" says Starr King. Yes, they seem so, even if they are not altogether permanent. Already by a slide here, by erosion there, their lines are imperceptibly changing. They are always on the march. In a million million years, Sir James Jeans tells us, they will have almost reached the level of the plain. But that is a long time ahead. We think it is safe to say that they will be on display for tourists for some time to come. It is even quite probable that long after the doughty and flippant guides of the nineteenth and twentieth centuries are dust and ashes the mountains will still remain.

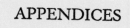

APPENDICES

APPENDIX A

HOTELS OF THE WHITE MOUNTAINS

Note: Hotels of this region range from ordinary roadside places to the most sumptuous establishments, and the rates are, accordingly, made to suit every pocketbook. Many of the great hotels command superb views and offer every luxury. The list is scarcely selective, and naturally the charges are subject to change.

Where rates are given, the first column is by the day, second, weekly.

IMPORTANT REFERENCES

Hotels marked § are open the year round.
Places marked (A) have American Plan.
Places marked (B) send illustrated booklets on request.
Places marked (E) have European Plan.

The list, arranged alphabetically, follows:

BARTLETT (Altitude 680 feet):

	DAILY	WEEKLY
Hotel Howard AB	$5.00 up	$25.00 up
Maple Cottage §A	3.50	14.00 up
Sweet Farm Inn BAE	3.00 up	18.00 up
Thompson's Inn BE	2.00 up	18.00
The Pines ABE	3.50	20.00
Maple Dale Farm AB	2.50	14.00 up
Elmcrest Cottage AB	2.50	14.00

BATH (Altitude 521):

	DAILY	WEEKLY
Colonial Inn AB	3.00 up	20.00 up
Fairview Farm	1.75 up	12.50 up

BENTON (Altitude 580):

    (Railroad Station, Woodsville, N. H.)

	DAILY	WEEKLY
Captain Nixon's Log Cabins	$3.00	$18.00

BERLIN (Altitude 1013):

Berlin House §E	Apply	Apply
New Revere Hotel §A	3.50 up	21.00 up

BETHLEHEM (Altitude 1470):

Sinclair Hotel AB	5.00 up	35.00 up
Upland Terrace AB	5.00	35.00
Howard House AB	6.00 up	40.00 up
New Agassiz Hotel AB	6.00 up	40.00 up
Park View Hotel AB	5.00 up	35.00 up
Highland Hotel AB	6.00 up	42.00
Central House-Hillside Inn AB	5.00	28.00
The Strawberry Hill House AB	5.00 up	35.00 up
Maplehurst AB	6.00 up	40.00 up
Buena Vista Hotel ABE	2.50 up	15.00 up
The Arlington AB	5.00 up	35.00 up
Turner's Tavern AB	6.50 up	32.50 up
Columbia Hotel AB	4.50 up	27.50 up
The Alpine AB	5.00 up	35.00 up
The Reynolds BA	5.00 up	Apply
Lovejoy's Inn ABE	4.00 up	25.00 up
The Sunnyside AB	3.50	Apply
Grand View Cottage AB	4.00	21.00 up
(Post-office, Littleton, N. H.)		
Terra Nova Farm AB	3.50	18.00 up
(Railroad Station, Littleton, N. H.)		
Valley Home §A	3.00	16.00
(Railroad Station, Wing Road, N. H.)		
Valley View Farm AB	3.50	20.00 up
Goodwin's Log Cabin A	7.00	45.00
Hill Crest Inn AB	4.00	22.00 up
Mount Washington Hotel AB	6.00 up	35.00 up
Colby Inn AB	4.00	25.00
The Way Side Inn AB	4.00	25.00

	DAILY	WEEKLY
Rocky Birch Inn AB	$4.00 up	$25.00 up
Beech Hill House A	2.50	15.00

(Post-office, Pierces Bridge, N. H.)

BRETTON WOODS (Altitude 1587):

The Mount Washington AB	9.00 up	Apply
The Mount Pleasant AB	6.00 up	Apply
The Bretton Arms AB	5.00 up	35.00 up

CAMPTON (Altitude 597):

Maple Cottages AB	2.50	15.00
Hatetoquitit Farm A	2.00	14.00
Sandwich Notch Camp	....	35.00

CANAAN (Altitude 942):

Lucerne Inn AB	6.00	25.00 up
Canaan Inn AB	4.00 up	15.00 up
Camp Calumet (Boys) B	Season	300.00
The Cobb House AB	4.00 up	18.00 up

CENTER CONWAY (Altitude 466):

Eaton Hall	3.00	18.00

CENTER SANDWICH (Squam Lake):

(Reached by Auto from Mt. Whittier, or Meredith)

"Top o' the World"	3.00	15.00
Diamond Ledge Camp and Lodge	4.00 up	18.50 up

CHOCORUA (Altitude 530):

(Auto from Mt. Whittier)

Chocorua Inn and Annex AB	5.75 up	31.50 up
Hayford House AB	3.50	20.00 up
Chocorua View House §AB	3.00	18.00
Maplehurst AB	3.50 up	18.00 up

COLEBROOK, Dixville Notch (Altitude 1017):

The Monadnock AB	4.00 up	28.00
Camp Diamond AB	5.00 up	30.00 up
Colebrook House §A	4.50 up	28.00
Big Diamond Camp and Cabins AB	4.00 up	25.00 up

COLEBROOK, Cont.

	DAILY	WEEKLY
Elm Tree Inn §A	$4.00	$21.00 up
Polly's Place (Inn and Tea House) E	5.00	....
Monadnock Gift Shop or Hough's Inn ABE ...	3.50	21.00 up
Private House A	2.50	14.00
The Meadows A	2.75	12.00 up
Willow Farm A§	2.50	12.00

CONWAY (Altitude 466):

Camp Wonalancet (Boys) B	Season	275.00
(Post-office, Eaton Centre, Conway, N. H.)		
Waukeela Camp (Girls) B	....	38.00
Presidential Inn and Cottages B	5.00	32.00 up
Pequawket Camps (Boys) B	Season	250.00
Evans Camp (Adults) AB	4.00	25.00
(Post-office, Eaton Centre, Conway, N. H.)		
Pine Knoll Camp (Girls) B	Season	350.00
Hillside Dairy Farm AB	3.00	14.00
Woodward Farm AB	3.50	18.00 up
(Post-office and Railroad Station, Fryeburg, Me.)		
Hanson Cottage §A	3.00	14.00
Wing's Tavern AB	4.00	25.00

CRAWFORD'S, Crawford Notch (Altitude 1891):

Crawford House AB	7.00 up	42.00 up

DIXVILLE NOTCH (Altitude 1990):

(Auto from Colebrook)

The Balsams	Apply	Apply

EAST CONWAY (Railroad Station, Fryeburg, Me.):

Woodward Farm AB	3.50	18.00 up
Bethlehem Cottage, E	Apply	Apply
Sumac Lodge A	2.00	12.00 up

ERROL (Auto from Berlin, N. H.):

Umbagog Camp AB	4.50 up	28.00 up
Akers Pond Cottage E	3.00	21.00
The Elite	Apply	Apply

FABYAN (Altitude 1058):

	DAILY	WEEKLY
Fabyan House AB	$7.00 up	$42.00 up
Fabyan House Annex AB	5.00 up	35.00 up
White Mountain House AB	4.50 up	26.00 up

FRANCONIA (Altitude 990):
(Auto from Littleton)

Forest Hills Hotel AB	6.00 up	42.00 up
Pecketts-on-Sugar-Hill AB	Apply	Apply
Spooner House AB	4.00	21.00 up
Pleasant View AB	3.00	17.00
Profile Farm Inn and Cottages AE	3.00 up	21.00 up
Mt. View House §AB	4.00	20.00 up
Pinestead Farm AB	2.50 up	14.00 up
Auto Rest A	3.00	20.00
The Riverside §A	2.50	16.00
Green Shutters AB	5.00	25.00 up

FREEDOM, N. H.
(Auto from Mountainview, N. H.)

Loon Lake House A	3.00	16.00 up
The Mills Farm §A	2.25	15.00

GORHAM (Altitude 812):

Mt. Madison House AB	7.00 up	Apply
Willis House & Cottages A	4.50	21.00 up
Glenn House AB	5.00 up	30.00 up

HOLDERNESS (Squam Lake):
(Railroad Station, Ashland, N. H.)

The Asquam Inn	3.00 up	21.00 up
Holderness Inn and Camps AB	4.50 up	28.00 up
Camp Aloha (Boys) B	Season	300.00
Hillside Cottage BA	3.50	18.00 up
Camp Algonquin (Boys) B	Season	300.00
Big Squam Inn §AB	4.00 up	20.00 up
Holderness Camp BE	4.00 up	Apply
Little Squam Lodges (Boys) B	Season	250.00
Lakeside Camps AE	3.50	23.00

INTERVALE (Altitude 544):

	DAILY	WEEKLY
The Bellevue AB§	$5.00 up	$28.00 up
Pendexter Mansion AB	4.00 up	21.00 up
Emwood Inn and Cottage AB	4.00	18.00 up
Maple Villa A	4.00 up	21.00 up
Rest-A-Bit Inn A	3.50	18.00 up
Smith's Tavern AB	3.00 up	21.00 up
Fosscroft Inn AB§	4.00 up	21.00 up
Pittman Hall AB	4.50 up	28.00 up

JACKSON (Altitude 757):

Wentworth Hall and Cottages A	10.00 up	Apply
Gray's Inn AB	5.50 up	32.50 up
Eagle Mt. House AB	4.50 up	28.00 up
(Open February to March to accommodate Winter Parties)		
Iron Mt. House AB	4.50 up	28.00 up
Jackson Falls House AB	4.50 up	25.00 up
Wilson Cottages AB	3.50 up	18.00 up
The Hawthorne AB	4.00	21.00 up
Spruce Mt. Bungalow Camps AB	3.00 up	20.00 up
Moody Farm §A	2.25	13.00 up
Fernald Cottage §AB	3.50	18.00 up
Thorn Mt. Summer School (Boys) B	Season	400.00
Oak Lea A	3.00	21.00
The Nestlenook A	3.00 up	20.00 up
Brookmead Cottage §A	3.50	Apply
Pleasant Hill Cottage §A	2.50	15.00 up
Duck's Head Cottage §A	3.00	15.00
Meserve Hall AB	4.00 up	24.50 up
Evergreen Cottage §A	2.50	14.00

JEFFERSON (Altitude 1437):

New Waumbek System AB	7.00	42.00
Pliny Ridge House AB	4.00 up	22.00 up
(P.O. Jeff. Highlands)		
Bois Mt. Farm A	3.00 up	18.00 up
(P.O. Jeff. Highlands)		
Gray Gables Motor Inn A	5.00	25.00

	DAILY	WEEKLY
Cloverdale Cottages	$4.00	$22.00 up
(P.O. Starr King)		
Hillside Farm AB	4.00	22.00 up

JEFFERSON HIGHLANDS

Highland House AB	4.50 up	28.00 up

KEARSARGE (R.R. Sta., North Conway):

Russell Cottages AB	5.00	30.00
Kearsarge Mt. Inn AB	2.50 up	18.00 up
(Railroad Station, Intervale, N. H.)		
Mountain View Farm A	2.50 up	14.00 up
(Railroad Station, Intervale, N. H.)		
Abbott Farm	3.00 up	18.00 up
(Railroad Station, Intervale, N. H.)		
Sunnymeade B	4.50 up	23.00 up
Birchmere Farm A	3.00	16.00
(Railroad Station, Intervale, N. H.)		
Hamilton Villa AB	2.50 up	15.00 up
(Railroad Station, Intervale, N. H.)		

LAKEPORT (Lake Winnipesaukee):

Camp Idlewild (Boys) B	Season	300.00
(Railroad Station, Weirs, N. H.)		
Camp Samoset (Boys) B	5.00	....
(Railroad Station, Lake Shore Park, N. H.)		
Ames Farm AB	3.50	16.00 up
(Railroad Station, Ames, N. H.)		
Mt. Belknap Hotel §	4.00 up	20.00 up
Camp Acadia (Girls) B	Season	250.00
(Railroad Station, Weirs, N. H.)		
Mt. View House AB	3.00 up	16.00 up
Winnipesaukee Farm and Annex §AB	3.50	16.00 up
Camp Lynnholm (Girls) B	....	25.00
Chanticleer Inn AB	4.00 up	25.00 up
Pleasant Valley Farm A	2.50	15.00
Locust Farm A	3.00	15.00
(Railroad Station, Weirs, N. H.)		

LAKEPORT, Cont.

	DAILY	WEEKLY
Elmcroft Farm A	$3.00	$18.00 up
Barramy Acres	3.00	16.00 up
Lake View Farm A	2.50	15.00
Springdale Farm §A	2.50	15.00
(Railroad Station, Meredith, N. H.)		
The Ranch Farm A	2.50	14.00
Lake Shore Farm AB	3.00	18.00
(Railroad Station, Weirs, N. H.)		

LANCASTER (Altitude 864):

Lancaster Inn §AB	4.50 up	25.00 up
The Elms §A	3.50	15.00 up
Granite State Stock Farm AB	2.25	15.00
Elmwood Farm	....	15.00

LINCOLN (Altitude 1400):

Lincoln Hotel AB	4.00 up	21.00 up

LISBON (Altitude 598):

Camp Ogontz (Girls)	Season	350.00
Pleasant View AB	4.50 up	18.00 up

LITTLETON (Altitude 700):

Chiswick Inn AB	4.00 up	25.00 up
Maple Cottage §A	2.50	15.00 up
The Grand View AB	3.00 up	21.00 up
The Burgess Place A	2.50	15.00
Wallace Farm AB	4.50 up	30.00
The Twin Pine Farm §	2.50	15.00

LYME (Auto from Thetford, Vt.):

Camp Pinnacle (Boys)	Season	300.00
Alden Tavern A	4.00 up	15.00 up
Union St. Farm	2.00	12.00
Lock Lyme Cabins	4.00 up	25.00 up

MAPLEWOOD (Railroad Station, Bethlehem):

Maplewood Club AB	6.00 up	42.00 up

NORTH CHATHAM (Railroad Station, Fryeburg, Me.):

	DAILY	WEEKLY
Royce House A	$3.00	$16.00 up

NORTH CONWAY (Altitude 715):

Hotel Randall AB	7.00 up	42.00 up
New Robertson Inn AB	4.00	21.00 up
Kearsarge Hall and Cottage §AB	3.00 up	20.00 up
Lucy Farm House §AB	3.50	16.00 up
Edgewood Cottage AB	3.50 up	18.00 up
Highland Villa A	3.50	....
Moat Mt. House	3.00	15.00 up
The Elmwood AB§	3.50	20.00
Mountain View House B	3.00	18.00
Nereledge §AB	3.50	20.00
The Maples AB	3.00 up	18.00 up
The Further Residence §A	3.00 up	21.00 up
Brookside Inn	3.00 up	16.50 up
Woods Cottage A	2.50 up	15.00 up

NORTH STRATFORD (Coös County):

Hotel Stratford	Apply	Apply

NORTH WOODSTOCK (Altitude 809):

Hotel Alpine AB	6.00 up	40.00 up
Deer Park Hotel AB	5.00 up	23.50 up
Mountain View House AB	3.50	17.50 up
Fairview AB	3.50 up	19.00 up
(Post-office and Railroad Station, Fairview, N. H.		
Mt. Adams Hotel AB	4.00 up	18.00 up
Russell House §AB	4.00	21.00 up
Mountain Park House BA	3.50	18.50 up
(Railroad Station, Mountain Park, N. H.)		
Maplewood Cottages AE	3.00 up	17.50 up
The Greenleaf Inn AB	4.00 up	23.00 up
Sunset Farm Inn AB	2.50 up	15.00 up
Woodstock Inn	5.00 up	Apply
Hilltop House	3.00	18.00

PASSACONWAY (From North Conway):

	DAILY	WEEKLY
Swift River Inn AB	$3.50 up	$20.00 up

PIKE (Altitude 749):

Lake Tarleton Club AB	10.00 up	63.00 up
Camp Tahoma, sr. (Girls)	Season	350.00
Camp Tahoma, jr. (Girls)	Season	350.00

PLYMOUTH (Altitude 483):

Pemigewasset House AB	7.00 up	42.00 up
Plymouth Inn §A	4.00 up	25.00 up
Mt. Prospect Lodge AB	5.00 up	Apply
Travellers' Inn	5.00 up	Apply
Greenwood Lea AB	3.50	18.00
The Manuel Farm AB	2.50	15.00
Bayley's Tourist Home	1.00 up	....

RANDOLPH (Altitude 1203):

Ravine House AB	5.00 up	35.00 up
Mt. Crescent House AB	4.00 up	22.00 up
Coldbrook Camp	Apply	
Mountain View House	....	14.00 up

ST. JOHNSBURY, VT. (Altitude 711):

New Avenue House A	5.00 up	Apply
St. Johnsbury House A	5.50 up	Apply

SANDWICH (Auto from Meredith):

Red Hill Lodge	2.00	12.00

SHELBURNE (Altitude 704):

The Gates Cottages A	3.00	18.00 up
Evans Cottages A	2.50	Apply

SILVER LAKE (Railroad Station, Madison, N. H.):

The Lakeside AB	4.00	21.00 up
Camp Allegro (Girls)	Season	300.00
Silver Lake House AB	3.50	20.00 up

STARR KING (Railroad Station, Highlands, N. H.):

	DAILY	WEEKLY
Starr King A	$3.00	$20.00
Elm Cottage A	3.00	18.00

SUGAR HILL (Altitude 1650):

Sunset Hill House AB	7.00	45.00 up
Hotel Lookoff AB	Apply	

TAMWORTH (Auto from Mt. Whittier):

Vraimont Cottages (Adults) AB	5.00	25.00 up
Camp Chocorua (Boys) B	Season	300.00
Camp Larcom (Girls) B	Season	300.00
Edgehill and Camps §AB	4.50	21.00 up
Swift River House	2.50	14.00
Whittier Lodge §AB	3.00 up	16.00 up
The Maples §	2.50	14.00 up
Hotel Tamworth AB	4.50	21.00
The Gray Camp	2.50	15.00

THORNTON (Post-office, Campton):

The Outlook	2.50	14.00

TWIN MOUNTAINS (Altitude 1450):

Twin Mountain House AB	5.00 up	28.00 up
Rosebrook Inn AB	4.00 up	22.00 up
Grand View Hotel AB	4.00 up	21.00 up
Carroll Inn and Camps AEB	4.00 up	21.00 up
U-Auto-Rest A	3.00	18.00
Supreme View Inn ABE	Apply	Apply
King Cottage AB	3.00	18.00
The Maples AB	4.00	16.00 up
The Homestead A	2.50	16.00
Hillside Lodge AB	3.50	20.00 up
The Riverside AB	3.00 up	21.00 up
Pleasant View Cottage	Apply	Apply
Cherry Mt. Farm House A	2.50	16.00 up
Cold Spring House §A	2.75	16.00

TWIN MOUNTAINS, Cont.

	DAILY	WEEKLY
Willow Farm A	$2.50	$16.00
The Rox Mere AB	Apply	Apply
(Post-office, Whitefield, N. H.)		

WARREN (Altitude 847):

Moosilauke Inn AB	5.00 up	30.00 up
Bailey's Tavern E	4.00	....
Hillside House AB	2.50	12.00 up
Sunrise Farm AB	2.00	12.00 up

WEST THORNTON

Algonquin Farm Inn	3.00	20.00
Pleasant View Farm AB	3.00	16.00 up
Tecumseh Lodge B	2.50	15.00

WHITEFIELD (Altitude 950):

Mountain View House BA	8.00 up	56.00 up
Hotel Spruces AB	4.50 up	25.00 up
Lindsay Inn §AB	4.50	28.00
Locust Cottage BA	3.00	17.00
Spalding Inn AB	5.00 up	35.00 up
Greystone Lodge ABE	5.00 up	25.00 up
Phoebe Ann Inn A	5.00 up	35.00 up
Hillcrest A	3.50	20.00
Cherry View Cottage A	2.50	15.00

WONALANCET (Auto from Mt. Whittier):

Ferncroft and Camps AB	4.50 up	25.00 up
Wonalancet Farm A	4.00 up	....

WOODSTOCK (Altitude 649):

Van Allen's Inn AB	3.50	15.00 up
Fern Hills Farm A	3.00	15.00 up
Camp City Lodge & Cabins	1.00 up	10.00 up

APPENDIX B

SUMMER CAMPS IN NEW HAMPSHIRE

Note: Where possible the name and address of the director are given.

(FOR BOYS)

Camp Algonquin, Squam Lake (Railroad Station, Ashland, N. H.) Edwin DeMerritte, 11 Willow St., Belmont, Mass.

Aloha, Squam Lake (Sta., Ashland). E. W. Ogden, 60 State Street, Boston.

Bay State, Tilton, N. H. E. J. Mellen, 20 Slade St., Belmont, Mass.

Calumet, Canaan, N. H. R. C. Callard, 134 Crescent Avenue, Plainfield, N. J.

Camp Belknap, Lake Winnipesaukee (Sta., Weirs, N. H.). E. P. Conlon, Concord, N. H.

Chocorua (Sta., Mt. Whittier). S. G. Davidson, Tamworth, N. H.

Contoocook, East Jaffrey, N. H. F. W. Moses, Carnegie Tech., Pittsburgh, Pa.

Contoocook, Contoocook, N. H. LeRoy Morand, Contoocook, N. H.

Granite Lake, (Sta., Keene, N. H.). Albert Loewinthan, 838 West End Avenue, New York City.

Idlewild, Lake Winnipesaukee, Lakeport, N. H. (Sta., Weirs). L. D. Roys, 334 Otis Street, Boston.

Lawrence, Lake Winnipesaukee, Bear Island (Sta., Weirs). Henry B. Coleman, Y. M. C. A., Lawrence, Mass.

Little Squam Lodges, Little Squam Lake, Holderness (Sta., Ashland). F. D. Aldrich, Worcester Academy, Worcester, Mass.

Mascoma, Enfield, N. H. Thomas J. Dent, Hanover, N. H.

Mohajo, Washington, N. H. (Sta., Hillsboro). Mr. and Mrs. J. H. Dell, Washington, N. H.

Monadnock, Thorndike Lake, Jaffrey (Sta. East Jaffrey). Frederick S. Ernst, 59 Cottage St., Wellesley, Mass.

Namaschaug, Lake Spofford, Spofford, N. H. (Sta., Keene). J. P. Maloney, 27 William St., New York.

Passaconaway, Bear Island, Lake Winnipesaukee, N. H. (Sta., Weirs).
A. G. Carlson, 51 Beaconsfield Rd., Brookline, Mass.

Passumpsic, Lake Fairlee, Ely, Vt. David R. Starry, 27 Drummond Ave.,
Chevy chase, Md.

Pemigewasset, Wentworth, N. H. D. B. Reed, University of Chicago,
Chicago, Ill.

Penacook, North Sutton, N. H. (Sta., Bradford). R. B. Mattern, Dobbs Ferry,
N. Y.

Pequawket, Pequawket Pond, N. H. (Sta., Conway). Eugene I. Smith,
Conway, N. H.

Samoset, Lake Winnipesaukee (Sta., Lake Shore Park). Thomas E. Freeman,
24 Maple Street, West Roxbury, Mass.

Spaulding, Penacook (Sta., Riverhill). R. E. Crowell, Y. M. C. A., Concord,
N. H.

Sunset, Lake Sunset (Sta., Greenfield). M. Agnes Boyle, 64 Hartford St.,
Dorchester, Mass.

Thorn Mountain, Jackson (Sta., Glen & Jackson). G. A. Bushee, 3 Hammond Street, Cambridge, Mass.

Twin Lake Camp, Sutton (Sta., Bradford). R. C. Blodgett, Box 1, Glen
Ridge, N. J.

Wallula, Twin Lakes (Sta., Potter Place). B. A. Hoban, St. George's
School, Newport, R. I.

Waubanaki, Lake Winnipesaukee (Sta., Meredith). Dr. Matthew O'Brien,
517 Clapier St., Philadelphia.

William Lawrence, Lower Beech Pond (Sta., Wolfeboro). F. W. Lincoln, Jr.,
1 Joy Street, Boston.

Winaukee, Lake Winnipesaukee, Center Harbor (Sta., Weirs). I. S. Abrahams, 976 E. 10th St., Brooklyn.

Wonalancet, Eaton Center (Sta., Conway). E. M. Moore, 15 Howard St.,
Arlington, Mass.

Wyanoke, Lake Winnipesaukee (Sta., Wolfeboro). Walter H. Bentley, 14
Beacon Street, Boston.

(FOR GIRLS)

Camp Acadia, Lake Winnipesaukee, Lakeport (R.R. Sta., Weirs). Dr. and
Mrs. J. H. Quimby, Lakeport.

Adeawonda, West Ossipee (Sta., Mt. Whittier). Miriam L. Spaulding, 755
Boylston St., Boston.

Allegro, Silver Lake (Sta., Madison). Mrs. Blanche Carstens, 212 Garden Apartments, Forest Hills, N. Y.

Anawan, Lake Winnipesaukee (Sta., Meredith). Abigail P. Hazelton, 28 Whitefield Road, Somerville, Mass.

Beau Rivage, Portsmouth, N. H. (Sta., Portsmouth), Frances E. Deverell, 1105 Park Ave., New York.

Billings, Fairlee Lake, Ely, Vt. A. C. Hurd, White River Jct., Vt.

Carter, Andover, N. H. (Sta., Andover). Maynard Carpenter, Lebanon, N. H.

Eagle Point, Lake Stinson (Sta., Rumney). A. L. Richman, 10308 Adams Ave., Cleveland, Ohio.

Forest Vale, Franklin, N. H. Ethel B. Mayall, 12 Aiken Ave., Princeton, New Jersey.

Greggmere, Gregg Lake, N. H. (Sta., Antrim). Mrs. Morris Klein, 609 West 114th St., New York City.

Idlepines, Bow Lake (Sta., Rochester). Mrs. S. Evannah Price, 40 High Street, Springfield, Mass.

Interlaken, Lake Sunapee (Sta., Newport). Ida L. Dudley, Hanover, N. H.

Kehonka, Lake Winnipesaukee (Sta., Wolfeboro). Laura J. Mattoon, Wolfeboro, N. H.

Khoo-Khoo-Khoos, Lake Winnipesaukee (Sta., Wolfeboro). Rev. and Mrs. B. L. Yorke, Route 1, Box 74, Alton, N. H.

Larcom, Tamworth (Sta., Mt. Whittier). S. C. Davidson, Tamworth.

Lynnholm, Lake Winnipesaukee (Sta., Lakeport). Clara A. Osgood, 37 Baltimore St., Lynn, Mass.

Monauke, Lake Sunapee. Mrs. Marguerite S. Fowler, 1395 Church Street, Indiana, Pa.

Oahe, Munsonville, N. H., (Sta., Keene). Sara R. Carter, 600 Lexington Ave., New York City.

Ogontz, Lisbon, N. H. (Sta., Sugar Hill), Miss Abby A. Sutherland, Ogontz School P. O., Pennsylvania.

Opechee, New London, N. H. (Sta., Potter Place). Miss F. F. Hockaday, 37 Temple Place, Boston, Mass.

Owaissa, Lake Winnipesaukee, Wolfeboro, N. H. Mrs. Gertrude M. Stevens, 419 Boylston St., Boston, Mass.

Pine Knoll, Conway, N. H. Mrs. J. C. Bucher, Peekskill, N. Y.

Shore Acres, Province Lake (Sta., Purleyville). Miss Laura E. Young, Province Lake, N. H.

Spaulding, Penacock (Sta., Riverhill). R. E. Crowell, Y. M. C. A., Concord, N. H.

Swastika, Granite Lake (Sta., Keene). Mr. and Mrs. R. E. Hodgdon, 436 Broadway, Cambridge, Mass.

Tahigwa, Lake Tahigwa (Sta., Laconia), Etta A. Lavine, 44 Waverly St. Roxbury, Mass.

Tehoma, Lake Armington (Sta., Pike, N. H.). Miss Anna W. Coale, 30 East 42nd Street, New York City.

Tall Pines, Bennington, Evelina Reaveley, Elmwood, N. H.

Wabasso, Bradford, Christine H. Smith, Bradford, N. H.

Waukeela, Conway, N. H. Frances A. Davis, 30 Bay State Rd., Boston, Mass.

Wi-Co-Su-Ta, Bristol, N. H. Mrs. Anna Rothman, 277 West End Ave., New York.

Wihakowi, Northfield, Vt. Arthur E. Winslow, Northfield, Vt.

Winnemont, Ossipee Lake, West Ossipee, N. H. (Sta., Mt. Whittier). Rae Frances Baldwin, 14 Beacon St., Boston, Mass.

Winnetaska, Asquam Lake, N. H. (Sta., Ashland). Mrs. George Whitehouse, 12 Huntington Ave., Boston, Mass.

Wotanda, Meredith, N. H. C. W. Ledley, Glen Ridge, N. J.

GOLF COURSES

Berlin	Androscoggin Country Club	9	Holes
Bethlehem	Bethlehem Golf and Tennis Club	18	"
Bradford	Pleasant View Golf Club	9	"
Bretton Woods	Bretton Woods Golf Club	9	"
Bretton Woods	Bretton Woods Golf Club	18	"
Claremont	Claremont Country Club	9	"
Colebrook	Colebrook Golf Club	9	"
Concord	Beaver Meadow Golf Club	9	"
Crawfords	Crawford Notch Golf Club	9	"
Dixville Notch	Balsams Country Club	18	"
Dover	Cochecho Country Club	9	"
Dublin	Dublin Lake Club	9	"
Exeter	Exeter Country Club	9	"
Fabyan	White Mountain Golf Club	9	"
Farmington	Farmington Country Club	9	"
Franconia	Forest Hills Hotel Golf Club	9	"
Franconia Notch	Profile Golf Club	9	"
Franklin	Mojalaki Country Club	9	"
Gorham	Androscoggin Country Club	9	"
Hanover	Hanover Country Club	18	"
Hopkinton	Dustons' Country Club	9	"
Jackson	Gray's Inn Golf Club	9	"
Jackson	Wentworth Hall Golf Club	18	"
Jefferson	Waumbek Golf Club	18	"
Kearsarge	Russell Cottages Golf Club	9	"
Keene	Keene Country Club	9	"
Laconia	Laconia Country Club	18	"
Lake Spofford	Lake Spofford Hotel Golf Club	9	"
Lake Sunapee	Soo-Nipi Park Golf Club	9	"
Lake Sunapee	Lake Sunapee Country Club	18	"
Lebanon	Carter Country Club	9	"
Manchester	Amoskeag Country Club	9	"

GOLF COURSES, cont.

Manchester	Manchester Country Club	18 Holes
Maplewood	Maplewood Country Club	18 "
Mont Vernon	Mont Vernon Country Club	9 "
Moultonboro	Bald Peak Club Colony	18 "
Nashua	Nashua Country Club	18 "
New Castle	Wentworth Hotel Golf Club	9 "
New London	Lake Sunapee Country Club	18 "
New London	Willow Farm Golf Club	9 "
Newport	Newport Golf Club	9 "
North Conway	Kearsarge Country Club	9 "
North Sutton	Maple Leaf Golf Club	9 "
North Woodstock	Alpine Hotel Country Club	9 "
Peterboro	Peterborough Golf Club	9 "
Pike	Lake Tarleton Golf Club	9 "
Pittsfield	Pittsfield Country Club	9 "
Plymouth	Plymouth Golf Club	9 "
Portsmouth	Portsmouth Country Club	9 "
Rochester	Rochester Country Club	9 "
Rye Beach	Abenaqui Golf Club	18 "
Sugar Hill	Sunset Hill Golf Club	9 "
Sugar Hill	Hotel Lookoff Golf Club	9 "
Sunapee	Granliden Hotel Golf Club	9 "
Twin Mountain	Twin Mountain Golf Club	9 "
Walpole	Hooper Golf Club	9 "
Warren	Moosilauke Golf Club	9 "
Waterville	Waterville Valley Golf Club	9 "
Whitefield	Mountain View Golf Club	9 "
Wolfeboro	Kingswood Golf Club	18 "

MISCELLANEOUS INFORMATION

Persons requiring more detailed information than is given below may address D. D. Tuttle, Director of the New Hampshire State Bureau of Publicity, Concord, N. H.

SYNOPSIS OF MOTOR VEHICLE LAWS

Non-resident Owner. A non-resident owner of a motor vehicle which is used solely for pleasure and is not used for carrying passengers or property for a profit or for hire, and which has been duly registered for the current year in the state or country of which the owner is a resident, and in accordance with the laws thereof shall not be required to register such motor vehicle in this state.

Operator's License. No owner of such motor vehicle and no non-resident chauffeur or driver of such vehicle who is the holder of a license to drive such vehicle in the state or country in which he resides shall be required to purchase a license to drive such vehicle within this state.

Registration fees are based on gross weight of vehicle and load. The Motor Vehicle Department, State House, Concord, N. H., will gladly and promptly give full information.

Operators' licenses are granted to persons over 16 years of age.

Professional Chauffeurs' licenses are granted to persons over 18 years of age.

SPEED RESTRICTIONS

No greater speed than is reasonable and proper:

Open country ....35 miles per hour
Thickly settled or business district ....15-20 miles per hour
Suburban ....20 miles per hour
Around curves, at intersections, etc., unless view is
    obstructed ....15 miles per hour

FISH AND GAME REGULATIONS

All persons of sixteen years or over are required to have a license to fish or hunt and the license money is all used in propagation and protection work. The fee for non-resident fishing licenses is three dollars and fifteen cents; for hunting and fishing licenses, fifteen dollars and fifteen cents.

A synopsis of the laws regulating such sports is given below but owing to the limited space cannot be complete. Inquire from the local agent to get a copy of the complete laws or write to the Department of Fisheries and Game, Concord.

OPEN SEASONS

FISH

Brook Trout—6 inch minimum and 5 lbs. daily limit. Coos, Carroll and Grafton Counties, May 1 to Sept. 1; all other counties, April 15 to August 1; lakes and ponds, 7 inch minimum and 5 lbs. daily limit, April 15 to Sept. 1. (See law-book for trout law regarding ponds and other exceptions.)

Lake Trout—15 inch minimum, Jan. 1 to Sept. 1; 20 lbs. and 6 fish daily limit.

Aureolus Trout—12 inch minimum, April 15 to Sept. 1; not more than 6 in one day.

Rainbow Trout, Brown Trout and Steelhead Trout—Same as brook trout.

Salmon—15 inch minimum, April 1 to Sept. 1; 6 in one day—Exceptions, see chapter 200, par. No. 2.

Bass—6 inch minimum, July 1 to Jan. 1; except bass may be taken with a fly in Sunapee Lake June 15 to January 1.

Pike Perch—10 inch minimum, June 1 to March 1.

White Perch—7 inch minimum, June 1 to Sept. 1; 10 lbs. daily limit.

Pickerel—12 inch minimum, June 1 to Jan. 16; 10 lbs. daily.

Shad and Whitefish—Jan. 1 to Oct. 1.

Pout—June 1 to Nov. 1 except Coos County and Connecticut River. Limit—not more than 40 a day.

Lobsters and Oysters—Not to be taken by non-residents.

PUBLIC CAMP GROUNDS

The State Forestry Department maintains a free camping ground opposite the Willey Cabins in Crawford Notch

(Roosevelt Highway). The State forest ranger, located at the Allen Spring Ranger Station a half mile below the camping grounds, allots space and issues camp fire permits. The Society for the Preservation of New Hampshire Forests maintains log cabins at Lost River, for which a charge is made. Many other camps are scattered over the whole region, and campers are urged to observe the usual decencies in leaving the camps clean, and exercising the utmost precaution about fires. A carelessly thrown match or untended, or unextinguished, coals may work terrible devastation.

The State maintains official tourist information booths at Berlin, Colebrook, Concord, Keene, Lake Sunapee, Lancaster, Lebanon, Littleton, Manchester, North Woodstock, Plymouth, and Rochester.

FEDERAL CAMP GROUNDS

The Federal Government, through its Forestry Service, maintains six camp grounds along the main highways. Pure water, the necessary sanitary facilities, central fireplaces, and free fuel wood are supplied and forest officers, who visit the camps on regular inspection, are ready to assist the public whenever possible.

The Dolly Copp Camp Ground is six miles south of Gorham along the Peabody River, just off the Pinkham Notch Highway.

Glen Ellis Camp is twelve miles from Gorham on the same highway and is a favorite spot for picnics.

Zealand Camp Ground, situated between Twin Mountain

and Fabyan, lies between the Roosevelt Highway and the Ammonoosuc River.

Gale River Camp Ground is between Twin Mountain and Franconia Notch, on the Daniel Webster Highway.

White Ledge Camp Ground is just off the main highway from Boston, near Mount Chocorua.

Oliverian Camp Ground is two miles north of Glencuff.

No charges are made at any of the camps, the only restrictions being that the users leave them clean and undamaged. No fires may be built without a permit (free) from the nearest ranger, or from the Forestry Service Supervisor, at Laconia, N. H.

BIBLIOGRAPHY

BIBLIOGRAPHY

"The White Mountains, covering roughly an area somewhat less than forty miles square in northern New Hampshire, with but nine mountains over five thousand feet in height and only one peak above six thousand, have had more written about them, probably, than any other mountains, the Alps alone excepted."

—Allen H. Bent: *Introduction to a Bibliography of the White Mountains,* published for the Appalachian Mountain Club by Houghton Mifflin Company, 1911.

Belknap, Jeremy. *The History of New Hampshire*. Vol. III. 1792.

Child, Mrs. Lydia Maria. *"Chocorua's Curse,"* The Token. Carter and Hendee. Boston, 1830.

Crawford, Lucy, Wife of Ethan Allen Crawford, Esq. *The History of the White Mountains from the First Settlement of Upper Coos and Pequaket*. 1846.

Oakes, William. *Scenery of the White Mountains*. 116 plates. 1848.

Spaulding, John H. *Historical Relics of the White Mountains*. 1855.

Ball, B. L. *Three Days on the White Mountains*. 1856.

Willey, Benjamin G. *Incidents in White Mountain History*. Nathaniel Noyes. Boston, 1856.

Eastman, Samuel C. *The White Mountain Guide Book*. 1st ed., 1858.

King, Thomas Starr. *The White Hills.* 1860.

Hitchcock, C. H. and others. *Mount Washington in Winter.* Chick and Adams. Boston, 1871.

Powers, Grant L. *Historical Sketches of the Discovery, Settlement, and Progress of Events in the Coos Country and Vicinity.* 1st ed., 1840. Reprint, 1880.

Drake, Samuel Adams. *The Heart of the White Mountains.* 1881.

History of Coos County. 1888.

Ward, Julius H. *The White Mountains.* 1890.

Bolles, Frank. *At the North of Bearcamp Water.* Houghton Mifflin Company. Boston, 1893.

Rollins, F. W. *Tourists' Guide Book to the State of New Hampshire.* Rumford Press. 1902.

Bent, Allen H. *Bibliography of the White Mountains.* 1911.

Packard, Winthrop. *White Mountain Trails.* Small, Maynard. Boston, 1912.

Sweetser, M. F. *Chisholm's White Mountain Guide Book.* Portland, 1913.

Goodrich, A. L. *The Waterville Valley.* Revised edition, 1916.

Kilbourne, Frederick W. *Chronicles of the White Mountains.* Houghton Mifflin Company. Boston, 1916.

Sweetser, M. F. *Guide to the White Mountains.* Houghton Mifflin Company. Boston, 1918.

Goldthwait, James W. *The Geology of New Hampshire.* Rumford Press. Concord, 1925.

Atkinson, J. Brooks. *Skyline Promenades.* Alfred A. Knopf. New York, 1925.

O'Kane, Walter Collins. *Trails and Summits of the White Mountains.* Houghton Mifflin Company. Boston, 1925.

Brown, George W. *Franconian Gateway and Region of Lost River.* 1926.

Harrington, Karl Pomeroy. *Walks and Climbs in the White Mountains.* Yale University Press. New Haven, 1926.

Washburn, H. B. *Trails and Peaks of the Presidential Range.* W. M. Davis Press. 1926.

The A. M. C. White Mountain Guide. 1928.

The indebtedness of the authors to the White Mountain "classics"—to the Crawford *History,* Spaulding's *Relics,* Willey's *Incidents,* and King's *The White Hills*—will be apparent. Mr. Kilbourne's *Chronicles of the White Mountains* is by all odds the most comprehensive account of the mountains from a historical point of view and has been invaluable to us. We are especially indebted to Mr. Kilbourne for his account of the casualties on the Presidential Range. A manuscript account of casualties since the publication of Mr. Kilbourne's book by R. S. Monahan has also been useful. Mr. Monahan's article will appear in a forthcoming number of *Appalachia.*

Mr. O'Kane's little handbook on *Trails and Summits of the White Mountains* is a very useful book, especially in planning trips.

The A. M. C. Guide is, of course, much more detailed. It is also supplied with many very carefully prepared maps. The real devotee of White Mountain trails will hardly want to be without it.

INDEX

INDEX

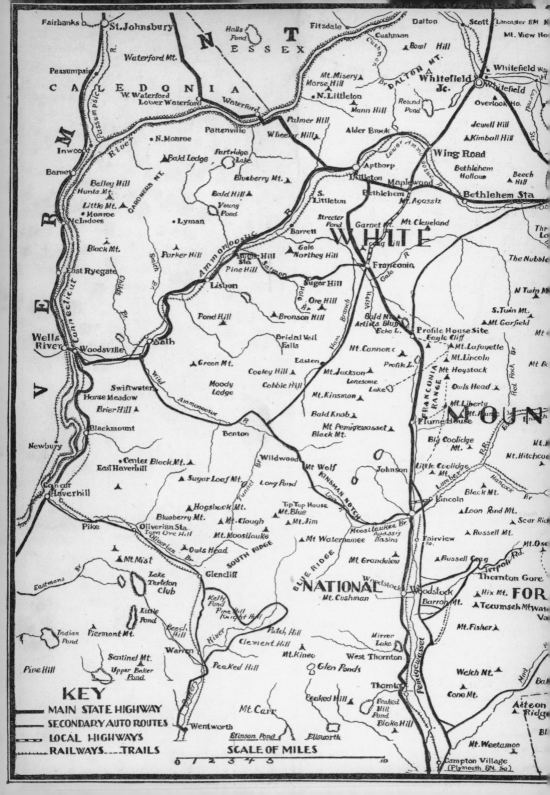